SELLING VERO BEACH

Florida in Focus

UNIVERSITY PRESS OF FLORIDA

Florida A&M University, Tallahassee
Florida Atlantic University, Boca Raton
Florida Gulf Coast University, Ft. Myers
Florida International University, Miami
Florida State University, Tallahassee
New College of Florida, Sarasota
University of Central Florida, Orlando
University of Florida, Gainesville
University of North Florida, Jacksonville
University of South Florida, Tampa
University of West Florida, Pensacola

Selling Vero Beach

Settler Myths in the Land of the Aís and Seminole

Kristalyn Marie Shefveland

Andrew K. Frank, Series Editor

UNIVERSITY PRESS OF FLORIDA

Gainesville · Tallahassee · Tampa · Boca Raton
Pensacola · Orlando · Miami · Jacksonville · Ft. Myers · Sarasota

Copyright 2024 by Kristalyn Marie Shefveland
All rights reserved
Published in the United States of America

29 28 27 26 25 24   6 5 4 3 2 1

Library of Congress Cataloging-in-Publication Data
Names: Shefveland, Kristalyn Marie, 1979– author.
Title: Selling Vero Beach : settler myths in the land of the Aís and
   Seminole / Kristalyn Marie Shefveland.
Other titles: Settler myths in the land of the Aís and Seminole | Florida
   in focus.
Description: 1. | Gainesville : University Press of Florida, [2024] |
   Series: Florida in focus | Includes bibliographical references and
   index.
Identifiers: LCCN 2023042343 (print) | LCCN 2023042344 (ebook) | ISBN
   9780813079035 (hardback) | ISBN 9780813080536 (paperback) | ISBN
   9780813070780 (pdf) | ISBN 9780813073286 (ebook)
Subjects: LCSH: Indians of North America—Florida—History. | Vero Beach
   (Fla.)—History. | Indian River (Fla. : Lagoon)—History. | BISAC:
   HISTORY / United States / State & Local / South (AL, AR, FL, GA, KY, LA,
   MS, NC, SC, TN, VA, WV)
Classification: LCC F319.V54 S54 2024 (print) | LCC F319.V54 (ebook) |
   DDC 975.9/2800497—dc23/eng/20231025
LC record available at https://lccn.loc.gov/2023042343
LC ebook record available at https://lccn.loc.gov/2023042344

The University Press of Florida is the scholarly publishing agency for the State University System of Florida, comprising Florida A&M University, Florida Atlantic University, Florida Gulf Coast University, Florida International University, Florida State University, New College of Florida, University of Central Florida, University of Florida, University of North Florida, University of South Florida, and University of West Florida.

University Press of Florida
2046 NE Waldo Road
Suite 2100
Gainesville, FL 32609
http://upress.ufl.edu

For

Tom Telenko
The Pirate

CONTENTS

Preface ix

Introduction 1

1. Vero Man to the Aís: The Indian River Lagoon's Early History through the Early American Republic 15

2. Settlers and Settler Colonialism of the Eighteenth and Nineteenth Centuries 40

3. The Indian River Farm Company's Booster Dreams of a Colonial Past 64

4. Citrus and Pineapple Dreams: Settler Memory and History 90

5. Memory and the Built Environment 111

6. Guinea Cows, Landscape Paintings, Waldo, and Zora 141

Conclusion 158

Appendix: From the Sexton Family Records, A Typewritten Rough Draft Copy of Hurston's Article "Double Muscle and His Pappy Too" 163

Acknowledgments 171

Notes 173

Index 201

PREFACE

Clevelanders dream of Florida. Especially when the sky turns gunmetal gray, and the lake effect snow starts to pile up on the interstate. The beginnings of the tradition of Clevelanders turned snowbirds to the balmy subtropics of Florida can be pinpointed right to the late nineteenth century when other Midwestern Yankee adventurers and entrepreneurs turned their attention south to find new products, plant citrus dreams, or, in the case of most travelers, escape the doom and gloom of a Cleveland winter. In the case of my family, it's a little bit of all the above. My father, Thomas Telenko, grew up with memories of trucking goods down to Vero Beach with his father in the early 1950s and his grandmother settling south after years of Cleveland winters. Their Vero Beach was a quiet and sleepy beach town along A1A, the old Jungle Road bustling with citrus trucks and tourist traffic along US1, what folks now remember as quintessentially "Old Florida." A descendant of Hungarian and Slovenian immigrants, my dad liked to tell stories of Old Cleveland and Old Florida. Tales of making Hungarian chicken paprikash, *Csirkepaprikás,* with the quip that "first, you steal the chicken" followed by an anecdote of the old country and mentions of horse thieves. When his attention would turn to Florida, he'd talk about the old roads, the Jungle Road especially, and the roadside attractions along the highways, the fruit stands, and the self-taught artists the Highwaymen who would sell their brightly colored landscape paintings out of the trunks of their cars. Of each trip he'd made as a child, how he once attempted to ride his bike with a group of friends from W 99th Street, how they made it all the way to Medina (25 miles) before turning around, and how he would retire there one day, which he did, in 2005.

When my father was diagnosed with esophageal cancer, our conversations about the old roads and the past became more important. While I had visited Vero as a child, after my parents finally retired there, my trips became more frequent, and it became a space that I knew yet had so many questions about. With his illness, I selfishly wanted to preserve his stories for myself and my daughter, for those tales to remain in this world, but I also wanted to talk with him about anything but the reality at hand. So, we began a research project. We'd talk about Old Vero. "Say, why did they stop growing pineapples along the Atlantic Ridge off Oslo," he'd ask, or "Whatever happened to Waldo Sexton's pyramid?" I'd head out to the Indian River County archive and come back armed with facts about the rise of Cuban pineapple imports, and we'd veer into conversations about the Cuban missile crisis before heading back to legends about Northerners and Clevelanders in Vero like Arthur McKee and Waldo Sexton. Sexton is most responsible for the kitschy "Old Florida" that Vero Beach is famous for. Buildings made from cobbled together driftwood and decorated with pilfered Spanish mission bells and tiles. And his pyramid, meant to be a roadside shrine. All that's left of the pyramid these days are memories. Natural erosion, tropical storms, and the passage of time have battered and, at times, erased, many of these settler landmarks on the built environment of Vero Beach. But the stories remain.

Introduction

Collective memory is a representation of the past shared by a group or community, however, "remembering is not only a personal mental function locked in the human brain. What we remember, it is argued, extends beyond what we have personally experienced." Our memories are directly connected to the communities that we are a part of, our families, our organizations, our kin and networks, "individuals are able to acquire and preserve their memories through their membership in social groups." A community of memory or, "mnemonic community" sustains the collective memory, "relics from the past, for example, provide vital bridges between past and present signifying that how and what we remember is objectified in material forms."[1] Preexisting interpretations or "knowledge" of a place primes visitors, settlers, and tourists, to see the landscape as they want to see it. Historical debris, myths, and traditions affect and distort the lens through which individuals view the past. Settler memory is a collective identity that often erases Native peoples from the past and present, intellectually reframing the past to remove Native history. While Vero is no exception in this process, examining this community and its use of settler memory allows for an intriguing analytical history that raises questions about how we all tell our stories and present ourselves and our past to the world.

Rather than embracing the fascinating and tantalizing history of the region itself, and its Native peoples, boosters and settlers chose to import stories and imprint them onto the region, reflecting less about Vero as a place and more about the settlers themselves. The volume that follows is the story of these acts of memory, particularly settler memory, of the town of Vero Beach, from the colonial record through the mid-twentieth century. These deliberate acts of misremembering and firsting/lasting have a direct impact on Indigenous peoples of Florida who face the ramifications of stereotypes and the false narrative of settler innocence.

"Hauling Indian River Oranges in Florida." Courtesy of the Matheson History Museum, https://ufdc.ufl.edu/mh00000458/00001/images.

"Old Florida" is a catch-all phrase that references the pre-Disneyfication of the state, the Florida before the theme parks and the interstates. This Florida of the popular imagination was a tourist destination but references to this bygone era are framed within a lens of authenticity—of sleepy beachside hamlets, Spanish- and Mediterranean-inspired architecture, cowboys driving herds throughout the interior, vast orange groves, and hammocks draped in Spanish moss. This "real" Florida is also a manufactured space, a Florida conceived by northern émigrés who settled in the region throughout the late nineteenth century. Calls to a Native Florida as the "real" Florida are also constructs of settler imagination, framed within the lens of stereotypes and the grand American narrative of Manifest Destiny and tropes about Native identity, like the noble savage. Lost within these conceptions of Florida are the realities that all of Florida is a manufactured space, a cultivated space, and each generation actively carves from the environment the Florida that suits their interests.

Vero Beach has a history that dates back thousands of years when the area was inhabited by powerful Native polities, including the Aís people. These tribes thrived in the rich marine ecosystem of the Indian River Lagoon until the arrival of the Spanish in the sixteenth century, which ushered in an era of violence, displacement, disease, and enslavement. Sporadic attempts for European and American settlement allowed the remaining tribes of South Florida to retake the lagoon and coalesce into other polities, including the Seminole. It was not until the late nineteenth century that American settlement of the region expanded into the hammocks of the Seminole as Northerners, including Henry T. Gifford, founder of Vero in 1891, purchased land in the area for a citrus farming community and began promoting the region to potential settlers. He planted groves of citrus trees and built a railroad line to transport the produce to markets in the north. The Indian River Farms Company played a significant role in the development of Vero Beach and the surrounding area. It was established in 1919 by a group of investors who recognized the region's potential for agriculture and land development.

For the last 150 years, citrus farmers and cattlemen on the Indian River have sat astride fertile plots of reclaimed marshland. While the town of Vero Beach and its surrounding farms are relatively new settlements in the oldest European colony of North America, the Indian River settlers of the 1880s actively sought to connect themselves to Florida's colonial and Indigenous past. To this end, Indian River architecture and produce advertisements reflect imaginative and fanciful views of the colonial and Indigenous world of Florida. This "Old Florida" motif includes idyllic jungle scenes that reference the Garden of Eden and connect to the Indian River Lagoon with advertisements for citrus that include friendly and noble Indians.

Florida's Indian River Lagoon is a remarkably diverse ecosystem that includes the settlement of Vero Beach, a modest-sized town along the Atlantic Ocean, as the pelicans fly, midway between Cape Canaveral and Miami. The Indian River is not a river, rather, it is an estuary and lagoon, where saltwater and freshwater meet to form brackish water that flows through mangrove wetlands and salt marshes wedged between the barrier islands of Florida's Atlantic coast and the mainland. Its currents are dependent upon the wind, flowing south one day and north the next. To that end the modern lagoon is a 156-mile-long estuary with the main bodies of water: the Banana River, the Indian River, and the Mosquito Lagoon. Five inlets interconnect the Indian River Lagoon with the Atlantic Ocean. The Indian River Lagoon is home to 685 species of fish; 370 species of birds; 2,200 animal species; and 2,100 plant species. The barrier islands of the lagoon region attract high numbers of nesting sea turtles each year and the lagoon is located along the Atlantic Flyway, a biological highway for

"Florida—the tropical wonderland," 1941. State Archives of Florida, Florida Memory, https://www.floridamemory.com/items/show/157526, accessed 30 March 2023.

migratory birds. According to Florida State Parks, "The lagoon has been called 'the cradle of the ocean,' acting as a refuge for countless species."[2]

Vero lies in the heart of the lower Indian River Lagoon, in a section of south central Florida referred to as the Treasure Coast, a nickname that references numerous Spanish treasure fleets wrecked offshore whose gold and silver bounty still occasionally ends up on the beaches of the region. Coastal reefs, shallow shores, and hurricanes made this section of Florida particularly dangerous for the Spanish fleets. The history of the Treasure Coast provides a host of opportunities for legend and myth: epic adventure sagas of Indigenous peoples, European pirates, Native and Settler scavengers/wreckers, as well as American boosters, truckers, dreamers, and farmers—some stories are true, some embellished, some far stranger than fiction could ever dream to be. In this case, the act of naming and storytelling actively capitalize on Yankee fascination with global Indigenous pasts, and the dream of a settler Manifest Destiny pioneering into Edenic frontiers—a booster dream.

First discovered, last settled. First peoples, last of their kind. Throughout Florida history one can see the themes of Edenic paradise juxtaposed against a progress narrative that privileges Anglo-American settlement myths that have a long national history. While Native peoples often have a role in settler origin stories, as Ojibwe historian, Jean O'Brien explains, firsting in the historical narrative can be seen in the creation of origin stories that continue to downplay Indigenous presence and history. When settler origin stories do acknowledge Indigenous peoples, they incorporate them only as the preface for non-indigenous history, relegating their story to a distant past and denying them contemporary or future presence.[3] Thus the result, O'Brien argues, "is the successful mounting of the argument that Indian peoples and their cultures represented an 'inauthentic' and prefatory history."[4] Firsting, therefore, is that legitimate, or authentic, history, which begins with European settlement. In the case of Florida, the argument could be made that it begins with Anglo-American settlement. Lasting is another common element of settler histories, emphasizing so-called Native lasts in contradiction to settler firsts. For example, the discourse of the Vanishing Indian or the last of their kind reflects a "rhetorical strategy that asserts as a fact the claim that Indian can never be modern." By that definition, Native peoples are placed into cultural stasis, residing in an "ahistorical temporality in which they can only be the victims of change, not active subjects in the making of change" whereas settlers are afforded progress narratives.[5] Settler usage of lasting is often employed in naming practices, organizing a territory in a way that amplifies a message of extinction, in a pattern of replacing/removing. By situating the settler at the heart of the narrative, the story becomes about a preordained inevitability of replacement whereby previous Indian histories of a region become a "dead end" and the settler claims the region as their own.[6] This message of replacement is found in monuments, place names, and archaeological sites. This is interconnected with themes of Divine Providence, Manifest Destiny, and American expansionism that characterizes American history.

On the topic of Eden and the history of Florida, many early explorers characterized the New World as an earthly paradise or a recovered Eden. While some of these descriptions can be interpreted as attempts to secure funding for new explorations, many of these reports reflect the awe-inspiring abundance of the Americas and a historical fantasy about Eden not as an idea but a literal place that a worthy explorer could reclaim. Western literary tradition has emphasized the idea of an earthly paradise in Judeo-Christian works on the Garden of Eden and also in Plato's description of the doomed island of Atlantis, and explorers often returned with fantastic tales of Atlantic islands that could be Atlantis or Eden. Legendary adventures and myths characterize the early Modern World. As Jean Delumeau explains,

> ... until the emergence of the fact of evolution and of the slow and difficult rise of the "human phenomenon," many civilizations believed in a primordial paradise that was characterized by perfection, freedom, peace, happiness, abundance, and the absence of duress, tensions, and conflicts. In that paradise human beings got on well together and lived in harmony with the animals. They also communicated effortlessly with the divine world. This belief gave rise in the collective consciousness to a profound nostalgia for the lost but not forgotten paradise and to a strong desire to recover it.[7]

Thus, the theme of Eden played an integral part in the exploration era and was "an important stimulus to voyages of discovery."[8] Many regions of North America had Garden of Eden themes, and "this persuasion and identification played no little part in the history of the United States and in the pushing back of its 'frontier' to the West."[9] Within the theme of Eden, one can find the two tropes of Florida history, the divine paradise and the tragedy of the fall.

In the case of Vero, one is presented with acts of remembering, or rather, more importantly, deliberate misremembering and firsting/lasting of not only Florida's history but also the settler history of the Americas more generally. In a 1963 speech, famed African American writer James Baldwin notes, "Part of the dilemma of this country is that it has managed to believe the myths it has created about its past, which is another way of saying that it has entirely denied its past."[10] In the end, modern Vero cannot imagine an Indigenous presence because the narrative of erasure has been so successful, yet there is obvious Indigenous history that gets replaced by the settler narrative as they misappropriate the narrative to their own needs.

To be fair, however, unrealistic settler narratives of Florida and its Indigenous inhabitants have a long history that encapsulate the issue of Eden and paradise juxtaposed against a hellscape of the fall of humanity. Since their first encounters with the Indigenous population of Florida, European descriptions of the territory have held elements of the fanciful and picturesque, filled with either dreams of fortune, grandeur and glory, or the extreme opposite—a hellish landscape, a malarial and festering swampland of grim misfortune. In 1563, Jean Ribault, the doomed French

Huguenot colonizer dreaming of a way to garner favor from the French crown and Catherine Medici, wrote of North Florida as a land ripe for French colonization that could cure melancholy, "the fairest, frutefullest and plesantest of all the worlde," a veritable cornucopia, "honney, veneson, wildfoule, forrestes, woodes of all sortes, palme trees, cipers, ceders, bayes, the hiest, greatest and fairest vynes in all the would with grapes," and the "sight of the faire medowes is a pleasure not able to be expressed with tonge."[11] From that same attempt to colonize, one can see the other trope in Florida descriptions, the festering cesspool of miasma and malaise. As a survivor of the failed French colony Nicholas Le Challeux wrote in 1565, "Whoever wishes to go to Florida, Let him go where I have been, And return dry and arid, And worn out by rot. For the only good I have brought back—A single silvery stick in my hand. But I am safe, not defeated. It's time to eat; I die of hunger."[12] These encounters set the stage for the Florida historical narrative: Edenic paradise or an earthly hell to test the will of men.

These tropes soon reflected the entire Florida peninsula and played out in colonial literature and throughout the nineteenth century. Florida is the exotic Eden, where the promise of man can also be met with his downfall in the verdant jungles. The book that follows focuses on the lower Indian River Lagoon region that surrounded the town of Vero Beach, including parts of Sebastian, Fellsmere, and north Fort Pierce. This section of the lower Indian River Lagoon is a place of continued and sustained settlements by Native peoples and European/American settlers. Based on existing physical records, Native occupation of the site dates as early as the Pleistocene era. Repeated attempts by the Spanish to colonize the area proved fruitless but the coastal Aís utilized the Spanish shipping industry to their advantage, salvaging and plundering the numerous ships wrecked off the coast. Their treatment of shipwreck survivors led Governor Pedro Menéndez de Avilés to write to Madrid in 1573 and list "five Spanish ships that had recently washed ashore on the middle east coast. The Indians, he reported, had captured or killed nearly all of the survivors." For this, Menéndez petitioned for permission to enslave. Throughout the seventeenth century, an uneasy and often violent relationship persisted between the Spanish and the Aís, and while Menéndez's wish was not granted, the Aís did fall subject to attacks by English-allied Native enslavers throughout the eighteenth century as coalescent Native Floridians regrouped in the interior and became known as the Seminole.[13]

Shallow waters and shoals off the coast of Florida led to numerous shipwrecks resulting in the loss of life as well as treasure. Examining Menéndez de Avilés's writings on the topic provides a window into the Aís's repeated and continued resistance to colonization. Menéndez alleges in his correspondence to the crown that the Aís regularly murdered shipwreck survivors and were generally violent opposed to the Spanish missionaries. English records corroborate the remaining size and presence of the polity as in 1696, a Quaker named Jonathon Dickinson survived a shipwreck south of Vero near Port St. Lucie and traveled through the territory on his way to St. Augustine, leaving behind the most detailed account of the Aís people. The Atlantic side of the Lagoon opposite Vero Beach, called Orchid Isle by settlers and the site of Riomar, was once a paramount village of the Aís, visited by the Jece with the Dickinson party in 1696. Between the seventeenth and nineteenth centuries, however, the written European record of the Indigenous peoples of south central Florida is a fragmented record; there is no lasting European written record of permanent and sustained settlement of the Indian River until the nineteenth century when American settlers created Mosquito County in 1824 (the whole eastern coast had been known as Los Musquitos since the 1500s). Despite the lack of written records, however, physical evidence and oral histories highlight that coalescent Seminole people lived throughout the Florida peninsula and the Indian River Lagoon in the seventeenth and nineteenth centuries as Spanish, English, and then American forts slowly came to their territory. Like other Indigenous communities in the Americas, the Seminole people are diverse in both ancestry and culture. Seminoles hold that they have always been in Florida, drawing upon their ties to their Calusa, Tequesta, Aís, Apalachee, and Timucua ancestors who claimed the peninsula before the arrival of European conquerors in the sixteenth century. They also hold true to communities of Hitchiti- and Muskogee-speaking ancestors who established themselves on the north central highlands and panhandle regions in the latter half of the eighteenth century. Maintaining a sense of cultural independence but political affiliation, these assorted communities eventually banded together to confront American expansion into Florida in the nineteenth century, known as the Seminole Wars. The survivors of this conquest eventually reformed into three units in Florida: the Seminole Tribe of Indians, the Miccosukee Tribe of Indians of Florida, and the independent Seminoles.

There was very little European settlement activity throughout the eighteenth into the early nineteenth century until Americans moved into the peninsula. This changed after the Seminole Wars (1817–1818; 1835–1842; 1855–1858). Encouraged and emboldened by the 1842 Armed Occupation Act that subsidized white settlement in Seminole territories, settlers moved into the territory, resulting in the creation of Fort Vinton, thirteen miles southwest of president day Vero Beach. To the north of Vero, settlers established a community named Susanna near the Sebastian River and the first permanent white homesteaders near Sebastian were Gottlob Kroegel and Augustus Park.[14]

Florida's history became an area of focus with American expansion as settler writers attempted to figure out how the region would fit into the American republic and how to remove Native peoples, both figuratively and literally, in the Seminole Wars. While Florida became a state in 1845, the lower half of the region remained relatively unsettled by Europeans or Americans. In the late nineteenth century, with the first generation of Florida professional histories came equal parts tall tales, promises, legends—all without much hint at Florida's longer history of Indigenous presence or experiences of colonization. Indeed, one must carefully examine most of the nineteenth-century historians as they were often interconnected with boosterism. What is boosterism you might ask? Nineteenth-century boosterism was a phenomenon of Anglo-American settler expansion into the West and the South, combining extravagant sales tactics with public relations campaigns, including published histories, to sell spaces to American settlers. Booster literature of the Gilded Age and Progressive Era was energetic, jingoistic, and wildly optimistic of the potentials for Florida as a Edenic garden—one with the potential to restore health to white Americans through leisure and connecting to themes of the Anglo-American Protestant work ethic, that they would reap the rewards tilling of the soil and expanding American settlement. For example, Sidney Lanier wrote an 1876 guidebook history filled with ominous foreboding about the past, but enthusiastic proclamations about the potential for subtropical Florida. Decrying a past akin to a "bowl of blood . . . death and disappointment," he chronicled the colonial past and the Seminole Wars "like a bill of mortality . . . almost on a formula." After briefly recounting Spanish expeditions, missionary occupations, attempts at colonial and federal settlements, wars with the Seminole, he opined, "Surely it ought to give us a great many oranges, a great many bananas, and a great many early vegetables, after having been so bloodily fertilized for such a time. Surely it ought to restore to us a great many sick men,—it has swallowed up so many well ones!"[15] To that end, this quote neatly summarizes the settlers belief in Manifest Destiny and Divine Providence, the settler is owed bananas and oranges, he has toiled through hell and deserves an earthly paradise.

Boosters in both the nineteenth and twentieth centuries cast Vero as either remarkably ancient or dazzlingly modern. That bloody and violent past, a point of great focus for scholars of the three Seminole Wars, virtually disappears in the booster literature of the early twentieth century when these crafty writers sought to cast Indigenous peoples (who still lived in active communities all along the Indian River Lagoon, north and south of Lake Okeechobee, and in the Everglades) as picturesque assets and tourist commodities (if they mention them at all). Beginning in the booster literature of the nineteenth century and continuing through twentieth century heritage projects that focus on pioneer and frontier settler memoirs, one can see the casting of former enemies as tragic heroes and reframing of Indigenous peoples and stories to fit into and justify American settler ambitions. We tend to associate this narrative of American settler ambitions with the West, but it remains deeply relevant to the South as well. As one scholar of the West and memory has described it, we must consider the construction of memory and how they are not merely "recollected or reproduced" but at times, "even invented." Settlers of the West and Florida have both selectively created memories that highlight the stories and events they want to remember, "pioneer reminiscences, like the promotional literature, can be most profitably used as a mirror to reflect the outlook of those doing the reminiscing, rather than as a clear window on the actual events that are described between the covers of their accounts."[16] Once again, framing an Indigenous past to fit a settler narrative, replacing an Indigenous history for a settler colonial memory project.

In the introduction to a late nineteenth-century history of Florida, then Governor John W. Martin made it clear that he viewed Florida as still a pioneer state and employed firsting/lasting, "oldest of all in its history, it is the youngest of all in its development."[17] Referencing Spanish colonization, another Florida essayist, Frank Parker Stockbridge wrote, "A new world had been discovered, and adventurous men flocked to it in search of—what? Wealth, freedom from the restraints of the old civilization, excitement, novelty, all the things that make adventurous men go adventur-

Pekad Brand. Jerry Chicone Jr. Citrus Crate Label Collection, Special and Area Studies Collections, George A. Smathers Libraries, University of Florida.

ing . . . The migration to Florida to-day is another such great movement of peoples, unparalleled in our generation. Here is history in the making, the drama of a world movement being enacted before our eyes . . ."[18] Booster advertising journals for Vero Beach, like the *Indian River Farmer*, enthusiastically agreed that all men (referencing Anglo men) despite the century, were great pioneers, harkening to past explorations, and all they wanted was health and wealth. Despite the passage of time, human nature remained consistent. By viewing the Gilded Age and Progressive Era and booster literature through the lens of the deep-rooted colonial past, one can see that an active reimagining was taking place, at odds with the realities at hand. In some cases, white Americans simply pretended that Seminoles no longer existed in Florida after Seminole isolation following the three wars.

Scribner's Monthly: An Illustrated Magazine for the People published a series of travel narratives and articles throughout the post–Civil War period of the late nineteenth century, depicting both in prose and in remarkably detailed illustrations, a defeated South as an exotic travel locale for their curious northern audiences. In November 1874, as part of "The Great South," series, Edward King described his journey to Jacksonville, a 263-mile trip via rail from Savannah, Georgia, "the rendezvous for all travelers who intend to penetrate to the interior of the beautiful peninsula."[19] Writing in romantic prose, he asked his readers to "pause with me at the gateway of the great peninsula and reflect for a moment upon its history. Fact and fancy wander here hand in hand; the airy chronicles of the ancient fathers hover upon the confines of the impossible."[20] Describing a winter paradise, King chastised the cynical reader who might "murmur incredulously" at the tales of Florida, yet, "what poet's imagination, seven times heated, could paint foliage whose splendors should surpass that of the virgin forests of the Oclawaha and Indian rivers?"[21] King shares in effusive praise that the Indian River may be:

> ... difficult of access, but swarms of travelers are now finding their way there ... with a little renewed attention, be made one of the richest garden spots in America ... Hardly a thousand miles from New York, one may find the most delicate and delightful tropical scenery, and may dwell in a climate which neither Hawaii nor Southern Italy can excel.[22]

By 1890, white settlers established additional communities at Orchid, Roseland, Wabasso, and Vero Beach. These communities benefited from Henry Flagler's railroad that connected them to markets to the north and created the community of Gifford, a labor camp for the railroad construction companies.[23] With these fledgling settlements established, the area grew in popularity throughout the late nineteenth century and began to flourish as an agricultural community by the early twentieth century.

Writers imagined Florida and created myths surrounding its bounty all throughout the waves of exploration, tentative settlements, wars, and finally, agricultural success. Thus, the chapters that follow explore a chronological timeline with areas of focus on settler and colonial memory from Spanish conquistadors and their first encounters with the Aís through the mid-twentieth century marvels championed by booster Waldo Sexton. Chapter 1 begins with the early physical and written history of settlement

Two women looking at a painting of Native Americans in the Driftwood Inn, 1967. Photo by Nancy Brower. State Archives of Florida, Florida Memory, https://www.floridamemory.com/items/show/84310, accessed 30 March 2023.

with an emphasis on the discovery of Vero Man and Indigenous polities in the region through the period of the Early American Republic. Chapter 2 considers the era of the first entrenched settler movements in the lower Indian River which was part of the Armed Occupation Act following the First Seminole War. An era of violence and upheaval, indeed a total bloodbath on both sides, this chapter examines the settlement of the lower Indian River Lagoon and the aftermath of war as Seminole adapted to permanent American settlements in the region. Chapter 3 examines the Gilded Age and Progressive Era. This chapter analyzes the early citrus efforts of the Indian River Farms Company and how settlers and boosters utilized Native peoples as motifs for their expansion and settlement. Chapter 4 provides a case study of a settler family, the Hallstroms, detailing the south Vero settlement of Viking and their legacy and the Florida Ridge pineapple plantations. Chapter 5 continues the story of the Indian River Farms Company and northern settlement. This chapter is a study of

Florida mythmaking by Cleveland industrialist Arthur McKee and Indian River Farms salesman Waldo Sexton, the men most responsible for the vision of "Old Florida" that the city of Vero Beach is known best for. Finally, the last chapter concludes with the story of Waldo Sexton and Zora Neale Hurston who worked with Waldo on an article about his Spanish guinea cows, a breed that he claimed had origins in Spanish colonization. Settler colonialism and memory misappropriated Florida's history, and Florida's actual history is in stark contrast to the narrative of "Old Florida," the following chapters examine these cases of collective memory, settler memory, and how Vero's Native history is often hidden in plain view.

1
Vero Man to the Aís

The Indian River Lagoon's Early History
through the Early American Republic

How do narrators craft a Florida history and why does it matter? This chapter emphasizes the regions Native history and how settler narratives from the Spanish to the Americans portray Florida. Throughout the literature on the settlement of Florida, from the contemporary sources of Spanish, French, and English attempts to colonize through the American experiment in the nineteenth century, to the protohistories of the Gilded Age, and even the more recent scholarship, a prevailing theme remains in which Native peoples of the coast are described as "fierce" and "resistant" to the Spanish before dying off in the mid-eighteenth century, leaving a depopulated peninsula. However, these narratives rely heavily on the biased and fragmented written record as well as a fundamental misreading of the 1763 removal of Spanish colonists and mission Indians to indicate that *all* Native peoples left for Cuba. A recent history by Alejandra Dubcovsky improves our knowledge of the era, highlighting that "the Aís seem to burst into Spanish, French, Dutch, and English sources like lightning, brightly and rapidly illuminating the geopolitics of south Florida, and then just as quickly disappear into one of the many lacunae of the colonial archive."[1] More detail about the lower Indian River Lagoon's Indigenous history can be found by viewing the physical records of the region and consulting Native oral histories and epistemologies. The physical record of the Indian River Lagoon tells a remarkably rich history. Vero's Indigenous history brings into question many long held stereotypes about Native peoples and their settlements in North America. Physical evidence of human settlement in the Indian River Lagoon date back at least to the late Pleistocene era as physical evidence from what came to be known as the Vero Man site indicates occupation some 13–14,000 years ago.[2] By examining the remaining physical evidence, including Clovis and Folsom points that highlight the presence of hunters in the region, one can see continuous occupation of the marshlands of the lagoon. Eventually these groups culminated into complex polities in the Mississippian Era throughout Florida.

The group that inhabited the region that became Vero were the Aís, a polity of several thousand people that controlled the lower Indian River Lagoon in a large territory that ranged from Cape Canaveral south to Jupiter. When the Spanish arrived in 1513, they named the territory Rio de Aís, or Indian River, after the group. The first European-recorded history of the Aís came from that encounter, and as Robert Davidson notes in the only book-length history of the Aís, they have "the dubious honor of being the first native tribe encountered by Europeans in what became Spanish Florida. The hostility they displayed to Ponce de León and his small band of explorers would be the standard policy of the tribe for the next 200 years in dealing with European trespassers."[3]

The Aís maintained an array of differing relationships with other people in Indigenous Florida and might have been tributaries of the Calusa, whose primary settlement was in the Port Charlotte region of the southwest coast. They were certainly trading partners of the Calusa, Jeaga, Mayaca, and other groups of southern Florida. Debate continues about the location of the Aís's principal town. Some point to remaining physical evidence at Fort Pierce's Old Fort Park, which includes mounds with human remains and other details of human occupation dating back around 500–1,000 years. Others point to Riomar on the Atlantic side of Vero Beach as the primary settlement of the Aís, and two Palm Bay archaeologists have more recently suggested that the Aís town was located on the lagoon side near the Kroegel homestead along US 1 and Indian River Drive.[4] Eugene Lyon surmised that the principal town was likely closer to the Sebastian inlet. All these potential sites indicate long-term Native settlement and development in the region. And written records from the Spanish highlight the wealth and power of the Aís people and their settlements. That is not to say, however, that the Spanish records and subsequent interpretation of those records are without concern as a significant point of focus for the region has been less on the history of Indigenous peoples of Florida or the depth of colonial records in Seville and more on bragging rights related to first European encounters.[5]

While the written histories of north Florida and its Indigenous residents have been combed by scholars and armchair historians alike, less is known about the Indian River Lagoon. Renewed interest in Florida's colonial Spanish past had direct correlations to St. Augustine's rise as a tourist destination in the late nineteenth and early twentieth centuries and booster attempts to build picturesque spaces, however, by the late twentieth century, scholars began to reexamine the colonial record more critically. With this analytical lens, more details emerge on Native Florida and their experiences with the Spanish. Esteemed Florida historian, Eugene Lyon, author of *The Enterprise of Florida: Pedro Menéndez de Avilés and the Spanish Conquest of 1565–1568* (1976), was one of the first to undertake extensive translations of the Spanish archive to better understand the history of *La Florida*. Taking that Spanish history into consideration, most scholarship focused on North Florida with brief mention of the rest of the Florida peninsula, placing significant emphasis on the failures experienced by the Spanish in South Florida. "Indeed from the very beginning, the most difficult and enduring problem for the Florida conquest was that of the Native Americans. Spain's Indian policy wore two conflicting faces," Lyon opined in *Pedro Menéndez de Avilés* (1995), "the dark side was the treatment of Florida Indians by de Soto and other conquistadores. But there was also the rhetoric of good treatment, which was backed by royal edict." Referencing the New Laws of 1542, which ostensibly outlawed enslavement of Indigenous peoples, Lyon reflected on the goals of the Spanish government versus the realities faced by the conquistadors, "in Florida as in the other Indies, officials, soldiers, and settlers often changed drastically the terms of dealing with the native Americans," by imposing heavy trade levies, engaged in forced labor of Native peoples, and forcing Christianity upon them which "threatened not only their own religions but their whole cultural structure." Attempts in South Florida often proved a disaster, tense from the very beginning, "the Jesuit missionaries failed to win converts in south Florida," as the Spanish retreated north to their outposts in St. Augustine and Santa Elena.[6]

What emerged from these failures, however, built an image within the European colonial mind of South Florida and its Native peoples, hostile and negative as one scholar describes, "in terms of material wealth or glory, the land failed to meet the expectations of Spanish, French, and English immigrants. Similarly, Indians failed to live up to settler expectations as civilized humans or as being capable of assimilating to civilization . . . in response, colonists constructed images of Indians to rationalize their misfortunes and define their own identity."[7]

As the Spanish explored north of the Caribbean they skirted south along Florida's Atlantic coastline before spotting the outcropping of land that they named Cabo Canaveral (Cape of Canes) because the "reeds reminded them of sugarcane" and anchored near a river they called Santa Cruz in what might have been the Jupiter Inlet encountering El Cabo de las Corrientes, the Gulf Stream. While no "chronicler recorded the exact time, place, and details... perhaps the inhaling of strange body smells, the pain inflicted by Toledo steel—or stone-tipped spears, or the unintelligible words marked Florida's chapter of genesis."[8]

Spanish historian Antonio de Herrera y Tordesillas wrote of these Castilians going ashore along the Atlantic coast in April 1513, "Here Juan Ponce went ashore, being called by the Indians, who they tried to take the boat, the oars and their arms. In order not to break with them, they suffered the attack, not wanting to scandalize and have trouble in the land." Eventually the Aís knocked a Spaniard unconscious, Herrera continued, "they had to fight with them; they with their arrows and lances armed with points of sharp bones and spines of fish," the Aís wounded at least two Castilians while suffering no injury themselves.[9] By most European accounts, the Aís were the first to encounter the Spaniards in La Florida and their hostility to the encounter and further intrusions would forever impact their reputation and history. Adding to the stereotypes of their ferocious nature were rumors of their scavenging Spanish wrecks that hit the reefs that lie close to the shores of the lower Indian River region and their propensity to kill any Spanish survivors. Having found no evidence of gold, other precious metals, or minerals, the Spaniards backed off momentarily until slavers began to move into the peninsula.[10] Later in 1521 when explorer Francisco Gordillo and slave trader Pedro de Quexos moved through the coastal Southeast, some accounts included the Aís firing arrows upon the slave raiders.[11] Known expeditions to regions of Florida included Diego Miruelo (1516); De Ayllon (1520); Pedro de Quexos (1523); Panfilo de Narváez (1527); Hernando de Soto (1539); and Don Tristan de Luna (1559).[12] Disease followed where the explorers and slavers traveled as trade took pathogens well outside the regions of direct contact: a typhus outbreak in 1585; various "pests and contagions" between 1613 and 1617; yellow fever in 1649; smallpox in 1653; and measles in 1659.[13] Thus the Spanish reshaped the Aís and their territory through their introduction of slavery and disease.

Ponce de León believed that Florida's Indigenous peoples deserved their misfortune, connecting once again to European conceptions of humanity and original sin, the fall from paradise, justifying conquest through the Doctrine of Discovery and Christianity. De León explained, "inasmuch as everything went wrong . . . it is believed that God was not served nor the time come for conversion of that land and province to our holy Catholic church, since he [God] permits the devil still to keep those Indians deceived . . . and the population of hell to be augmented with their souls."[14] In between his first and second voyage, he was enslaving Natives in Trinidad before coming back to Florida in 1521 with two ships outfitted for settlement of the southwest coast. He brought with him a herd of cattle, sheep, and pigs. Potential settlers brought seeds and plants for their planned agricultural invasion.[15]

Historically, early Spanish exploration and settlement of Florida foundered repeatedly, from the doomed Panfilo Narváez and Hernando de Soto expeditions, to Pedro Menéndez de Avilés's attempted mission settlements. Most written accounts of the Aís come from Menéndez de Avilés (Governor of La Florida) 1565 attempt to establish a mission named Santa Lucia in the region. A major reason for the Spanish interest in the polity came from their wealth and prestige. His failure in the region led to designs to depopulate the region via enslavement and take their territory by force. Hernando d'Escalante Fontaneda was a Spaniard shipwrecked in south Florida around 1545 at the age of ten and wrote an account detailing the Calusa and the Aís. Indicating the trade between the two, he wrote, "I desire to speak of the riches found by the Indians of Aís, which perhaps were as much as a million . . . or over, in bars of silver, in gold, and in articles of jewelry made by the hands of Mexican Indians, that they brought to the Calusa whose principal chief, Carlos, then divided among the Aís, Jeaga, Guacata, Mayajuaco, and Mayaca."[16] Dreams of finding another Cuzco or Tenochtitlan inspired both Narváez and de Soto (who was also driven by rumors of cities of gold told by Narváez survivor Cabeza de Vaca) but Menéndez, at times a rumored pirate and other times, a loyal soldier of the Spanish crown, had more complicated motivations for being in Florida. Menéndez was certainly in search of riches, but he also believed in the Northwest passage, rumored to be somewhere between Newfoundland and the Chesapeake.[17] His opportunity to prove his loyalty and further his own ambitions came with the desperate French Huguenot settlement in north Florida, Fort Caroline.

The French colonists posed two threats: first, they were Protestants and a threat to Catholic hegemony in the New World and second, some mutinous Frenchmen had taken advantage of their location near the Caribbean to attack and pillage Spanish ships. French corsairs began threatening Spanish and Portuguese hegemony on the seas in the 1490s when they were off the coast of Brazil and by 1510 were actively working against the Spanish in the Caribbean, once holding the town of Cartagena ransom in 1544. By the first half of the sixteenth century, the Spanish lost hundreds of ships laden with goods to French corsairs.[18] René de Laudonnière arrived in 1562 exploring parts of Florida and Carolina in the hopes of creating a Huguenot colony. He settled Fort Caroline along the St. Johns River in 1564, a colony that he hoped would bolster the Huguenot position in France. Settling on a bluff near what is now Jacksonville, Florida, he said the site was so pleasing that "melancholics would be constrained to change their nature." His hopes for an Edenic paradise would soon sour dramatically as food shortages settled in. Supported by Englishman Thomas Stucley, famed privateer/pirate John Hawkins visited the colony in 1565 and found it in deep disarray, in want of provisions, and in a state of chaos. Hawkins offered to take survivors back to France, but Laudonnière refused, allowing that his colonists could purchase a ship from Hawkins if they wanted to return to France.[19] Eventually his men mutinied and sailed to Cuba where the Spanish captured them and learned of the colony. French Admiral Jean Ribault made his way to Florida to bring reinforcements and provisions to Fort Caroline and took two shipwrecked sailors from the Aís as well as some silver they had looted from the wrecks.[20] Soon after, Menéndez and his fleet arrived at what would become St. Augustine and destroyed the French settlement with the intelligence and assistance of the Timucua.[21] Tensions from Europe spread throughout the colonial world, ensnaring Native allies into colonial ambitions while Native polities sought pathways to respond to European incursions. Lost in many of the narratives are the wide variety of motivations for all parties.

Further complicating Menéndez's ambitions and motivations to settle the region were rumors regarding the welfare of his son, Juan, a shipwreck victim that might have survived somewhere in the South Florida coast. Accused of piracy, Menéndez petitioned King Philip and relayed the tale of his lost son, telling the king he must "coast all of it if necessary, and go ashore to ask the Indians by signs if there were any bearded men among them or upon some neighboring island." With the king's permission, Menéndez received additional instructions to "survey the entire coast of Florida, exploring its inlets, harbors and bays, drawing them in detail" to prevent further wrecks as "the loss of so many ships, people, and treasure en route to and from the Indies, and even of the royal fleets which had gone to the settling and conquest of the land, was ignorance of the mysteries of the coast."[22]

One learns about Pedro's attempt to find Juan Menéndez from the records of the failed French settlement at Fort Caroline. Stefano de Rojomonte of Paris was one of the mutineers who broke away from René de Laudonnière in 1564 to raid Spanish Caribbean settlements. Captured by Spanish forces, he stood for interrogation in Havana Cuba. In his testimony, they asked about the fate of Juan and the others on the ship *Concepcion*. Through a document by Hernando d'Escalante Fontaneda, a shipwreck survivor, we learn even more. Fontaneda wrote a memoir (published in 1575) of his seventeen-year experience among the Natives along Florida's southeast coast:

> Other vessels have been lost, among them the armada of New Spain, of which it was said the son of Pedro Menéndez was general, for the Indians took a Spaniard that reached the shore whom they found starving. And I saw him alive and talked with him. He told us that they came from New Spain, and were going to Castile; that the general was the son of Pedro Menéndez, the Asturian; that he came as a sailor in another vessel; and that the people of neither knew any thing of what had befallen other, until the Indians [Calusa] armed themselves to go to the coast of Aís, when he saw them go and return with great wealth, in bars of silver and gold, and bags of reals and much clothing.[23]

In his memoir, Fontaneda alludes to the Aís as powerful tributaries of the Calusa, sharing loot plundered from Spanish shipwrecks with the Calusa as well as the Jeaga, Mayaca, and others.[24]

Once Menéndez destroyed the French settlement, he set to exploring the rest of Florida including the lower Indian River Lagoon, setting south with a "poorly provisioned army with 70 prisoners of war," to look for his son and to capture territory for the Spanish crown. Outlining his plan to King Philip in an October 15, 1565, report, ". . . the sea is like a river, I will search with the boats along the islands of Canaveral all Los Martires for the best harbor and fittest place to erect a fort." Spanish settlements traditionally thrived in densely inhabited Native lands and the Aís had the highest population on the Atlantic coast south of the Timucua settlements.[25] Along their journey south, the Spanish passed through a number of Native settlements, leaving behind "mirrors, knives, scissors, and bells, as a sign of good will."[26] Menéndez's plan was to erect forts all along the coast so that "at no time, within these 150 leagues that are between here and Havana, will the enemy be able to attack or fortify themselves; or lie in wait for convoys or ships from the Indies."[27] His plan for the Native Aís and others in South Florida included placing 150 soldiers, "for they are needed to keep watch over the (Aís) Indians who are very warlike."[28] His ultimate goal for the future Santa Lucia and Tequesta forts was to place a garrison of 300 men at each fort outfitted with small shallow-draft brigantines from St. Augustine and Havana. While the Spanish, alongside Indigenous allies, held North Florida, their influence in South Florida would prove more difficult to establish, highlighting the power of Native polities like the Aís.

Seeds of the failure could be found early in the disastrous expedition south into the Aís territory that began the Spanish settlement. Men suffered from hunger and fatigue, "in the course of this march, men dropped dead while still going forward," pushing eight leagues a day, gathering only "palmetto buds, cocoa-plums and prickly pears to eat and carry."[29] Arriving near what would become Vero Beach on November 4, 1565, Menéndez sent two captains to the Aís village on the barrier island, arriving before the cacique who "kissed them both on the mouth, which is the Indian's surest token of amity."[30] This unnamed cacique wore a piece of gold on his forehead, "worth more than 50 pesos," and his men wore smaller pieces of gold.[31] Menéndez left Captain Juan Vélez de Medrana in charge as civil governor and military commander of the district.[32] The friendly encounter lasted for a short time as the Spaniards built Santa Lucia further south in the Indian River Lagoon. During a few attacks shortly after the establishment of Santa Lucia, the Spanish estimated that warriors numbered between 500–1000 men, "the attacks continued daily, with the result that the men were no longer able to search for food and they began to starve." When a supply ship arrived, the desperate soldiers attempted to escape to Havana but were intercepted by Menéndez in the Straits of Florida. What happened to the mutineers is not known, however, Menéndez was determined to establish a mission and subdue the Aís.[33]

At issue for the Spaniards and the Aís were disagreements over shipwrecks and trade in salvaged materials from the many shipwrecks that dotted the lower Florida Atlantic coast.[34] The Aís, along with other Native polities of the Americas, did not need the Spanish at St. Augustine for survival, for they "had built a long and stable culture organized almost entirely around the sea. Their life was sustained by turtles, fish, and shellfish from the river, inlets, and ocean." What the Spanish provided, in the form of shipwrecks, was access to prestige items that the Aís could use in barter with other Native groups.[35] Menéndez hoped to subdue the Native Timucua, Surruque, Aís, Jeaga, Calusa, Tequesta, Mocama, Guale, and Orista by establishing missions and eventually build a school in Havana for the children of Native caciques while building forts and missions throughout the peninsula and west toward Mexico.[36] Indeed the Aís posed a great threat to Spanish dominion over the region as another fear emerged with rumors that the Aís provided refuge for runaway Black slaves. Menéndez found a shipwrecked mulatto living with the Calusa named Luis who at one point had partnered with Cosme Farfán, the commander of the Spanish treasure fleets of 1540, 1554, and 1555. Luis became fluent in the language of Aís and worked with Menéndez to negotiate the release of shipwrecked captives, including a Black woman and a mulatto "who had lived among the Calusa since they were children and who could hardly speak Spanish."[37] One anonymous shipwreck survivor wrote scathingly about his experience, "I dressed myself in their fashion and in every way adapted myself to their circumstances. My appearance soon took the form of a slovenly and idle Indian." Continuing on his condition, "My soul was like my body—miserable and ugly and I was always ready for the pleasures of vice. The Devil was my brother and I showed my fondness for him by defending him on all occasions when I sinned for pleasure and believed the ways of evil to be most glorious."[38] Once again, the colonial record reflects a narrative of paradise lost and the tenuous precarity of the human condition.

The Aís had greater access to Spanish shipwrecks than any other Florida Natives, the location of their settlements near a particularly treacherous stretch of the coast where many Spanish treasure ships on their way from the Caribbean back to Spain foundered on the reefs close to shore. Too far away from the Spanish settlements at St. Augustine to be under full Spanish control, nonetheless, "the Aís were subject to considerable Spanish influence but unlike many of the Timucua, they retained their independence and tribal culture."[39] The location of the Aís polity along the routes of the treasure fleet proved advantageous for them, as one shipwreck captive remembered, "they never lack silver, pearls or gold. The

Spaniards pay well for the use of the Florida passage; some losing there, even as I did, their shame and others going to their deaths."[40] The Aís would parcel out the gold and silver found in the ships to the Calusa and Timucua and present captives to other neighboring Native groups, for example the Jeaga might give a captive to the cacique of the Aís and the Aís might present a captive to the Tequesta. Evidence of this is present in both the Fontaneda narrative as well as the journal of Quaker shipwreck survivor, Jonathan Dickinson.[41]

Rather than understanding the violent response of the Aís, Tequesta, and others to the Spanish invasion as "acts of self defense," Spanish officials concluded that the Tequestas deserved conquest because they had "'blood lust for killing Christians.'"[42] Menéndez grew exasperated and violent toward the Native Floridians, encapsulated in his 1573 report entitled, "Damages and Murders Caused by the Coast Indians of Florida," where he described the territory as "full of danger and where many ships are lost coming from the Indies to these kingdoms." He recommended that "It is needful that this should be remedied by permitting that war be made upon them with rigor, a war of fire and blood, and those taken alive shall be sold as slaves; removing them from this country and taking them to neighboring islands."[43] King Philip and his council refused the request and Menéndez abandoned plans to settle South Florida, "the continual disturbances confined the settlers, and Menéndez himself to the poorer coastal soils. The Spaniards could not safely reside in the interior, where the land was well suited to pastoral and agricultural enterprises."[44] From there the legend of the Aís as "murderous wrecking and salvaging operations" as well as rumors of cannibalism would grow.[45] These presentations as an example of colonial rhetoric on Native Florida have deep repercussions, variances of these characterizations of the Aís and other Native Floridians reemerge in later colonial and American settler narratives.

Gonzalo Méndez de Canzo was the governor of La Florida from 1596 to 1603 and visited the coastal villages on his way to St. Augustine from Havana in 1596. Along the path he visited with caciques and provided gifts as he sought to reclaim Spanish shipwreck survivors. It appeared at first that the relationship with the Aís had improved when the Aís asked the governor to send a translator for their settlement. When Juan Ramirez de Contreras arrived to his post, however, the Surruque and Aís killed him along with the two Spanish mission Indians that accompanied him south. The Spanish retaliated quickly and violently against the Surruque, killing sixty while capturing fifty-four women and children. The cacique of Surruque went to St. Augustine to plead for the return of his people and the governor demanded that the Surruque cacique bring him the cacique of the Aís to answer for the attack. The Surruque cacique complied and when he returned with the Aís cacique and some twenty-two men, the Spanish imprisoned them all. Then the Spanish parceled out the Native women and children to married soldiers as domestic laborers and sent the Native men to the fields and to unmarried soldiers. Eventually, in compliance with Spanish laws regarding Indian slavery, survivors gained freedom on January 31, 1600, but a dangerous precedent was in place, "pacification by terror."[46] All future attempts by the Spanish to assure Aís allegiance involved the forced compliance of caciques through capture and gift giving before returning the men to their home territories.[47]

The Aís relationship with the Spanish was nearly always hesitant and wary yet they actively traded with other rival European groups. Advantageously located, the Aís traded ambergris with French corsairs, and interacted with English and Dutch pirates moving through the region. Rumors abounded that the Aís actively aided Dutch pirates in 1627 that attacked a Spanish frigate near Cape Canaveral and anchored near an Aís village.[48] Harboring runaway enslaved peoples continued as well. Pedro de Ybarra was the Governor of Florida from 1603 to 1605 when the Aís had two runaway enslaved Africans in their settlements that they refused to return to the Spanish. Seven originally ran away, the Spanish recaptured five, but these two remained in Aís territory and had married Aís women.[49] Despite Ybarra sending gifts over several years, they only returned the enslaved men when Ensign Juan Rodríguez de Cartaya took the "Capitan Chico" (assistant chief) hostage and threatened to take the "Capitan Grande" (cacique) hostage as well.[50]

Despite their ambivalence about trading partners, the Aís did send some warriors north to St. Augustine to assist the Spanish against threats from the English, though rumors of the threat the Aís posed remained in the Spanish mind. A soldier, Alvaro Mexia, reported on the Aís territory in July 1605 to Governor Ybarra that he labeled as "A handy and useful guide which describes truthfully in every detail the rivers, channels, lagoons, woodlands, settlements, harbors, shoals, and camps from St. Augustine to the Bar of Aís."[51] As a result of Mexia's trip, the cacique of the Aís visited St. Augustine and the relationship between the two groups entered into a more tranquil period as Ybarra noted, "Since then the Caciques come and go as they please, and our soldiers do the same, by seas as well as by land, with the greatest Security."[52] The Aís utilized their location as an advantage, emphasizing their access to knowledge in their trip to St. Augustine, and their ability to act as "gatekeepers of information."[53] That the Aís were informed and aware of the game afoot surprised the Spanish at first and the Aís worked to maintain their role in the information networks of the Atlantic and American Southeast.

In 1696, English Quaker Jonathan Dickinson found himself shipwrecked in the land of the Aís. Detailing his more than 200-mile march north to St. Augustine, Dickinson provides the most significant English record of the Native peoples south of St. Augustine as he noted that he believed the Aís feared the Spanish.[54] Dickinson's account reads as an act of divine intervention, a quasi-hagiography propaganda of the hardships of this pilgrim into the wilderness, as the Quakers quickly published the journal in 1699, reissuing editions at least fifteen times, "often in little leather bound volumes tooled in gold to be treasure and handed down from generations."[55] Writing in the introduction, Leonard W. Labaree opines, "all should agree that this journal is a memorable account of hardship and suffering bravely borne, and of a stirring episode from America's early years."[56]

The Dickinson narrative is a classic example of the colonial gaze and settler memory. Dickinson, a Quaker merchant with Atlantic connections, sailed on the barkentine *Reformation* from Jamaica to Pennsylvania on September 2, 1696, with his wife and infant son, a family member, a Quaker missionary, eleven enslaved Africans and Indians, and nine mariners. A month into their voyage a storm struck, washing their hens, sheep, and hogs overboard as the vessel ran aground off the coast of Florida in the early morning of October 3. Twenty-four castaways made it ashore where they were soon met by two Native men that Dickinson labeled as Jobes. All told, the survivors would cross through the territories of Spanish mission Indians at Santa Lucia, the Aís polity, the Jeaga, and the Surruque. It was the Jeaga that would first encounter the Dickinson party and seek to salvage the wreck. Dickinson came with preconceived negative understandings of the Native people in Florida, reflected in his commentary on their treatment of survivors, "we communed together and considered our condition, being amongst a barbarous people such as were generally accounted man-eaters, believing those two were gone to alarm their people. We sat ourselves down, expecting cruelty and hard death, except it should please the Almighty God to work wonderfully for our deliverance."[57] Spanish colonial commentaries had a long-term effect and Dickinson's writings are an example of the literary tradition and form of the travel narrative, whereby, "the travel narrative would appear to be a literary form in which the possibility of fiction is inherent. To the extent that the point of view dramatizes itself through self-revelation and through the conscious structuring of material, the work becomes a dramatic entity."[58] And in this case, Dickinson is presenting his errand into the wilderness in the genre of settler innocence in a manner akin to a Christian hagiography, should he or his family become martyrs in the process.

Through Dickinson's deeply biased perceptions and understanding of Native people, terms like "bloody minded creatures" and "savage men" appear frequently as he documents in close detail the mistreatment the group received at the hands of Natives they called the Santaluces. North of the Jeaga, the Santaluces set upon the group and took their clothing and forced the group to walk a gauntlet of taunts, stones, and blows, "vehemently foaming at mouth, like wild boars, and taking their bows and arrows with other weapons, cried out *Nickaleer, Nickaleer.*" Nickaleer was their word for the English. Once at the Santaluces settlement, Dickinson alleged that they poured sea sand into his child's mouth.[59] These violent encounters played alongside frequent contradictions as Dickinson also wrote that the cacique's wife came to the aid of Dickinson's wife, pulling the sand from the infant's mouth. While Dickinson disparaged the living conditions of the cacique's house, noting spiders, scorpions, and vermin, he also noted the next day that the cacique was "looking on us pleasantly, made presents to some of us, especially to my wife; he gave her a parcel of shellfish, which are known by the name of clams."[60] Later in their journey, in a separate encounter, the cacique of the Aís showed the Dickinson party his "compassion on us," by washing and tending to Mary Dickinson's sunburned and injured feet.[61] A group of Spanish soldiers found the surviving party on November 12 and assisted them to the Surruque border as the survivors continued their long trek north to St. Augustine, five died from exposure on November 23 before arriving in St. Augustine where the "townspeople lodged, clothed, and fed them, and the governor kindly arranged for them to travel up to Charleston."[62]

Language and word choice is important within this narrative. To understand why Native people were initially hostile to the Dickinson survivors one must consider the lived experience of Florida Natives in the age of colonization. Indian violence and hostility could easily be attributed to naturally healthy fear of enslavement, destruction of their communities, and disease. Prior experiences with pirates and colonizers thus colored the treatment afforded interloping foreigners as Native peoples "were very knowledgeable about different European nations and distinguished between them. These distinctions greatly influenced the Native Americans' reaction to the English castaways huddled around the shambles of the Reformation."[63]

Native allies provided protection and support of the survivors, yet the Dickinson narrative provided an opportunity for a document of Christian resiliency, his "struggle in the wilderness, a release from bondage or a goal attained, thus became for the devout seventeenth century traveler such as Dickinson a significant demonstration of the workings of Divine Providence."[64] He discusses kindness and generosity but his underlying judgment and fear prevents him from seeing their humanity as Dickinson also crafted his tale like a captivity narrative, of redemption from submission to the ways of Native peoples, "beyond the fear that they were to be 'shot, burnt, and eaten,' Dickinson's major apprehension was the fate of his infant son if the parents were to die. 'One thing did seem more grievous to me and my wife than any other thing,' he wrote, 'that our child would be kept alive, and bred up as one of these people; when this thought did arise it wounded us deep.'"[65] Scholar Jason Daniels recently re-examined the Dickinson narrative and argues, "Native Americans did not treat the English poorly at all. In fact, the castaways simply experienced a complex expression of a standard protocol developed by the Native Americans after dealing with decades of shipwrecks." The Native Floridians "cowed castaways into submission regardless of national origin," following up by determining the cost/benefit analysis of keeping them alive and then finally, taking whatever of value they could salvage from the shipwreck and the survivors themselves for trade and barter.[66]

Native Florida would soon see an influx of war and violence as the various European powers struggled over their Atlantic holdings with the War of Spanish Succession that engulfed in Europe in late 1701 and soon spread to the Americas. Known as Queen Anne's War in the American theater, English troops armed with Native allies marched on Spanish St. Augustine from South Carolina and attacked Native Floridians. Hostilities between the warring colonists and their Native allies led to the destruction of the Apalachee missions (1704); attacks on Pensacola (1707); a siege on Charles

Town, South Carolina (1706); and minor skirmishes spreading as far west as French colonial trade in Mobile, Alabama (1709). For the Natives of South Florida like the Aís, the greatest threat were the armed Native polities moving south in a gore of rampant slave raiding and destructive assaults, disrupting the delicate balance these Florida groups maintained with European powers. As they and others faced displacement their traditional patterns of mobility, became "far more extreme and sudden."[67]

Between 1704 and 1711, the Aís polity were the victim of slave raids to waves of violence as the Yamasee they raided south through Florida enslaving Native peoples for sale to English traders in Charleston, South Carolina. A map from Carolina trader Thomas Nairne from 1711 indicates the Yamasee canoe landing, whereby, "Here the Car[o]line Indians leave th[eir] Canoes when they go to war against the Floridians." In a recent study of archaeological evidence, Alexander Y. Sweeney also documented the presence of a St. Johns pottery vessel at Altamaha Town, that may have come from the Aís and contained plunder from the raids.[68] While many early studies of the region indicated that enslavement depopulated the region, more recent studies have focused on the coalescent groups that emerged because of the upheaval, groups that survived the trade and continue to live throughout the American Southeast. Ponce de León was not the first European in the Florida peninsula, since 1492, Spaniards went throughout the greater Caribbean, Gulf of Mexico, and north along the coast of Florida in search of "slaves, fish, water, lumber and other commodities." Yet de León receives credit because of the doctrine of discovery.[69] Slavers likely knew for at least a decade that there was a large body of land north of Cuba that was inhabited by "numerous hostile natives."[70] Although Queen Isabella of Spain at first outlawed the enslavement of Native peoples in the conquest, the distance of the Atlantic Ocean, dubious interpretations of just war, and the lucrative nature of the trade allowed for large-scale enslavement of Native peoples of the Americas to thrive.[71]

The Aís towns numbered close to forty-five by the early eighteenth century as they maintained existing and forged new trade and kin networks throughout Florida, including with the Timucua to the north and Calusa to the southwest. The slave trade changed everything. Forced to disperse, some groups fragmented, others tried to coalesce with larger groups, others sought to live in much smaller communities. While the Natives of South Florida had enjoyed some degree of autonomy for generations of European contact, "the violence of Indian slaving collapsed distance and bridged space."[72] Beginning in the late seventeenth century with the efforts of Governor Ybarra, some of the Aís elite had softened their stance on the Spanish and sought their assistance during the slave raids, particularly the 1703 raid led by Captain Thomas Nairne of South Carolina directly into Aís territory. As a result of the chaos, some of the Aís and others moved to St. Augustine for safety, returning after the outbreak of the Yamasee War halted extensive slave raids south from 1715 to 1717.[73]

On July 31, 1715, eleven ships under the command of Juan Esteban de Ubilla, heavily laden with treasure destined for the coffers of Spanish, sank off the coast of what would become the town of Sebastian and the north edge of Vero Beach. The upheaval of the Spanish War of Succession and the subsequent American theater of Queen Anne's War halted the treasure fleets, known as the *Flota de Indias,* thus the eleven ships comprising the 1715 plate fleet were heavily overloaded with cargo and 2500 crew and passengers. This special treasure armada consisted of a combined fleet including the annual *Galeones de Tierra Firma* out of the port of Cartagena, Colombia led by Captain General Don Antonio de Echerverz y Zubiza, and the *Flota* out of Vera Cruz, Mexico. The fleet comprised accumulated wealth mined from the Americas (including the Native manned silver mines of Potosí in South America) for the last three years. The two fleets met in Havana where they were delayed for two months while officials carefully took inventory of the cargo including eight chests of gold and jewels: wedding gifts intended for the new wife of King Philip V of Spain, the Duchess of Parma. They finally set sail on July 24 in the middle of Atlantic hurricane season. A pilot ship captained by Antoine Darie, the French ship *Grifon,* veered off course and thus avoided the hurricane that destroyed the other eleven ships as over a thousand passengers perished off the coast of Florida.[74] Immediate salvage efforts and the archaeology these efforts left behind provides insight into the Aís polity during this crucial period.

Synthesizing the archaeology of the wreckage site with an ethnohistorical approach, historian Alejandra Dubcovsky explores the impact this site likely had for Native peoples and the role they played in salvage. Within just a few weeks of the wreck, the survivors put together a makeshift salvage camp to recover as much of the cargo as possible, working against the weather, pirates, and the ocean tides to recover "roughly half of the treasure . . . until rough currents pushed the exposed vessels too far from the coast and submerged the cargo too deep to reach."[75] Once they abandoned the site, the wreck became the stuff of legends in Florida, a "fable of lost riches" until 1942 when Charles D. Higgs, a retired astronomer and amateur historian, found the site. Due to the active threat of German submariners off the coast of Florida during World War II, little attention was paid to the wreckage site until Kip Wagner, a contractor, found Spanish coins along the beach and archaeologist Hale Smith formally excavated the site in 1946 (Site 8-IR-24).[76]

Research on the site has largely focused on the treasure and the Europeans involved. Dubcovsky's recent work, however, reflects on the important Native story present in the physical record.[77] Don Francisco Salmon survived the 1715 wreck and wrote two letters to Florida's governor, Francisco de Corcoles y Martinez, the first detailing the difficulties the survivors were facing and the second detailed the amount of treasure lost that needed to be salvaged immediately. The treasure was more important as "rather than asking for food or rescue, Salmon demanded pistols, axes, rakes, and shovels."[78] Havana officials received word of the disaster within two weeks and sent a mission led by Don Juan del Hoyo Solórzano to lead the salvage effort, bringing with him "grappling hooks, chains, empty chests, long handle rakes, and diving bells," and thirty experienced divers from the Caribbean that included Native workers.[79] The exact location of the wreck was known to the salvagers who began work in earnest, sending Natives into the depths "using rocks as weight belts" and a device called a "Bermuda tub" a primitive diving bell made from an open-ended wine cask that allowed for an hours' time at the wreck site, "until the air in the tub 'fouled' (exhausted its oxygen) and had to be hauled to the surface."[80]

The salvage site left behind a rich material record as it was in operation for "about two years and housed Cuban soldiers, Indigenous divers from the Caribbean, and some of the Indian militia from St. Augustine."[81] The site offers insight into camp life with fragments of wine bottles, remnants of iron tools, like knives and parts of flintlocks, dice, food waste including fish bones, and pottery. The pottery is of particular interest when considering the role of the Aís and their movement throughout Florida. Pottery sherds found at the site are San Marcos Plain and San Marcos stamped pottery, which was the traditional pottery style of the Guales who lived along the coast of Florida. Thanks to "trade, intermarriage, diplomacy, or some combination of these factors," the San Marcos style expanded among the Guales to Mocamas, Timucuas, Yamasee, and other Native groups of the Southeast. Other evidence of Native influence at the salvage camp included "several carefully punctured musket balls and modified Spanish coins," that Native actors repurposed as "decoration or jewelry."[82] The presence of San Marcos pottery as well as other items that indicate Native Floridian engagement "unsettle both the timelessness and the subsequent erasure of Native history from south Florida." The pottery was likely made by Aís who emigrated to St. Augustine and returned to the lower Indian River Lagoon.[83] Despite an attack by English pirate, Henry Jennings, in January 1716, two vessels heavily laden with salvaged treasure headed to Spain in August 1716.[84]

Documented European evidence of the Aís becomes sparce in the mid-eighteenth century, however, a 1737 Spanish royal engineer's report on the problem of defending Florida against other European powers recommended, "the expediency of establishing a colony of 200 at Aís."[85] In June 24, 1743, two Jesuit priests (Jose Maria Monaco and Jose Javier de Alana) set out from Havana to a mission among the Tequesta and heard tales that the Tequesta had gone north to Santa Lucia to celebrate a peace with "the chiefs of four or five villages of maimios, santaluzes, mayacas, and some other tribes." When the priests arrived, the Native Floridians were hesitant to accept the mission, accepting the provisions and goods from the priests, but wary of being tributaries to the King of Spain, thus sacrificing their autonomy. The priests built a mission raising a flag above the small fort on August 8, 1743. With little support for their effort from the government in Havana, the fort quickly failed as the Spanish feared the fort could be used by the English or Native foes and slave raiders. In about 1750, "a band of Creek Indians on a raid into south Florida passed up the St. Johns River to its headwaters and portaged through Aís."[86]

Some Spanish stayed in the lower Indian River Lagoon, fishing in the fall and winter, occasionally in danger of attack by Native raiders from the north.[87] Settler records during this time indicated that the Aís may have taken refuge with the Calusa, their former tributaries, in southwest Florida.[88] In 1738, the Spanish established Gracia Real de Santa Teresa de Mose (Fort Mose) as the first free Black settlement in North America, located north near St. Augustine. By 1740, General James Oglethorpe, of English Georgia, attacked northern Florida, centering his assault on Fort Mose and St. Augustine with the assistance of Creek allies, including their mico, Cowkeeper. At the end of the Seven Years' War in 1763, Spain traded Florida to England in exchange for Havana; the English subsequently divided the Florida territory into East and West Florida. Scholars of Florida and the Southeast have often erroneously claimed that the peninsula was depopulated in 1763 with the Spanish retreat to Cuba at the end of the Seven Years' War, one scholar going as far as to the say that "for the Florida Indians it was the end of time" and that "no descendants of the original Florida Indians have survived."[89] This is a common mistake referenced in Florida scholarship; however, the documents are referring merely to mission Natives at St. Augustine, not to all Natives of Florida. More recent scholarship by scholars such as Denise Bossy and Andrew Frank highlights the myriad ways that coalescent groups retained members of the original Florida Natives as they became new polities in response to settler and colonial movements. Frank argues against the extinction narrative for Florida Natives, "Floridians too frequently understand the modern Seminoles as migrants rather than as Indigenous to the region." Scholars have ignored the connections that the modern Seminole have to the Indigenous polities of precolonial and colonial Florida. The Seminole, for example, moved throughout South Florida in the eighteenth century into Aís, Jeaga, and Tequesta territory, on their way to trade with Cuba, and traded "deerskins, honey, beeswax, dried fish, and various fruits to fishers who offered guns, metal goods, rum, cloth, coffee and other items that they Seminoles could not produce for themselves."[90]

Some of the knowledge about the Florida peninsula in the late colonial era comes from English colonist and botanist William Bartram who began his four-year journey through the American Southeast in 1773 along with other European naturalists, surveyors, and entrepreneurs evaluating the territory and its people for commercial potential. There is often a gap in Florida history between the initial fall of the Spanish colony in 1763 and the American takeover of the region in the nineteenth century; however, late European settlement in the 1760s allowed for a series of failed British plantations to emerge in the upper Indian River Lagoon and explorations by William Bartram and Bernard Romans.[91] Bartram and Romans are the most extensive English chroniclers of the entire Florida peninsula in the eighteenth century, as British colonists and the empire sought to ascertain what they could gain from the soils and peoples of Florida. Bernard Romans was in the region in 1760 and mentioned the 1715 treasure fleet wreckage in his 1775 publication, *A Concise History of East and West Florida* where he described the Indian River as *Aísa Hatcha*, Deer River, exploring its topography, flora and fauna, in detail. "During the season," he wrote, "the loggerhead turtles land here in vast multitudes, to lay their eggs, which the bears profit by." Speaking of the multitude of deer and turkeys, he commented on his Spanish guide who informed him that, "he had formerly been taken by the savages, and by them carried a prisoner, in a canoe, by way of this river, to their settlements on the banks of the lake." Romans more than likely describes the region surrounding Lake Okeechobee.[92]

Bartram made his way throughout the Southeast between 1773 and 1777. An erroneously placed highway marker in Sebastian, Florida, noted that Sebastian was the southernmost point that Bartram traveled, although closer inspection of Bartram's travels places him farther north in the Indian River Lagoon with most of his Florida explorations centered around what was then known as East Florida and near Seminole settlements in what would become Payne's Prairie and areas around the Alachua and Suwanee Rivers. Visiting the capital of the Alachua Seminoles in North Florida, Bartram described a prosperous agricultural settlement with herds of cattle and beautiful horses.[93] While Bartram likely never came near the lower Indian River Lagoon, his Edenic writings on the natural landscape of the Southeast and Native peoples deeply influenced settler memory and the historiography particularly as it related to the idea of the noble savage as will be seen in later chapters. He certainly inspired Washington Irving, who not only sparked the Ponce de León myth but romantically wrote of the Seminole as "leading a pleasant, indolent life, in a climate that required little shelter or clothing, and the spontaneous fruits of the earth furnished subsistence without toil."[94]

British settlement of the lower Indian River and South Florida was tentative and fleeting. On May 18, 1803, Spanish East Florida resident John H. McIntosh, held grants for several parcels of land in the upper Indian River Lagoon but never pursued title because he participated in a rebellion against Spain. Loyal Spanish soldiers received similar grants that they never pursued in 1816 and 1818.[95] While the Europeans and Americans paid little attention to the Indian River Lagoon, coalescent Native communities thrived in the northern Panhandle and south of Lake Okeechobee, expanding their territories in the verdant landscape by raising cattle and continuing centuries-long traditions of the Native Southeast.

What is the impact of the Spanish colonial period on American settler memory? In the nineteenth century, American readers learned more about Florida from fictionalized myths and legends created by Washington Irving in his 1831 publication *Voyages and Discoveries of the Companions of*

Columbus, which was rather loosely based on Irving's analysis of Herrera's *Historia.* That Irving consulted the Spanish sources gave the myth a veil of authenticity, as he wrote eight chapters about de León's experiences in the Caribbean and later in Florida. His consultation of the primary sources, however, proved shallow, as "he was infamous for the liberties he took with the facts," and those liberties took root in the historical imagination of American chroniclers and settlers, "when it comes to New York, no one considers fictional characters like Rip Van Winkle or Ichabod Crane to be actual men who lived and breathed," yet, in the case of Florida, thanks to Irving and the Florida booster and tourist industry, the fictional account of the explorer searching for a fountain of youth becomes enshrined as "history."[96]

This influence and how entrenched it became in settler memory can be seen in the 1869 publication *A Guidebook of Florida and the South for Tourists, Invalids and Emigrants,* whose editor, William M. Goza, noted, "a rumor was abroad among the natives of the Bahamas, of Cuba, and even of Yucatan and Honduras, that in a land to the north was a fountain of water, whose crystal waves restored health to the sick and youth to the aged." Intrigued by this promise, Goza argued that many "credulous islanders, forsaking their homes," ventured north and speaking to the audience of his publication, he urged that "the tide of wanderers in search of the healing and rejuvenating waters still set thitherward . . . one returns to his own, restored to vigor and life. Intelligence now endorses what superstition long believed."[97] A latter-day settler of the Indian River Lagoon in 1891 agreed, "I dreamed, as all the weakly and all the woe-be-gone in physical suffering have dreamt, of the fountain of youth, of the garden of the Hesperides." Summing up the "glory of the Indian River climate, it is as sweetest honey kissed by beauty's rosy lips."[98] Enshrined with the barest hint of historical truth, a chronicler of the encounter for the Florida Historical Society opined in 1924, "Florida, a land of perpetual summer, began its historical existence wrapped in romance and adventure . . . The whole country decked in the fresh bloom of spring charmed his senses."[99]

What we know about the peoples of South Florida and the Indian River Lagoon has been limited to the fragmented and biased written record and remaining archaeological evidence. Unfortunately, development of settler Florida in the late nineteenth and throughout the twentieth century has led to the destruction of many of the Native shell middens and town sites. This included the use of the shell materials for the paving of roads and the

Indian mound on the property of J. R. Pierson, 1936. State Archives of Florida, Florida Memory. https://www.floridamemory.com/items/show/125339, accessed 30 March 2023.

leveling of shell mounds for the construction of houses, including the 1884 House of Refuge No. 5 built at the Indian River Inlet.[100]

Plainly speaking, the lack of European records of Native peoples does not indicate that Native history in the region is lacking, new scholarship that includes the oral testimony and history of Native peoples alongside the European record and the physical evidence has brought forth a more nuanced understanding of the entire peninsula of La Florida, its peoples, and the vibrant and lasting history of Native Florida. Within this framework, we must consider one of the most important discoveries in Florida, Vero Man, and the settler narrative and debate about Native Florida that ensued.

The discovery of material remains known as Vero Man quickly became enmeshed with the Garden of Eden and paradise. Indian River Farms Company workers dredging the region to reclaim the marshlands for agriculture discovered the site in 1913. In the process, these workers found late Pleistocene human and animal remains.[101] The first discovery in the main canal included a wide variety of megafauna: mammoths, mastodons, saber-toothed tigers, bear-sized mega-sloths, and an unknown species of tapir. State geologist Dr. E. H. Sellards, recognizing the importance of these discoveries suggested that the workers collect these bones and keep an eye out for any human remains as well, which the workers found in 1915 along the wall of the canal.

By 1916, Dr. Sellards was in collaboration with local Indian River farm workers and citizens of Vero—including Frank Ayers and Isaac Wells as they began to look for more human remains. Controversy soon followed the discovery as Sellards put forth his argument that this site of human and animal occupation was at least 14,000 years old, refuting accepted contemporary scientific beliefs that no humans were in North America before 4–6,000 years prior. The dispute over dates reflects another method of interpreting history as shaped by presentist goals and motivations, and in this case, Sellards's greatest antagonist was Aleš Hrdlička, the infamous curator of the Physical Anthropology department at the Smithsonian Institution National Museum of Natural History.[102] In a series of publications and private letters, Hrdlička and Sellards sparred divisively over the importance of the discovery, the dating of the site, and the way the workers preserved the canal site and recovered the bones.

Close-up of stratum no. 2 at Vero where human remains were found. Photo by Elias Howard Sellards, 1916. State Archives of Florida, Florida Memory, https://www.floridamemory.com/items/show/124621, accessed 30 March 2023.

At the heart of this debate for the boosters and Florida public, however, was the invigoration of the colonial era myth of Florida as an Edenic paradise and their opportunity to showcase Vero on the national and international stage. While Florida settlers were digging up evidence of Native Florida, instead of telling the story of Native Florida, they instead took this as an opportunity to erase the Indigenous past. Framing the remains to tell the story of a Judeo-Christian past and the Garden of Eden, one newspaper from nearby Fellsmere excitedly reported, "We stand by Vero in her contention that here in this part of the state was located the Garden of Eden and that the skeletons found at that point were those of Adam and Eve."[103] By highlighting the paradise to be reclaimed in Florida, developers were interconnecting to an older settler narrative of Florida, but as this volume highlights, they are contributing to a pattern of settler erasure of Native stories, while at the same time utilizing Native history for their own means. Lost in all this booster enthusiasm and showmanship is the history of the Native polities that came to inhabit and control the Indian River Lagoon in the centuries that followed, a story that deserves to be told in all its depth and fascinating detail. Rooted in these stories, however, is the Garden of Eden, paradises, and lagoons, all intertwined with the myths of settler Florida, the aforementioned legacy of Washington Irving's interpretations of a Spanish past, and a continuation of Native erasure from the narrative.

Another example of the legacy of mythologizing the Spanish past and Edenic natural Florida can be found in the Florida Historical Society and their celebration of the 500th anniversary of Ponce de León's landing. Celebrations included a staged reenactment and debate of where he landed and settler memory performance of the landing. At issue was whether he landed closer to St. Augustine or Melbourne Beach, 147 miles distance, and the difference of landing in the territory of the Aís or the Timucua. The debate about landing has inspired popular conjecture and scholarship alike. Florida scholar Jerald T. Milanich undertook a reexamination of the Freducci map in order to ascertain possible Ponce de León landing sites, allowing for some interpretation over sightings between Matanzas Inlet and Mosquito Inlet to the north before moving along to the south to the Rio de Canoas, the Indian River, and the Cabo de Corrientes.[104] Unsurprisingly, the Florida Historical Society production contributes to the vanishing/lasting Indian narrative of Florida as the testimony of the fictional Aís queen laments, "when Ponce de León came here in 1513, it was the end of my people's existence," and stage notes include directions that "the audience should feel the tension between them." This portrayal of Native Floridians additionally factors in the environmental issues facing the state of Florida when the queen remarks on the vastly changed landscape, "All I can tell you is that he first landed to the north of where he encountered my people. Even if you could describe the area where he landed, who could find it today?" Continuing, she says, "You have changed the course of great rivers, chopped down expansive forest, . . . if you continue down this path, you will no longer be able to call this land the 'land of flowers.'"[105] While this could easily be interpreted as fitting into the Ecological Indian trope, a common stereotype of Native peoples as the first environmentalists, European and American settlers have significantly altered the landscape and Florida waterways.

Florida's narrative is often lost in myth and settler memory, with visions of Old Florida stripped of its Native past, and its natural environment shadowed by Edenic dreams. Invasive species such as Australian pine as well as reclamation projects dot the Indian River Lagoon region with canals and new farmlands that drastically changed the coastal environment. Runoff from sugar plantations into Lake Okeechobee has proven disastrous for the Everglades. Successive hurricanes, amplified by coastal erosion, have drastically altered the landscape as well, erasing barrier islands and shifting the coastline. Turbulence in Florida, for both settlers and Natives, has a long history, both natural and man-made. The British and American era of Florida history would be no different.

2
Settlers and Settler Colonialism of the Eighteenth and Nineteenth Centuries

In the late colonial period (1750–1775), the American Southeast experienced disruptive growths in trade, European settlement, Native migration and displacement, and the upheaval of the plantation economy emerging in the Atlantic colonial world. European engagements with Natives in the Southeast at first centered around trade in goods and skins, eventually leading to the exchange of enslaved Natives that provided the labor for further trade and the Atlantic plantation economy. Native peoples adapted to the arrival of Europeans and instigated trade relationships, acting as powerful brokers and intermediaries with European parties throughout the Atlantic woodlands and adopting new modes of production in their communities as they became cattle herdsmen and at times owned enslaved peoples to produce crops and goods like their European neighbors.

European movement and settlement of the Southeast included a constant influx of goods and traders, meaning that involvement in the trade had dramatic effects on Native populations. Trading increased long-distance Indian migrations. Some groups moved to more advantageous regions to coalesce with others due to population loss or sought protection by joining a more powerful polity, typically with a known tributary or familiar ally. Trade throughout the colonial period became a weapon that Native peoples and colonists could use against one another in a series of hostilities. European trade radically restructured the physical and political orientation of the Native South.

At the heart of several conflicts was the trade in Indigenous peoples. While present from the beginning of English settlement, by the 1660s the English escalated the process in the Southeast, selling thousands of Native peoples into enslavement. Traders shipped most of the enslaved peoples to the Caribbean sugar islands, like Bermuda, Barbados, and Jamaica. Armed with European guns, raids began locally in Virginia but soon spread throughout the Southeast. The 1670 settlement of the Carolina colony ushered in several decades of massive enslavement with the assistance of Native allies such as the Westo and Yamasee, armed by a group of Carolina settlers called the Goose Creek Men.[1] Indian slave raids led to conflicts such as the Susquehannock War in Virginia in 1676, showcasing how Native peoples sought to push back against European settlers throughout the seventeenth and eighteenth centuries in a series of violent conflicts.

Due to these Native pushbacks and increasing colonial wars between the English and Spanish, most European settlement in Florida during the eighteenth century clustered around St. Augustine. North of the Florida settlements, violence erupted once again because of the Native slave trade and settler encroachment. Throughout the colonial period, waves of migration took place in the Native South due to the destabilizing effects of the trade era, especially Native slavery. From 1710–1715, the Tuscarora War in North Carolina resulted in the destruction of many settler plantations and the death of naturalist, trader, and writer, John Lawson. The Tuscarora eventually left North Carolina and emigrated north to join the Haudenosaunee alliance in upper New York. Meanwhile in 1715, the Yamasee War began in South Carolina because of Yamasee trade debts in a corrupt market, treaty violations by English traders and settlers as well as enslavement. This war involved the Yamasee, Creek, Catawba, Apalachee, Apalachicola, Yuchi, Savannah River Shawnee, Congaree, Waxhaw, Pee Dee, Cheraw, and more. Hundreds of colonists died in the war and many Native and European settlements burned including the trade town of Pocataligo. The Yamasee War ended when Cherokees entered the fray against their Native rivals in early 1716, turning the tide of the war in favor of the colonists. Remnant Yamasee dispersed into the lower Southeast, including Florida. To the west in 1729, the Natchez revolted against the French in Mississippi because of French seizure of sacred land (White Apple Village) and the enslavement of Natchez and later Chickasaw peoples that they sold to French sugar plantations in the in the 1730s. All these events, while seemingly peripheral to Florida, had deep impacts on both Native and Settler societies in the American South, conflicts that would soon further threaten Indigenous Florida.

While the English and French colonies grappled with Native wars and the creation of plantation economies, the Spanish empire and its Atlantic world holdings fell into deep decline by the seventeenth century. St. Augustine was a faltering outpost, a poorly equipped garrison unable to prevent the English encroachments from the north nor the French encroachments from the west. As discussed in the previous chapter, the English-sponsored Indian slave trade deeply affected the Native Southeast and Florida in particular. During Queen Anne's War (1702–1713, War of Spanish Succession) Native polities of the Southeast set clear alliances, the Spanish with the Apalachee and Timucua; the English with the Yamasee, Creeks, and Chickasaws; and the French with the Choctaws. The Creeks came out of this alliance as one of the most powerful Native confederacies in the Southeast. Themselves a coalescent group of Muskogean speakers, the Creeks made peace with the French, maintained a loose alliance with the English, and later even sent a delegation to Mexico City to establish a peace treaty with the Spanish.[2] For the next several decades, Native peoples and settlers kept an uneasy peace until the Seven Years' War (1756–1763) broke open new hostilities in the South as trade agreements and boundaries of settlement once again fell asunder to greed and avarice culminating in the Cherokee War that devastated the western settlements of the Carolina colony in the 1760s.

The late eighteenth century saw several futile attempts by Anglo settlers to move into Florida and expand beyond the region of St. Augustine and the Panhandle. A few Anglo settlers considered moving into South Florida and the Indian River Lagoon to plant cash crops such as rice, indigo, and sugar. Andrew Turnbull founded New Smyrna, Florida, in the upper Indian River Lagoon in 1768 with grand plans to produce indigo on his 40,000-acre grant. While settlers found fledgling success in the production of indigo, hemp, and sugarcane, these crops soon fell to disease and settlers faced attack by Native raiders throughout the region, keen on protecting the territory for themselves. Turnbull's plant production also brought with it deep changes to the natural environment, including imported cochineal insects and an "extensive network of canals that crisscrossed the settlement, drained 3,107 acres of wetlands, and established a precedent that would characterize the Indian River for over 200 years," setting the standard of land reclamation that would allow the region to thrive in the nineteenth century. By 1777, however, the colony failed entirely. It would be two hundred years before Florida's agribusinesses would dominate the market.[3]

Understanding the history of trade and violence helps to illuminate settler motivations and narratives that they brought with them into the Early Republic and into the new American state as they sought to expand into La Florida. It is at once a history of the prosperity of the trade and a history of misalliances, whereby leaders on both sides not only failed to prevent the outbreaks of violence and to mediate peace when violence erupted—they failed to agree and uphold treaty relationships that could prevent further violence and chaos. A major part of the problem was the settlers who flagrantly disregarded treaty obligations, trade regulations, and settlement boundaries, dating to the first European settlements in the Atlantic woodlands. With American independence from Britain, settlers consistently pressed the boundaries of settlement west into Indian territory resulting in a series of conflicts from the Appalachian plateaus, the Ohio River Valley south into the lower Mississippi River valley, and, eventually into Florida in the three Seminole Wars. And as land replaced the slave and skins trade as the most valuable commodity in the American Southeast, settlers had little incentive to keep positive relationships with Native peoples.[4]

Plans to settle Florida hit a standstill during the American Revolution as Florida remained loyal to England. In the Treaty of Paris, 1783, England ceded Florida back to Spain and the flamboyant and ambitious William Augustus Bowles arrived in south Florida in 1783 and in 1788 proclaimed himself the "Director General of the State of Muscogee."[5] The American Revolution had completely disrupted trade in Native territories. In the Southeast, many white traders who had professional and personal alliances with powerful Native polities sided with England and the Loyalists. When the American Rebels won, only one British trade company remained in the Southeast. Panton, Leslie and Company stayed on at Pensacola in Spanish territory, changing their name in 1805 to John Forbes and Company. All trade with Native nations in the new American state would be a part of the Factory System in the US Treasury Department, a plan to establish government-controlled forts in Native territories to maintain Native allegiance to the United States rather than to European powers and expand American-held territories in the Native South.[6]

These settlers desired more Native land in the South because of the development of the cotton gin and the introduction of short staple cotton that could grow in the interior lands of Georgia, Alabama, Mississippi, and Tennessee. To aid in the process, governmental programs sought to fulfill settler land desires and at the same time, figure out what to do with Native populations. What has come to be known as the Civilization Program began with federal agents sent to the various southeastern polities to teach Native peoples to be yeoman farmers on diminished plots of land. Assigned as the Indian agent to the southeastern groups, Benjamin Hawkins exemplified the sentiments prevalent at the time. While he "attributed to Creek men and women the same human traits and intelligence as any other people," he also was "ethnocentric and condescending." As a man inspired by the Enlightenment, Hawkins "believed that Western civilization was the pinnacle of human achievement and that through science, human reason, and habits of thrift, sobriety, and hard work, humankind as a whole could be lifted to this higher plane." To Hawkins, he was making a pledge to guide "the Indians along the path to U.S. citizenry."[7] The promise made to Native leaders was that they would retain their diminished lands and progressively intermarry and join Anglo-American culture. After the Louisiana Purchase in 1803, however, officials in the federal government increasingly began eyeing those western lands as an answer by removing Native peoples from the Eastern Woodlands entirely, including Florida.

Some Native groups adopted the Civilization Program while others were split into factions within their communities. Nativist revitalization and millenarian projects within Native polities started to gain momentum as early as the 1760s when Pontiac (Ottawa) in what became Michigan, rejected the influence of European powers, particularly the British government and the colonists, in a series of attacks throughout the Great Lakes. In 1799, Handsome Lake (Seneca), in what became New York, had a vision and set about sharing his revelations and the "Good Message." Handsome Lake advised his followers to give up alcohol and to return as soon as possible to older ways, utilizing the ways of the settlers only as necessary to best negotiate with them. It is now known as the Longhouse Religion.[8] By 1805, another Ohio Valley revitalization movement was underway in the Indiana Territory in the Shawnee settlement under the leadership of Tecumseh and his brother, Tenskwatawa, the Prophet. They began to preach their ideas of Native renaissance and committed their followers to the expulsion of Anglo-Americans from Native territories. Among their beliefs was that no individual nor Native polity could relinquish title to land held in common by all Natives in a region. In short, their Native revitalization teachings rejected the civilization project whole cloth and became a program of confrontation with the ever-expanding settler movements. Beginning with only 140 followers, the Prophetstown settlement along the Tippecanoe Creek in Indiana at times swelled to thousands of Native families and followers. Tecumseh actively sought to recruit Creek followers as well as other Southeast Native groups, visiting the Creek in 1811. In 1811, Peter McQueen, the clan grandfather and great-uncle to Osceola (William Powell) heard Tecumseh's speech and returned north to learn more. All of this was inflamed by the War of 1812 and several scholars argue that Tecumseh's visit had direct correlations to the Red Stick War of 1813–1814.[9]

William Weatherford led the anti-settler movement among the Creek in a faction called the Red Sticks who destroyed frontier settlements in western Georgia and Alabama throughout 1813–1814 culminating in an attack at Fort Mims in Alabama where they killed hundreds of settlers, Creeks, and militia members. Red Stick Creeks opposed the Civilization Program and supported traditional leadership as well as the preservation of communal lands. Creeks of the Lower Towns, however, were closer to the settlers, with more mixed families of Creeks, Blacks, and Americans. General Andrew Jackson, the commander of the military forces south of the Ohio River mustered together an army of 5,000 militia that included settlers as well as loyal Creeks, Choctaws, Cherokees, and Chickasaws to campaign through Creek Country to avenge the attack at Fort Mims. By March 27, 1814, Jackson and his army surrounded a Creek town in the battle of Horseshoe Bend, killing at least 550 of the insurgent Red Stick Creeks. Convening with Creek leaders later that year on August 9, the defeated Creeks present at the treaty signed over 22 million acres of land in southern Georgia and central Alabama as reparations for the Red Sticks actions. Importantly, some of the leaders of the Red Sticks were not present to sign the Treaty of Fort Jackson, having escaped to Florida where they joined forces with the steadily coalescing Seminole to resist the United States government and settler encroachments.[10]

Following the War of 1812, Americans sought to expand into the Florida territory for a variety of reasons: some wanted revenge for the Red Stick Creek Wars, some sought to capture enslaved African runaways, and still others sought to grab land for the expanding plantation system. With designs of American takeover of Florida, American settlers in Florida in 1812 formed the Republic of Florida and in 1814 Andrew Jackson seized Pensacola. As an outgrowth of settler expansion into the territory, the First Seminole War began in 1817 with Andrew Jackson's next invasion, correlating to a continent-wide era of violence and upheaval in the post–War of 1812 world as settlers sought to determine how Florida would fit into the expanding American republic.[11] Efforts to take over Florida had begun with the first American incursions into Seminole territory in the Patriot War (1812), a filibustering attempt to incite an insurrection against Spanish colonial rule in the territory.[12] With the success of American occupations of the Panhandle, coupled with the rise of Andrew Jackson and American takeover of the territory in the First Seminole War, American occupation and forced removal of the Seminole was inevitable. Jackson and his forces destroyed Seminole settlements and captured Spanish forts at St. Marks and Pensacola. The First Seminole War (c. 1814–1818) took place largely in North Florida but after the Spanish cession of Florida to the United States in the 1819 Adams-Onís Treaty (effective 1821) Native communities in South Florida grew.[13]

The first American attacks on Seminole lands resulted in a diffusion of Native communities southward. American sentiment at the time favored the removal of Native people in Florida as well as the rest of the Eastern Woodlands. Americans justified their actions as for Native interests, framing their intents opposite the British who were the real enemy, as one popular scholar selectively quoted General Edmund Gaines in light of an American attack on Fort Gadsden, "Those who offer them 'care and kindness' are the guilty parties. It is their acts of 'pretended' kindness, not American knives, guns, and bullets that 'effect the destruction of these wretched savages' by causing the Americans to kill so many more of them than would have been killed in the course of an unresisted American takeover."[14] These are active narratives of settler innocence and dispossession by words and memory that preserve an inaccurate portrayal of settler innocence, just as settler movement from the colonial and national period sought to dispossess these groups of their physical land. In crafting their settler memory and history of the region, these American settlements have justified expansion through the literary genocide and forced removal of the Native history of the region by venerating a false narrative that celebrates the historicizing and mythologizing of Native peoples while at the same time physically forcing Native peoples from their land.

In the new territory of Florida, removal played out in "a series of events," with Americans first promising Native Floridians a place in central Florida and then calls for total removal. This resulted in several outbreaks of violence. Seminole leader Osceola instructed his people to stockpile guns,

Post Office mural by Lucille Blanch, Fort Pierce, Florida, circa 1938. State Archives of Florida, Florida Memory, https://www.floridamemory.com/items/show/27150, accessed 30 March 2023.

powder, and supplies, in response to calls that they leave Florida for Oklahoma. Forced removal of the Seminole would be costly and deadly, with Major General Thomas S. Jesup and a young William Tecumseh Sherman both opining that the Florida swamp was not worth it. After a brief reprieve, large-scale violence between settlers and Native peoples in Florida exploded again in the 1830s although the precedents for this violence and removal originates with provisional Governor Andrew Jackson requesting permission to attack Red Stick Creeks and free Black communities along the Peace and Manatee rivers as early as April 2, 1821. Destruction to communities and dislocations due to drought led to "desperate" Seminole raids on white settlements for food in what would become the Alachua and Volusia counties in northern Florida.[15] Following the First Seminole War, the Americans established reservations north of Lake Okeechobee in south central Florida per the 1823 Treaty of Moultrie Creek forcing the Seminole to give up their claims to the region in the north. Andrew Jackson became president of the United States in 1829 and quickly set to work on removing all Native peoples from the Great Lakes and Native South. American lawmakers in Congress and the White House formalized the removal of Eastern Woodland groups to Oklahoma with the Indian Removal Act of 1830.[16]

The conflict over Native polities in the Southeast would eventually come to the lower Indian River Lagoon in the Second Seminole War (1835–1842). In the lower Indian River Lagoon, armed Seminole organized under the leadership of Coacoochee (Wild Cat) and violently resisted American efforts. Spurred to action by Seminole attacks on settler outposts, Jesup did not relish the task. "Distinction," he wrote, "or increase of reputation is out of the question; and the difficulties are such, that the best concerted plans may result in absolute failure, and the best established reputation be lost without a fault."[17] As federal policy shifted to total removal, Army scouts searched for Seminole to remove to Oklahoma, they also began to build the first permanent American settlements in the region from Fort Capron in the hammocks near Vero south to Fort Pierce along the Indian River Lagoon, and on to Fort Jupiter Loxahatachee and Lake Okeechobee. Americans also built a series of lighthouses along the Indian River at Jupiter, Cape Canaveral, and Mosquito Inlet. Eventually, under the guise of a white flag, Jesup and his men captured Creek leader Osceola on October 21, 1837, and the war straggled on under the leadership of Coacoochee (Wild Cat). American forces captured Coacoochee later in October 1837, but he and nineteen other Seminoles escaped from Fort Marion and went on to battle the American forces at the Battle of Lake Okeechobee. Wild Cat eventually negotiated for peace in 1841 and he, along with two hundred of his followers, surrendered for transport to Oklahoma.[18]

Through an examination of nineteenth-century popular literature one can surmise how Americans made a hero of Osceola while downplaying the role of Coacoochee and maintaining the myth of settler innocence.[19] While contemporary Anglo-American narratives of the Seminole Wars often focused on Indian depredation, massacres, torture, and intense violence, later accounts transformed Osceola and the Seminole into the myth of the noble savage, a doomed hero and freedom fighter. As one scholar describes it, "Osceola's story has provided fertile ground for any and all; tiny would-be truths have been used, discarded, and reshaped to accommodate the point of view of the reporter."[20] Washington Irving contributed heavily to how the American public and later generations viewed the Seminole people by justifying American dispossession of Native polities' rights to Florida in his "The Conspiracy of Neamathla."[21] Nineteenth-century literary responses to the Seminole Wars highlight and magnify settler fascination with Indigenous Florida. Of these four contemporary examples, only one, Dr. Weeden's report on the death of Osceola in American captivity, reflects any firsthand knowledge of Florida and its Native inhabitants. It is also likely another work of fantasy, written to appease settler and popular conceptions of the doomed and tragic hero. In all these writings, one can see the influence of earlier settler travel narratives, literature, and the stereotypes of Indigenous peoples that became fixed in the American popular consciousness by the nineteenth century. Washington Irving had no direct knowledge of Florida but clearly read the travel narratives and prose of colonial explorer, William Bartram, quite closely, at times even quasi-plagiarizing the naturalists' depictions of the peninsula. In Irving's *Wolferts Roost* (1884), he employed the noble savage trope, a form of the last of their kind narrative, describing the Seminole as, "leading a pleasant, indolent life, in a climate that required little shelter or clothing, and where the spontaneous fruits of the earth furnished subsistence without toil, emphasizing a yearning for the lost paradise of Eden, where man and nature lived in perfect harmony."[22]

In an epic poem, *Twasinta's Seminoles, or the Rape of Florida* (1885), Albery Whitman, a formerly enslaved man from Green River, Kentucky, directly compares the plight of the doomed Seminoles to African experiences in enslavement. In Canto 1, Verse X, he writes, "Fair Florida! whose scenes could so enhance—Could in the sweetness of the earth excel!" It is not only the natural environment that Whitman sees as Edenic paradise, but the Native Floridians as well. Whitman saw the Seminole as beautiful children of the forest, doomed to destruction by the ferocious and rapacious greed of European settlement.[23] Central to Whitman's story are the characters, Atlassa, a noble warrior modeled on Osceola, and his beloved wife Ewald, and her father, Palmecho, all tragic and courageous, yet doomed heroes. According to one literary scholar, "Whitman saw in the plight and oppression of the Seminoles, who were joined by many runaway slaves, a metaphor for the exploitation of the black man who had been stolen from his native land and sold into slavery."[24] Writing on Atlassa's motivations and character, in Verse 2, Canto LXXVI, "A sense of wrong burned in Atlassa's veins, Flowed with his life, and like a fever eat; No Coward's act upon his hands left stains; He hated e'en the likeness of deceit."[25] To Whitman, Florida was Edenic before the Europeans came, a paradise spoiled by the greed of European men, yet he too employs the noble savage and last of their kind narrative, his prose aligning firmly with other settler accounts.

Contemporary accounts of the Seminole Wars are no less effusive in their portrayal of Osceola and the Seminole as noble savages, last of their kind. Soldiers praised Osceola's intelligence and physical appearance, mythologizing him in the American press and for the American public. This is most apparent in the attention paid to Osceola's capture and tragic death at Fort Moultrie, an event that enchanted the settler imagination. Dr.

Frederick Weedon, a contract physician working for the US Army, lionized Osceola in death. In his report to artist George Catlin (famed for his sensitive portraits of Indigenous leaders), Weedon paints quite a romantic death bed scene, in line with the lasting narrative, of settler conceptions of vanishing and doomed Indians valorized in fiction by authors such as James Fenimore Cooper:

> About half an hour before he died, he seemed to be sensible that he was dying; and although he could not speak he signified by signs that he wished me to send for the chiefs and for the officers of the post, whom I called in. He made signs to his wives (of whom he had two, and also two fine little children by his side) to go and bring his full dress, which he wore in time of war; which, having been brought in, he rose up in his bed, which was on the floor, and put on his shirt, his leggings and his moccasins—girded on his war belt—his bullet pouch and powder-horn, and laid his knife by the side of him on the floor. He then called for his red paint, and his looking-glass, which was held before him, when he deliberately painted one-half of his face, his neck and throat—his wrists—the back of his hands, and the handle of his knife, red with vermillion; a custom practiced when the irrevocable oath of war and destruction is taken.[26]

According to Weedon, Osceola eventually shook hands with everyone present before laying serenely down and dying while holding his "scalping knife" and "smiled away his last breath."[27] This death scene made its way to popular American literature via Walt Whitman, in his 1891 poem "Osceola" from *Leaves of Grass*:

> When his hour for death had come,
> He slowly raised himself from the bed on the floor,
> Drew on his war-dress shirt, leggings, and girdled the belt around his waist,
> Call'd for vermillion paint (his looking glass was held before him),
> Painted half his face and neck, his wrists and back-hands,
> Put the scalp-knife carefully in his belt—then lying down, resting a moment,
> Rose again, half-sitting, smiled, gave in silence his extended hand to each and all,
> Sank faintly low to the floor (tightly grasping the tomahawk handle,)

Fixed his look on wife and little children—the last:
(And here a line in memory of his name and death.)
In that poignant dying, he ensured his own life and the life of a courageous people.[28]

Whitman's lasting narrative, emblematic of the noble savage stereotype, and last of his kind was bolstered by Dr. Weedon who would play an integral role in settler memory of Osceola, not only for his prose about the dying warrior, but for the souvenirs he took from the man as he prepared the body for a death mask, for the act he would take alongside another physician (Dr. Benjamin Strobel) before they buried the man, headless.[29] Weedon preserved the head of Osceola in a homemade alcohol solution and according to family documents and oral history, had every intention "to make the head available for public scrutiny, or even for sale." It was on display in the family drugstore in St. Augustine and family stories recount how Dr. Weedon used the head to scare his adolescent sons into behaving by placing it in their bedrooms. Eventually Weedon gave the head to his son-in-law, Dr. D. W. Whitehurst, who then passed the head on to Dr. Valentine Mott who placed it with his collections of heads for the museum at the Medical College of the City of New York. No one currently knows where the head is now as a fire at the college may have destroyed it in 1866. Whitehurst opined on passing the head to Mott, "I am aware that the sentiment of the ultra philanthropist would be shocked at what would be [illegible] desecration of the grave, and much sympathy would be expended that a child of the forest with qualities commanding admiration and regard should be conveyed to the tomb, a headless corpse." Whitehurst brushed these concerns aside, finishing, "with the scientific and intelligent, such influences are of little worth, and in the preservation of the dead we do no violence to the feelings of humanity or even the stronger attachments of love." Here the Seminole once again are treated both as bodies and land, as part of the noble savage mythos, Native peoples are seen as part of the land, a resource to be used. It should be noted that the descendant Seminole do not share his feelings of detachment from their ancestor and kin, severing his head from his body as settlers sought to separate the Seminole from their land.[30]

While Weedon spoke effusively and affectionately about Osceola, he was the one who removed the warrior's head and kept it as a macabre relic and trophy. While settlers describe Weedon as Osceola's friend at St. Augustine, men of letters and science collected bones throughout the colonial encounter and into the twentieth century for a variety of reasons as it was a "commone intellectual, cultural, and social pursuit," salvage ethnology at its worst. These trophies were "presented as scientific commodities and tools for solving riddles connected to race and time, human remains briefly assumed great prominence in the American consciousness," playing important roles in the establishment of American scholarly traditions such as anthropology and history, academies rooted in racial science and colonial hierarchies.[31]

Dr. Weedon would later remove to South Florida and the lower Indian River Lagoon alongside a wave of aggressive settlers migrating into the region in response to the government's call to action to forcibly displace remaining Seminole from Florida. The 1842 Armed Occupation Act is an example of the aggressive American expansion in the nineteenth century into Native territories and throughout the so-called frontier and highlights the lengths to which settlers and American propagandists sought to frame the removal of Seminole peoples from Florida as "defensive policy to protect 'peaceful' settler families." These settlers appear frequently during the material from this era as "persecuted migrants, refugees seeking asylum, or hardworking pioneers," and in many cases, as settler women in South Florida who defended the American hearths of their domestic spheres.[32] Many settlers in Florida felt that total Seminole removal was the only solution and thus the Armed Occupation Act sought to encourage "arms-bearing pioneers to occupy land in the dangerous Indian areas" through federal land grants in four concentrated areas of settlement: Indian River from present-day Sebastian south to S. Lucie Sound through what became Fort Pierce; a settlement near present-day Jupiter; a colony in the interior at Lake Worth; and a settlement further south near the Biscayne Bay. The settlement of Florida as an act of Manifest Destiny and Divine Providence squarely aligns with narratives typically reserved for the American West. Utilizing settlers as what one scholar has called the "leading edge of American civilization," the Armed Occupation Act became a blueprint for latter federal acts in support of settlers against Native peoples in the 1850 Land Donation Act (Oregon) and the 1862 Homestead Act.[33]

Hoping for at least 50,000 settlers within three years so that they might petition for statehood, proponents of the Armed Occupation Act program advertised East Florida's soil, climate, and potential for would-be settlers to dabble in tobacco, sugar, and cotton. However, citrus production was a primary interest from the start. Dr. Frederick Weedon applied for 160 acres near the abandoned military post at Fort Pierce and moved there with his sons, John and Frederick Jr., to begin the process of clearing the land. His settlement became the "general stopping place for everyone who travelled through the region of country, and a favorite resort for all who located on St. Lucie and Indian River."[34] Captain Mills Olcott Burnham was among the first to develop citrus groves and he might have been the first to grow pineapples along the Atlantic Ridge at his settlement on Ankona Bluff for commercial purpose. Burnham also eventually purchased a boat called *The Josephine* that he used to capture sea turtles for trade.[35] Further analysis of the Burnham account highlights a cordial but tense relationship with the Seminole and the Burnham family, coming to his settlement to trade and borrow utensils, which they always returned, "spotlessly clean" and when cautioned by Captain Burnham that his wife did not like their visits when he was away, they obliged, returning only when he did, bringing "presents of game, and again borrow the family cooking utensils."[36]

Inevitably, settler memories of the Seminole Wars played a distinct role in how settlers of the lower Indian River Lagoon saw themselves. In a July 13, 1843, article published in the *St. Augustine News,* an idyllic portrait of settler life along the Indian River appears, "This notable sheet of water is now constantly whitened by the ail of the emigrant in pursuit of land, and the stillness of its solitude broke by the splash of the oar and the merry songs of the boatmen." Continuing along this refrain, the article speaks to the "camp-fires of the adventurer" and settlers that were "vigorous in frame and sanguin in spirit" as the "land north and south of Fort Pierce are rapidly filling up" with settlers "in the enjoyment of the best of health—doctors being at a discount and forming the least useful article on the river." In language that boosters would adopt for later commercial settlement, these sources played dual roles, to counteract fears of disease that were ever present in soldiers' accounts of the region and to emphasize the Edenic qualities of the region, common themes for settler literature of Florida.[37]

Caleb Lyndon Brayton claimed 160 acres in June 1843 when he came south to Florida to improve his physical health while seeking a fortune and his account highlights settler erasure of a Native presence in the region while delighting in the potentials for agricultural paradise. Affectionately detailing his life in correspondence to his wife, who remained in New England while he set up their homestead, he planted over 140 acres with pumpkins and arrowroot while catching green sea turtles and fish for sale to Key West. Like Burnham, he dabbled in citrus and pineapples.[38] Opining on his crops, Brayton relayed to his wife Marian, "I have seen no Arrow Root that looks better than mine & from that we are sure it will grow on the Bluff. I brought a sample of tobacco to Augustine and had segars [sic] made of it, & the segar maker pronounced it equal to the best Cuba Tobacco."[39] Continuing in another letter, "Dearest, I have now no doubt of ultimate success in this delightful country. Oranges, lemons, Pine Apples, Figs, Bananas, Plantains, Ginger, Arrow Root, Indigo, & indeed almost all the tropical fruits can be raised here." Hoping that his wife and family would join him, Brayton aspired to a home that would be "one of the most delightful in the world." Speaking of pineapples, Brayton said "if there is anything that looks beautiful it is them," and boasted that his crop "look better and bear larger fruit than any in the West Indies & from those I already have, I can in 3 years have an income of from 5 hundred to 1000 [dollars]."[40] Other accounts of the region also describe a bucolic situation for settlers and of further Native erasure, "On the Indian River some of the best hammocks in the Floridas are to be met with, healthy and elevated. The occasioned breaks of pine bluffs are rather advantageous than otherwise as presenting better sites for settlements."[41] These early Anglo settlers wrote of limited connections with the Seminole as the Seminole largely chose to keep themselves separate from the white settlers, thus, an accounting of the true Seminole population eluded many white accounts for generations, even into the mid-twentieth century. Despite this, settler mythology remained rooted in powerful caricatures of Seminole people as "fierce savages."[42]

The perceived threat of Native peoples, however, continued to play a significant role in settler memory narratives. Take for example the "red-nosed Savannah cobbler" known as Cobbett. Cobbett was allegedly a "very poor workman . . . white-haired and red-nosed and could detect the aroma of whiskey more than a mile away." At the very scent, with a moments' provocation, Cobbett would drop his work and "come charging through the woods to get his share," a man known to "descend on the clearings or fields of persons serving spirits at 'grogtime' with such 'swift goat-like leaps that at first all hands would rush for their rifles, fancying that fifty painted Seminoles were at his heels, eager for white scalps.'"[43] What this imaginative narratives reveals, however, is that while the American government encouraged settlement as the first wave of expansion, the very real threat of Native resistance to the takeover of their territory loomed within the settler mind. Real violence erupted in July 1849 when the Seminole attacked several settlements, including one of a storekeeper named Barker near the Sebastian River. According to one settler account, the violence was not unwarranted, affording a rare moment that breaks away from settler narratives of innocence. Barker "had on several occasions cheated them on their trades" and while his brother-in-law, Major Russell, organized a retreat, the attack later proved to be only the work of four to five Seminole men rather than an orchestrated assault. This same account did not hold Major Russell in high esteem, opining, that he was "heartily disliked by the Indians" and that was why they took a parting shot at him as he led the settler retreat. This same account alleged that Russell accidentally poured ink over his wounded arm instead of salve and though the arm did not need to be amputated, Russell insisted upon it.[44] Governor William Moseley called to muster the state militia and settlers quickly abandoned their homes to go north to St. Augustine. These same Seminole warriors also took their violence to the Peace River settlements to the west.[45] Caleb Brayton wrote to his wife about the attacks, opining, "You will now not make any calculation to come to Florida till the Indians are exterminated. Government I presume will immediately establish a garrison at Indian River." He later claimed $2000 in losses although his home was not burned, further speculating on what should be done with the Seminole, ". . . I think unless some treaty is soon made with them, that a war of extermination will ere long be waged. Poor deluded creatures: they had better take their papooz's [sic] on their backs & bid adieu to Florida; for if they resist, no mercy will be shown them . . ."[46] Brayton presents himself as innocent in the face of Seminole removal and the Seminole as a doomed race, the last of their kind, yet the Seminole persevered and Brayton's wife would only join him in 1854 when his life was near its end, dying from complications resulting from tuberculosis.

Robert Ranson, the son-in-law of Captain Mills Olcott Burnham, also collected a series of stories about a lower Indian River settlement south of Vero Beach, near the St. Lucie River, from 1845 to 1849. Ranson's purpose in writing was to highlight "evidences of the manner in which both the men & women of former days met such trials & perils as are the inheritance of all pioneers who, in advance of civilization, fight their way through trackless wilds in order to fit the Earth for future safe & habitable conditions."[47] Within this narrative of settler progress and prosperity,

Ranson stitched together a settler history of the Seminole Wars and early settlement from "an old diary . . . very badly mouse-eaten" and clearly edited his takes on the events through his own nationalist and jingoistic settler lens of American innocence, ". . . and though in retrospect it would seem that these old-timers suffered many hardships and dangers, life was probably quite as enjoyable and at times quite as miserable, as in this year of Grace 1926, except for the constant dread of marauding and hostile Indians."[48] This lauding of the pioneer spirit can be found in narratives throughout the Indian River Lagoon from Cape Canaveral south to St. Lucie, interconnecting the Florida narrative to the national myth of Manifest Destiny and settler progress.

The Seminole Wars impacted the national and local consciousness deeply as American writers romanticized and mythologized the events throughout the nineteenth century and the legacy of those fictionalized accounts can be seen throughout Florida to this day. The third Seminole War, sometimes referred to as Billy Bowlegs' War after its principal leader, ended in 1858 as the United States forced some of the captured Seminole to go west to the Oklahoma territory; those who remained in Florida did so under the leadership of Sam Jones (Abiaka) in the region surrounding the Big Cypress Swamp. Thanks to the 1862 Homestead Act, the American population of the region surrounding the Indian River Lagoon swelled to 1,216 by 1870 in communities from Cape Canaveral to the north to Jupiter Inlet in the south.[49] Many Northerners flocked to Florida in the postbellum era as they toured the former slave states and sought to find adventures in territories they viewed as the frontier. The Indian River came to be known as an "untamed" space with "restorative effects" for folks suffering from physical and mental concerns, again connecting Florida to Eden and paradise, the world before the fall of humanity. Settlers sought these spaces to escape from the industrial and rapidly growing spaces of the North.[50]

For many settlers, Florida was "the last frontier." One historian opined on the Bell family's motivation for heading into the Indian River Lagoon from a settlement in Illinois near Vincennes, Indiana, "the Wild West was fast yielding to settlement and civilization," so this family descended from French and English settlers, "possessing the pioneering instincts of its ancestry; this family sharing the empire building characteristics of its associates, the Beechers, the Lincolns, and the Grants, 'came south' to our Florida, the last frontier." In this case, the frontier is less a place and more a process and perception, it was there that their family "strove mightily, endured privations, suffered hardships."[51] The Bell children saw wondrous sights, "old live oak trees with their veils of Spanish moss" and in the glittering river lagoon, "thousands of roe mullet," but they were also desperately lonesome, "we children cried an ocean of tears" while they were living in New Smyrna. Alongside loneliness, the Bell family had to learn how to adapt to farming the region, "we didn't know how to raise cow-peas and sweet potatoes like the natives did, but learned later," utilizing Native knowledge to conquer the landscape.[52] Excitement came when the Bells moved further downriver closer to Fort Pierce and visited with other settler families who shared stories to scare the children about Native attacks.

On a trip south in 1878, they met Captain Armour and his family. The Armour children began to cry as sand flies descended and bit incessantly, Captain Armour told his children, "Hush, children, the Indian will hear you and come on the boat." Emily recalled that she was very frightened to hear that, "I, of course, was green, thinking maybe they might come," adding that "if the Indians were a mile away they could have heard my heart beating." His wife chastised him, saying, "Old Man, the joke is on you" and he began to sing a sailor's alphabet song for the children to allay their fear of Indians and calm them from their lamentations over the biting flies. It calmed the children as they fell asleep, but the flies continued to bite at Emily who remembered, "I would have given anything to have been home."[53]

The Bell family account chronicles their experiences in the region between Titusville and Jupiter as Emily's husband, Jim, became the station keeper at the Indian River House of Refuge. Waves of settlers brought additional buildings along the coast in the form of the Houses of Refuge, ten built between 1875 and 1886 at intervals below St. Augustine to act as lifesaving stations for shipwrecks and they established a "governmental presence and a framework to which pioneer development clung," outposts of settlement but often spaces of frontier themselves. These stations joined lighthouses at Mosquito (Ponce de León Inlet); Cape Canaveral; Jupiter Inlet, Cape Florida; and Hillsboro Inlet Lighthouse built in 1907. In the region near what became Vero Beach there were two stations: Indian River/ Bethel Creek House of Refuge built in 1876 and the Indian River Inlet House of Refuge built in 1886 south of the inlet.[54] Building the Houses of Refuge sometimes included acts of settler destruction of Native sites as they actively leveled Indian mounds to prepare for the construction of the stations, quite literally erasing the past.[55] Keepers and their families were responsible for taking care of themselves through home garden plots, fishing, hunting, raising cattle, and collecting shellfish. Living in a tenuous situation, keepers had to provide for any shipwreck victims or settlers who came for protection at the station, and this placed a strain on their food supplies as very little was provided by the government. The houses were often far away from the main settlements and at times difficult to access to provide supplies. In many cases, the Seminole came to these stations to trade, bringing with them much-needed supplies for the station keepers.[56]

There Emily played host to visitors and tourists as well as would-be settlers as she tended to her home and raised their children. This account also addresses some of the remaining concerns that settlers had regarding Seminoles while at the same time highlighting the everyday experiences that settlers and Seminoles shared, including acts of friendship. Bell recalled the situation at Fort Pierce and trade between Captain Hogg and the Seminole. Brandied peaches and cherries were sold in most mercantile stores during this era, but Bell noted fears of the Seminole when she opined that Mrs. Hogg would not keep the brandied fruit in stock "until she had some protection, for the Indians might get wild."[57] The Hogg family built a trade with settlers and Natives in what would become P. P. Cobb's mercantile store in downtown Fort Pierce, building a small clientele into "a large business of all the latest and the best."[58]

Eventually Emily Bell came into regular contact with the Seminole as her husband and brother-in-law frequently traded and worked with Seminole men, including Henry Parker, and her children Madge and Charles would play with Seminole children, "they were their first playmates, friends, too." On Henry Parker, Emily shared, "He was a fine large Indian and a favorite with the whites," who unfortunately died by accident at the age of twenty, "they all mourned for him."[59] Recalling baking syrup cookies in her kitchen one day in 1882, Emily said that Polly Parker, Lucy, three children, and Nance (wife of Tuscanuga) were at her kitchen door. The Seminole had an encampment along the river. Emily was horrified when she offered the pan of cookies that instead of taking just a few of the cookies, Polly "took her dress up and poured the whole batch in her dress." Emily made her husband chastise Polly so that she would share the cookies with all the women and children, remarking, "she didn't like it." Emily made a point of saying, "I learned to never have anything, for they liked to beg, but never would steal."[60] That all being said, her mother acted as a nurse to the Seminole who visited, utilizing medicine that she brought from Titusville and Emily remembered, "they had great confidence in her. They loved her. They would bring her much meats and turkey, pumpkins and potatoes and even chickens." And Emily even shared a Christmas in 1883 with Dr. Johnnie and Billy Bowlegs.[61] One cannot miss the undertones of this friendly holiday meal, akin to the American popular imaginary of the first Thanksgiving.

Emily wrote this account in order to generate sympathy for her position in the Florida backcountry, however, the reality that emerges from the pages, is that her husband was interconnected and friends with important Seminole men who would protect the family if necessary. Billy Bowlegs III was the grandson of Osceola and the son of Nance, related to Lewis Tucker who played a major role in Vero's tourist industry (see Chapter 4) and Bowlegs was later a tribal historian. The Seminole who remained in Florida after 1858 increasingly came into conflict with the waves of settlers moving into the Florida territory throughout the latter half of the nineteenth century. After the three wars and several pieces of legislation, the Seminole remained, shifting from obstacles of settler progress to occasional pieces of history that some of settler groups sought to preserve. Throughout the 1870s and into the early twentieth century, several incidents involving theft of property, cattle, horses, and encroachment on Seminole land led to a wave of settlers who sought to protect Seminole interests, culminating in the creation of a group called the Friends of the Seminole. This group was part of a national trend inspired in part by Helen Hunt Jackson's 1881 book *A History of Dishonor* which chronicled the hardship and injustices that Native peoples of the United States had faced at the hands of settlers and the American government.[62] This progressive moment sought to perverse the "ancestors" of America and move toward capturing Native history as American history through the lens of firsting and lasting.

In the region near Vero, Emily Lagow Bell recalled a case involving the theft of cattle and hog killing where the Seminole were the aggrieved party and settlers took to hiding in the Houses of Refuge. The keeper's house held the "capacity sufficient for the residence of a family, and for the temporary shelter of as many as are likely to need it." This translated to "cots and provisions sufficient to succor twenty-five persons for ten days."[63] Keeping the houses were lonely affairs, and the remaining records of several keepers' families highlight deprivation and disease, often from bad water. When a crowd of settlers came to the house, Emily remembered one man saying, "We have come over here, as the Indians are on the warpath, their paints on and dancing around the fire. Say 'Killum all white man,' so we came here to see if you can't make a treaty with them. They said white men had stolen their hogs and driven all their cattle off and said they would killum all, in two suns." The next day her husband, her father-in-law, and brother-in-law, "all good friends with the Indians," yet the new power brokers of Florida, made their way over to Fort Pierce to raise money to pay back the aggrieved Seminole parties, they raised two hundred dollars but made it difficult for the thieves, "the rustlers got the cattle all right, but some of them had to leave the country."[64] This incident highlights the powerful position of the Bell family in both the white settlement and with their Seminole allies as two hundred dollars was half of a keeper's yearly salary, a princely sum in the fledgling settler community.[65]

Attitudes toward the Seminole shifted deeply in the late nineteenth century with settler perspectives on assimilation of the so-called last of their kind. Settlement of Florida often left Seminole communities and cattlemen prey to theft by settlers and these disputes caught the attention of a few progressive allies who sought to draw national attention to the situation. The Seminole cattle ranchers sometimes had to conceal their prosperity or risk theft from their white neighbors.[66] The Bell family were not alone in their pursuit of justice for aggrieved Seminole allies. Lilly Pierpont of Winter Haven to the north, later the first female Indian agent in Florida, wrote a letter to President Grover Cleveland's wife protesting the treatment of Seminoles at the hands of settlers, "they are at present inclined to be friendly, though they are often imposed upon by white settlers."[67] The Friends of the Florida Seminole, a humanitarian organization dedicated to progressive treatment of Seminole concerns, was organized on January 7, 1899, in Kissimmee, Florida. Instrumental in its creation was Minnie Moore-Wilson, author of *The Seminoles of Florida* (1896) who sought to bring national attention to the situation in Florida. The Friends of the Seminole was "similar to other benevolent societies of the period which were devoted to alleviating the 'Indian Problem' in the United States." The Friends hoped to purchase lands, provide educational opportunities, and seek legal protection for the Seminole people, particularly the Cow Creek band. These are national assimilation movements that have a longer history of paternalistic and deeply racial colonialist views about civility and society. Among the concerns the Friends put forth was a question, "Is it possible to stop these robberies? Is there no power anywhere, to give to enforce protecting orders for these Indians who cannot protect themselves? And if not are not some of our troupes needed to protect the homes of our own home-born oppressed race . . ."[68] Friends of the Seminole utilized paternalistic language, another example of the lasting narrative so prevalent in many settler histories of Native peoples throughout the nation.

Streams of settlers moved into the Florida peninsula thanks to booster companies, like the Indian River Farms Company and inspired by the successes of Henry Plant and Henry Flagler's railroad interests and development plans for the coast and interior. The Cow Creek band of the Seminole had territories surrounding the lower Indian River Lagoon and the Kissimmee River into the interior north of Lake Okeechobee. By 1879, complaints by settlers against the Seminole included the loss of $1500–$2000 worth of beef but at least one settler, R. H. Pratt, opined that "like offenses are committed against the Indians."[69] While it could easily be contended that the Friends of the Seminoles "fostered a paternalistic and naïve image of the Seminole people and their needs," at least one Florida scholar importantly has pointed out that the Cow Creek Seminole actively sought out the Friends for their help.[70] As the Friends sought to "protect" Seminole interests, however, one must also remember that their interest was informed by deeply flawed and damaging perspectives on Native Floridians and would contribute to themes of erasure.

The first major case the Friends would take on involved the theft of a horse from Captain Tom Tiger, brother of Tiger Tustenuggee, last war chief of the Cow Creek band. The Cow Creek had camps on the north and west shores of Lake Okeechobee with bands up toward the Kissimmee River and smaller encampments throughout the hammocks of the lower Indian River Lagoon. The Tiger clan were an important family all around, his sister Martha Tiger was the wife of Chief Tallahassee and kin of the Tiger family lived all throughout the hammocks of the lower Indian River Lagoon that would one day become Sebastian, Fellsmere, Vero Beach, and Fort Pierce.[71] Tom Tiger contacted the Friends to take up a case of horse theft. Tiger alleged that Harmon Hull had taken his horse from his camp near Fort Drum with the promise to return the horse in two months' time. Tiger claimed Drum signed a promissory note in late December 1897 on a cartridge box, however, due to a recent rainstorm, the writing was obscured and smeared. Hull, for his part, denied any wrongdoing and wrote to James M. Willson, Secretary of the Friends of the Seminole, "I don't no [sic] which you are for but I can tell you I believe some white man has put him up to claim and get me scared up best that he can do."[72] Many of the prominent settlers in the Fort Pierce region vouched for Tom Tiger including P. P. Cobb, James T. Gray, and R. A. Swearingen who noted that Tom was in dire financial need. Swearingen helped Tom out with fixing his wagon and asked that Willson do something soon to help Tom and his family financially. Although a jury eventually acquitted Hull of any legal guilt, this case provides some insight into the paternalistic nature of the Friends and the ways in which they memorialized and romanticized Seminole people. The Friends raised funds for another horse for Tom Tiger but allegedly the Seminole quipped back, "White men tell heap lies, and lawyer talkee, talkee to much all time [sic]."[73] Highlighting still simmering resentments and distrust, this incident came to be known as a "showcase trial of the plight of the Seminole in Florida," as Minnie Moore Willson contributed to the myth and fictionalization of the Seminole when she provided this romanticized noble Indian trope about Tom Tiger: "Captain Tom Tiger, Seminole chieftain, was the first Florida Indian that ever stood up in a white man's court, making, as the spectators remarked, the most imposing picture they had ever witnessed. The tall, magnificent looking savage, with uplifted hand, took the oath on the holy Book, with a perfect understanding of its meanings. . . . The Indian never swerved under the strongest cross-examination but told the story simply and direct."[74] Even as settler allies sought to assist Native Floridians, they could not help but play a part in the romanticization of Native peoples, once again interconnecting themselves to a lasting narrative, Tom Tiger as the last of a noble people on the brink of extinction.

These Friends of the Seminole would play a role in an important event after the death of Tom Tiger: the theft of his remains. At least one account of Florida describes Tom Tiger as a "natural hero for those in search of a Rousseauean noble savage," in part because of Tiger's physical appearance, well over six feet tall, "his eyes were black and fierce; his mouth—firm, but not cruel—was shaded by a small black moustache."[75] After losing his trial against Hull for horsetheft, "Tiger returned to life as before, trapping and raising hogs at his camp in the Bluefield district, north of Lake Okeechobee." While working on a dugout canoe he was struck by lightning and died. His family use the partially finished canoe as part of his grave, "a burial vault rather than build the traditional Seminole log-pen grave."[76] A white man came to the region in January 1907 alleging that he had plans to write a history of the Seminole. Claiming to represent the Smithsonian, John T. Flournoy took Tom Tiger's remains north on a train. In an oral history of early settlers of the Fort Pierce region, Tom King of the Southeastern Indian Oral History project for the University of Florida conducted an interview with Ada Williams whose story "conveys a feeling of respect and cooperation between the Seminole Indians and the early white settlers of Fort Pierce." Ada's father, William Lee Coates, had once lived with the Ruebin Carlton family west of the Indian River raising cattle in the hammocks adjacent to a number of Seminole settlements. Ada recalled fondly, "they were the Cow Creek Indians . . . they [the Carlton boys] would wrestle with them, they would hunt with them, they would go to their Green Corn Dances, and my father lived out there with them." As part of her interview, Ada spoke at some length about the incident involving the theft of Tom Tiger's remains. As to what she knew about Tom Tiger, she remarked, "He has been written up in the histories I have read about the Seminole Wars. Now, Tom Tiger was a very tall, handsome Indian, and he was very highly respected by the whites as well as the Indians." Dan Carlton was the sheriff at the time and when he was alerted to the theft, "because he had grown up in the woods . . . they came to him, and gave him just so many moons to get Tom Tiger's remains. It was solely because he had grown up with them as a boy, and wrestled with them and hunted, I suppose, that they didn't do some bodily harm to the settlers." Carlton and others contacted the Smithsonian who claimed no knowledge of the theft. Instead, the bones turned out to be on display at an amusement park in Johnston, Philadelphia, a letter from the Smithsonian noted that Flournoy had tried to sell the skeleton, but they wanted nothing to do with the issue. Settler allies successfully got Tiger's remains back, when they returned them to the Seminoles they waited until nightfall to take them, "then with torches they went with a long line of their people out into the woods. In the hammocks, they once again placed it in a tree where they thought that it would not be bothered."[77]

From the late colonial era through attempted removals and a new era of American settlement, Florida was a contested settler territory with the Native population under attack and on the attack throughout the region and era. Slavery, violence, settler incursions, and the power of Native polities are often lost in the settler narrative which privileges a progressive Anglo-American expansion and themes of Manifest Destiny and Divine Providence.

3

The Indian River Farm Company's Booster Dreams of a Colonial Past

Vero
(Tune, "Church in the Wildwood")

There's a town in Indian River Valley,
Where there's sunshine, fertile soil and ocean breeze;
You can spend your winters there,
Sleet and snow you need not fear,
And it's where you can remain long as you please

*

(Chorus)
Oh, come, come, come, come
Come to the little town of Vero,
That is full of "pep" and strictly up to date.
It is where the people come
To enjoy the southern sun,
It's the loveliest spot in the state.

*

There are churches, schools, banks, and club of commerce;
You can plainly see our motto's "Go Ahead!"
There are business buildings fine,
Good hotels where you can dine,
And you'll find that we are anything but dead.

*

The flowers never cease to bloom at Vero,
And the citrus fruit is surely hard to beat.
You can pitch your tent or build,
Of our lumber that's just milled,
And you'll find our little city quite complete.

*

If you'll come to make your home with us at Vero,
From the other states or nations far away,
You are welcome to the best,
But you'll have to show respect,
And never cease from boosting her throughout your stay.[1]

It was in the hammocks of Tom Tiger's land that Vero would flourish. As we have seen in the previous chapters, there certainly are examples of sporadic colonial and American settlements in the lower Indian River Lagoon, however, it was the late nineteenth-century settler expansion to the South and West that led to Vero. And at this time what made Vero famous, was the potential for citrus, "to own an Indian River orchard is to have title in the orange nobility. Smooth of skin, which is thin as a lady's glove, full of sweet juice to the bursting point, they are ne plus ultra, the last word in oranges," proclaimed the *Indian River Farmer*, a booster advertising journal linked to Yankee settlers and investors from the Midwest.[2] Orange history in Florida, has a much longer story than just the Indian River Lagoon as the earliest mention of oranges in Florida occurred in the late sixteenth century in an April 2, 1579, letter from Pedro Menéndez Marquis (nephew of Pedro Menéndez de Avilés) to the Audiencia of Santo Domingo. The Spanish introduced citrus to Florida and for two centuries, citrus consumption was local and limited in export until 1766 when the English began exporting two casks of juice and 65,000 oranges from groves around the St. Johns up to Lake George and orange districts south to New Smyrna.[3] Neither the Spanish nor the English placed any sustained emphasis on citrus cultivation for widespread commercial use and consumption, yet, thanks to the Spanish, citrus trees spread south throughout the Florida peninsula. Spanish missionaries and Bahamian mariners also cultivated many other crops for local consumption in South Florida including limes, oranges, coconuts, olives, and bananas.[4] Large-scale commercial growth would emerge when the United States acquired the territory in 1821 and settlers moved south seeking agricultural riches in the hammocks of the lagoon.[5]

By 1827, Floridians shipped more than a million oranges and established groves valued at between $5,000 and $10,000 with profits between $1000 and $3000. A deadly frost hit in February 1835, "a killing frost—which destroyed every orange, lime, and lemon tree" north of the 28th parallel in Florida, encompassing most of northern Florida and the Panhandle. This destruction was total as it included the roots of many of the trees. Recovery was slow-going as mandarin oranges that were brought in to replace the losses accidentally introduced purple scale insects that blighted the region on the St. Johns River until at least 1847.[6] Despite some domestic growth, Americans imported most of their citrus from the Mediterranean for consumption until the late nineteenth century, between 1874 and 1877 "annually importing about 200 million oranges with a value of more than 2 million dollars." General Henry S. Sanford eventually sought to build a domestic citrus empire in Florida with the horticulture of oranges, limes, and lemons. These included three primary varieties of oranges: Valencia, Pineapple, and Hamlin. Secondary varieties included Lue Gim Gong and Parson Brown. Tertiary varieties included Dream, Washington, Ruby, and Sour Jaffa. Satsuma oranges arrived in Florida in 1882.[7]

Farming Florida induced large-scale settlement. In the Gilded Age and Progressive Era, Northerners were fascinated by the economic potential of former states of the Confederacy and particularly with the prospects of Florida for investment and settlement. Perceived frontiers proved especially appealing to Midwesterners and Great Lakes Americans who saw Florida as the "embodiment of romanticism, with terror and tropical beauty, and menacing Indians. Wealthy tourists began coming to experience this wilderness from a safe distance, and often with a comfortable bed."[8] Steamboat tours up and down the St. Johns, Sebastian, and Indian rivers became a popular tourist endeavor. Journalists wrote guides and editorials on the American South in the 1870s, including Edward King's series, 'The Great South' in *Scribner's Magazine* and Julian Ralph writing for *Harper's Magazine* in the 1880s and 1890s. Several guidebooks, pamphlets, brochures, and articles about touring the South and Florida sated the curiosity of Yankee observers: "settlers, ex-soldiers, outlaws, drifters, sportsmen, naturalists, vacationers, and speculators all started finding their way down the Indian River, some finding what they were seeking, and others failing."[9] The short-lived early twentieth century advertising journal the *Indian River Farmer* boasted that Vero's summer climates greatly enticed northern visitors, "coming from sections of the country where they have been sweltering in the daytime and getting little relief at night, most of them expect to be fairly burned alive when they reach Florida." In Vero and the lower Indian River Lagoon they find, however, that "they are surprised to find weather conditions much similar to those of late spring at home."[10] Guidebooks were not the only ones popularizing Florida in the American imagination, novelists once again adopted these themes of paradise as well, imagining Florida to be an escape from northern winters, a paradise for health and a way to extend life.[11]

Very few writers wrote about the harsher elements of life in the south, including issues of race, economic inequality, or disease. For more than a century, "periodicals were the most significant advertising means by which Americans were enticed to the Sunshine State to enjoy its beauty and its mild winters . . . Americans who read of the wondrous Edenic qualities of Florida did not necessarily examine other articles dealing with the less than pleasant sides of the state's history and culture."[12] Guidebooks and journalists painted Florida romantically as one tourist remarked, "Florida! The very name is suggestive of sunshine and flowers, orange groves, and the sweet-scented air of 'Araby the blest.'"[13] These narratives are comparable to colonial travel writers, once again employing a theme of an exotic land to be conquered, whose Native history was merely a backdrop for progress and settlement. Travelers to Florida often took their time touring the South by steamship and railroads and later by automobile with the building of the Dixie Highway from Detroit to Miami.[14] Guidebooks focused on the positive elements of the Florida landscape for northern tourists as rapid industrialization at the turn of the twentieth century left many Americans yearning for a bucolic imagined past whose Native inhabitants played minor background roles to American progress and to that end, the American South was "frequently portrayed in popular culture as a region that was either primitive or exotic and was seen through the haze of moonlight and magnolias."[15] Guidebooks and journalists to Florida painted the region as a commodity, primitive tropics "but desirable areas awaiting Euro-American possession and cast the Indigenous peoples as idle and unthinking."[16]

In the late nineteenth century, town developers of the American South capitalized on settler imaginations and national mythmaking about the legacy of Pocahontas.[17] Southerners and Yankee settlers looked to older stories of conquest for inspiration as well, looking not only to the Spanish past as a theme for town building and resort architecture but to national Anglo–Indian experiences that justified conquest and their expansion into new territories. Examples of the use of the noble savage stereotype and the type of lasting that is present in the settler narrative can be found all over the country, from street names to monuments. One of the most popular is Pocahontas. For example, in rural Hinds County, Mississippi, there once stood a large western Plains-style teepee, part of a local barbecue joint, outside the unincorporated town of Pocahontas, in the shadow of the Pocahontas Indian mounds. Along the Black River in central Arkansas, the city of Pocahontas holds a statue to the Algonquian woman in their town center. And in coastal Vero Beach, a large Spanish mission-style building has a carving of Pocahontas with a basket that overlooks the town center.

A few recurrent themes emerge in settler memories and naming practices, including the use of "Pocahontas" in expansion and the memorialization of conquest stories. To begin with, these towns are part of a larger settler tradition of removal and erasure, obfuscating the Native history of these regions by replacing the elements that settlers wanted to forget with more "romantic" national narratives and a mixed bag of stereotypes, often playing upon the trope of the "Good Indian" and noble savage, but also reflect gendered conceptions of land and Indigenous peoples and rarely reflect any of the legitimate history of Pocahontas or the encounter period. They remain fertile sites for investigating the legacy of Pocahontas and the ways in which her story and identity are used to promote development and construct American identity in these new towns. In the case of Pocahontas, her story has become a part of the national narrative of American history, yet it is no longer her story. Instead she is wrapped in settler memory as an example of assimilation, interconnected with the land, as settlers describe the land yielding to progress, so too they describe the conquering of Pocahontas, connecting her name throughout the generations of settler expansion to places all over North America. In many of these regions, there are longer histories of Native settlements and oftentimes, violent encounters with settlers, as was the case for the Indian River settlements in Florida from first European encounter to the Seminole Wars.

Beginning in the booster literature of the nineteenth century and continuing through pioneer and frontier settler memory projects, one can see the casting of former enemies as tragic heroes and reframing of Indigenous peoples and stories to fit into and justify American settler ambitions. This is a narrative that again, we tend to associate with the West, but it is happening in the South as well as the settlement of Florida are two sides of the same coin of the post–Civil War South, where boosters selected national memories as they sought to block out the southern history they would like to forget. Certainly, this was not just a southern phenomenon, as scholar of the West and memory David Wrobel has described it, we must consider the construction of memories and how they are not merely "recollected or reproduced" but at times "even invented." Settlers of the West and Florida have both selectively created memories that highlight the stories and events they want to remember, "pioneer reminiscences, like the promotional literature, can be most profitably used as a mirror to reflect the outlook of those doing the reminiscing, rather than as a clear window on the actual events that are described between the covers of their accounts."[18] These are imaginative creations that both attempt to create a settlement and to hearken back to fantasies of the past that never fully existed. With often purposeful and selective constructions of memory, settlements chose Pocahontas because she molded to a settler dream of the Good Indian yielding to conquest as they sought a pliant and willing landscape that would yield mineral and agricultural riches.

These Yankees, calling themselves pioneers and colonizers, moved to the Indian River in South Florida in waves throughout the late nineteenth and early twentieth century and wealthy northern investors built their empires of citrus and sugar. Many of the Anglo settlers that moved south into Florida in the late nineteenth century "brought with them the ecological ethos of their time, having largely come to the Indian River from the land of the Erie, Ohio, and Pennsylvania canal systems," and according to one environmental historian, represented "a third wave of peninsular Florida Anglo culture, historically and culturally distinct from the southern inland 'cracker' and the Caribbean-derived 'conch' of the Florida Keys."[19]

The Indian River Farms Company of Davenport, Iowa, for instance, made some of the greatest strides toward conquering and reimagining La Florida. While Northerners began to settle the region in the 1880s, the Indian River Farms Company created a romantic narrative to sell land to potential Yankee colonizers. Herman J. Zeuch was the principal propagandist and organizer of this endeavor and stood to gain the most. In September 1912, Indian River Farms purchased 48,000 acres which expanded to 55,000 later that year. Most of the land, purchased at the bargain price of $3 an acre was underwater. Thus, the company first focused on dredging out a drainage canal into the Indian River north of the proposed sites. Once these wetlands were reclaimed, the company offered them at $150–$200 an acre. This endeavor was not his first foray into settler development, he was an insurance agent at one point in Denver and had stakes in the settlement of Alberta and Saskatchewan. Zeuch picked the Indigenous names. He renamed his hotel from the Bayhead Inn to the Sleepy Eye Lodge, a nod to a nineteenth-century Dakota chief known for his friendliness to white settlers. The name also recounted folk tales that Sleepy Eye had "never spilt a drop of blood of the white man." Zeuch likely unconsciously picked Sleepy Eye as a reminder of a frontier past, interconnecting his ambitious plans with earlier settler progress into the upper Midwest.

The company laid out the town of Vero in 1914, "with an eye single to modern development and improvement," while at the same time embodying older modes of colonization and themes of Edenic paradise.[20] Billed as "fountains of youth," artesian wells were a vital component of land sales, connecting the colonial fascination with Ponce de León, fueled by the well-known literary depictions of the Spanish colonial era by Washington Irving. Advertising the artesian wells as "fountains of youth" showcases continuous themes of a tropical paradise. The company drilled a well at Sleepy Eye Lodge, on the demonstration farm, and a settler home (the Barbers) and in the heart of town they drilled an artesian well at Pocahontas Park in January 1914.[21]

With settlement booming, the business block planned for downtown Vero was decidedly Spanish in origin, or, at least, a fanciful vision of Spanish colonization, one that would be on par with the new architecture for St. Augustine and Tampa. P. T. Burrows and Charles Grilk, Davenport architects, sought to "meet the requirements of a semitropical climate and at the same time harmonize with its surroundings," remarking upon the indifference that Florida has had for attractive buildings, "When the people of Florida begin to pay as much attention to the appearance of their buildings and environs as is done in California, a trip through Florida will be as great a delight to the eye as is presented by the western state." To this end, the architects of Vero and other Florida cities sought to recast Florida's Spanish colonial past with modern mission-style buildings they copied from California.[22]

California, for its part, was also susceptible to colonial nostalgia and historical reimagining of its past. By the late nineteenth century, promoters and boosters in California would explore the "social and cultural dynamics between Indians and Spaniards" in what one scholar refers to as the "Spanish colonial romance" that invigorated a celebration of San Diego beginning with a Cabrillo Celebration in 1892 and found its epoch in the 1915 Panama–California Exposition that built Balboa Park on 1,400 acres that had once been pueblo common lands. Matthew Bokovoy describes the building of southwestern historical memory related to the Spanish and Mexican eras as symbolic of an "Eden lost."[23] Evidence of California's colonial past thrilled tourists along the Pacific coast as they could tour old missions and see examples of haciendas. Florida had no remaining Spanish architectural history, because none of the wooden Florida missions withstood the test of time and the elements.

In an often-one-sided rivalry, comparisons to California occur frequently in the booster literature as Floridians sought to display their advantages over their western rivals. The *Indian River Farmer* published a story from M. E. Gillett who opined that Florida was best for oranges, "I think any Florida grower who will visit California and investigate conditions there carefully will come home feeling very much as I did—perfectly satisfied that his grove is in Florida rather than California. Everywhere I went I found people anxious to learn all they could about Florida, stating that sooner or later they hoped to make their home in the south and they felt that Florida had more to offer than any other southern state."[24] Whether this M. E. Gillett existed is up for debate. The sentiments, however, were part and parcel to the booster spirit of the age. In that same issue, another anonymous editorial had this to say about California citrus, "the oranges are thick skinned and tasteless, or too sour as compared with the sweet, russet-coated beauties that he finds in Florida. People eat oranges in Florida because they are delicious."[25] In an earlier editorial, an anonymous booster quipped, "I believe that Florida now has the whip-hand; that it is California that is in the corner—Florida holds the hand that is going to win."[26]

From their offices in Davenport, Indian River Farms focused on the east coast of Florida and the lower Indian River Lagoon with a series of booster advertisements and propaganda that called for white American settlers to prove their merit and succeed through honest labor and hard work, tied to the frontier ideology of pulling oneself up by their bootstraps, of opportunity for Anglo-Americans, "We want men who do things to join us in building a wonderful community. Remember we want No Drone. The bees kill their drones. Our human drones kill themselves . . . We're all workers. If you Are, Join us."[27] Zeuch was not exaggerating the labor ahead, the work would be hard but the return on investment enticed many settlers to the region. The Indian River Lagoon was a marshy, brackish, wetland that would need extensive reclaiming to produce profitable farmland, but Indian River Farms was determined in their task.

One of the most interesting buildings in this colonial memory project is the strange fusion of this romanticized Spanish mission past with the relief of Pocahontas on its second story. The Pocahontas Building, built in 1923 as a simple one-story city block, was only vaguely Spanish in its original construction.[28] In May, 1926, the second story was added alongside "23 efficiency, kitchenette apartments of the most modern type to be completely equipped and furnished," but according to one news report, "the most interesting things in connection with the project will be the modeling, in cement, of a life size Pocahontas, which is to be done by the sculptor, A. A. Thomas."[29] By September the "handsome building" was complete and decidedly more Spanish mission-style in its final version with elements of the revival architecture inspired by Moorish and Mediterranean traditions.[30]

Statues of Pocahontas and other Native peoples played into a post–Civil War sentimentality about US settler colonialism, including in the South. Scholars of memory have discussed the important differences between collective memory and history: "while history presents a neatly packaged version of past events, memory is an untidy process in which a mythical narrative is constantly negotiated."[31] It has long been the tradition that in schools throughout America, elementary teachers focus on "moral stories about past American heroes who struggled to create a national identity, forge and articulate enduring national ideals . . ." while promoting "American values" and Native history is often relegated to themes of inevitable demise.[32] This process can be tied back to the professionalization of history in the Gilded Age and the response Americans had to the dawning of the new century. Through commemoration, social clubs, and popular culture, Americans of this era often reacted against the influx of new immigrants, rapidly industrializing cities, and sought to create a connection to a uniquely American past while setting the stage for further development in places to the west and south.[33] In this way, the founders of Vero Beach projected their visions of the future by crafting an idealized past, a process that creates two very different types of histories, that of facts, and that of interpretation of those facts.[34] The myth of this Anglo–Indian encounter in the Chesapeake was of deep importance to Vero architects as a cherished national myth. Pocahontas plays the role of a founding mother in the settling of the American South and in the Midwest. For the settlers and architects of Vero Beach, this example of the mythical colonial past that the Indian River Farms Company and their Yankee boosters thought picturesque for their advertising journal but also represented a myth rooted in a national Anglo identity of the Algonquian woman nicknamed Pocahontas.

For these settlers, Pocahontas exists as a global icon, myth stripped of any historical fact, an icon that settlers can utilize with almost brand familiarity as Pocahontas became America's Indian. As literary scholar Philip Young noted in 1962, "Shopworn by sentimentality, Pocahontas endures and stands with the most appealing of our saints. She has passed subtly into our folklore, where she lives as a popular fable—a parable taught to children who carry some vague memory of her through their lives."[35] Treatments of Pocahontas fall into patterns, "dramatizing the story from the alleged facts, and filling gaps or inadequacies with invented material usually presented as fact," and settlers took advantage of public fascination with Pocahontas to lay claim to "virgin" territories while physically dispossessing Native peoples from their land and writing settler histories that bolster the American myth of settler innocence.[36]

Through plays, poems, novels, advertisements, and architecture, one can see the creation of an American myth and a claiming of Pocahontas as the model of what Rayna Green has called the "Pocahontas Perplex" a symbol of the Good Indian princess, "a Mother figure—exotic, powerful, dangerous, and beautiful—and as a representative of American liberty and European classical virtue translated into New World terms."[37] The Pocahontas narrative has been repeatedly manipulated by each successive American generation. Early settler narratives focus on her marriage to John Rolfe and the importance of her conversion while the nineteenth-century accounts place an emphasis on the rescue of John Smith, emphasizing her role as savior of the colony.[38] At some point, the historical figure of Pocahontas herself became this legendary character that could be used by settlers to suit their needs in creating a national myth, in the case of memorials, a physical reminder of their right to claim Indigenous land and space because Pocahontas had offered herself to the English. As Kevin Bruyneel explains, the myth of Pocahontas "is a form of American settler memory that disavows the role of gender, sexuality, and sexual violence in the foundation and functioning of settler colonialism—*of the taming of the continent.*"[39] This is what Philip J. Deloria has described as one of the "two contradictory and gendered story lines." In the case of Pocahontas, she has been "linked to the land itself . . . engendering a peaceful narrative of cross-cultural harmony in which whites became Indigenous owners of the continent through sexualized love and marriage stories." The second set of stories relied upon violent conflict and masculinity, which were certainly present in the narratives of the South with Native Floridians.[40]

At the start of the nineteenth century, US citizens participated in settler colonialism both across the continent and around the globe. In the process, settlers preferred two types of narratives when it came down to stories of the conquest of the land: the passive and the violent. In both cases, settlers and chroniclers made claims to the ever upward movement of their democratic experiment with a sense of innocence about their role in their violent encounters with Native peoples.[41] From the first encounter, Europeans represented the Native peoples of the Americas in a wide variety of venues: texts, woodcuts, paintings, sculptures, oral histories, marketing, and performances, part of a broader trend, as described by Deloria that "so-called savage Indians defined the boundaries and character of their civilization. Conversely, noble Indians allowed the romantic intellectuals of the Enlightenment to embody a critique of European social decadence."[42] The noble was an increasingly romantic view of Natives, a rational, moral stereotype of a people living in absolute harmony with nature who found their opposing reflection in the Ignoble or Demonic, another stereotype that was menacing, cannibalistic, and bloodthirsty.

The etymology of the word "savage" is revelatory. Rooted in terms that originally meant a state of nature, the noble savage became a peaceful people tied to a mythical past utopia like Arcadia, Elysium, and the Garden of Eden. The concepts of the good Indian and the noble savage were a part of the eighteenth-century Primitivism movement, a concept championed by Jacques Rousseau in his *A Discourse on Inequality* (1755) that men in their state of nature were essentially good or untainted by greed. This inspired nineteenth-century transcendentalists and novelists such as Ralph Waldo Emerson who encouraged readers to find their authentic, natural selves. The noble savage had natural wisdom, moral courage, and innocence. In the emerging popular literature, one can see this expressed in James Fenimore Cooper's *Leatherstocking Tales,* Herman Melville's *Moby Dick,* and Daniel Defoe's *Robinson Crusoe.* By the late nineteenth century, western novels would see further idealization of Indigenous peoples and caricatures of romantic Indian qualities.[43] Florida boosters most regularly turned to the noble stereotype of Native peoples as Florida itself became the site of modern-day Edenic fantasies of the Earthly Paradise.[44] The last "real" Indians of Florida left in the eighteenth century for Cuba, one recent

Pocahontas Building, Downtown Vero Beach, author photo, 2015.

popular history claimed. These types of settler stories help to justify Anglo racial classifications of the Seminole peoples, attempting to deny their claims to territory while claiming the Seminole were either not Indigenous to Florida or by focusing on their intermarriage with African Americans to deny their legitimacy. Scholar Jean M. O'Brien has argued that such a process of denying legitimacy to Indigenous peoples has "stubbornly remained in the consciousness and unconsciousness of Americans" and is a "toxic brew of racial thinking."[45]

Given the developers' Midwestern origin, the Sleepy Eye Lodge makes sense, and the inclusion of a Seminole building and Osceola Boulevard, as well as the 1926 Pueblo Arcade, are also logical inclusions to a town with a distant Spanish past for boosters seeking to create an investment opportunity for new "pioneers." But why choose the Algonquian Virgin-ian Pocahontas as the namesake for their headquarters? As mentioned earlier, while scholars of the contact period seek to understand the role of Indigenous women in their societies and their importance as cultural mediators, it is crucial to consider what these boosters thought Pocahontas represented and how these settlers used this Native woman as a justification for their conquest and settlement of the Indian River region.[46] The Improved Order of the Red Men was a popular fraternal organization for many of the Midwestern settlers of Florida. In 1885, the ladies' auxiliary of the Improved Order of the Red Men organized chapters of the Degree of Pocahontas throughout the country. Like the (mis)use of Native names and symbols by the Boy Scouts and many US summer camps to this day, these fraternal organizations had no connection to Indigenous people whatsoever; merely inspired by and patterned after their often-erroneous understandings of Indigenous beliefs and ceremonies. In the case of Pocahontas, tapping into longer settler narratives of removal, of lasting, and of conquering.

The example of Pocahontas described by these American settlers was one of "grace, beauty, and virtue as well as constant friendship to the palefaces." She was a woman of "remarkable grace, beauty, and kindness of heart," whose assistance to the English settlers "ultimately allowed the English colony to grow and flourish."[47] These Anglo-American settlers used the example of Pocahontas to demonstrate grace and continuing their manipulation of the Pocahontas narrative, the official history of the Improved Order of the Red Men, first published in 1892, included a poem by Miss F. N. Caulkins of New Haven, Connecticut, that includes the following lines:

Not thou, the red-browned heroine, whose breast
Screened the brave captive from the axe's gleam;
Not Pocahontas, lov'd, renown'd, caress'd,
But meek Rebecca, is my gentle theme.

. . . .

Star of Virginia, in her darkest hour,
Her joy, her theme of glory and of song;
Her wild red rose, that in the Stuart's bower
Shed grace—not took it—from the courtly throng.

. . . .

First Convert of the West! The Indian child

A matron stands—from whose sweet tongue
Flows the pure stream of English, undefil'd—
Flows the deep anthem, and eternal song.
. . . .
As Pocahontas, while these skies remain,
Still our Zodiac show the Virgin sign;
But, as Rebecca, when yon stars shall wane,
Yon Heavens roll by, she, as a star, shall shine.[48]

With lines like "First Convert of the West!" this poem clearly explains what Pocahontas meant to settler histories, interconnecting a Native woman with the yielding of the land, of conversion and progress, firsting and lasting. Pocahontas was not the only Native woman that Florida boosters would use to sell their settlements and products. Florida boosters of the Gilded Age and Progressive Era gendered the landscape and thus used women in a wide variety of advertisements to highlight the potential agricultural and citrus industries for would-be settlers. In marketing a semitropical land, Florida's advertisers sought to consistently play up the fertility of the area, a place of possibilities for the vigorous settler.[49] All told, at the University of Florida's collection of 3,147 vintage citrus labels, several hundred are vaguely "Indigenous" in theme and many are women. And their imagery buttressed what others settling there claimed: Florida was first discovered and last to be settled.

The cultural memory and myths surrounding the importance of Indigenous women allows some insight into settler construction of justified conquest and settlement of territory. Indigenous women played a significant role as cultural mediators and agriculturalists in nearly every sustained encounter between Europeans and Indigenous people in the New World and settler memory of these events highlight the settlement patterns of Florida.[50] The story of Pocahontas illustrates the importance of Native conversion to US settler narratives, as she turned away from her Indigenous beliefs to embrace the English, both figuratively and literally. She represents to settlers a promise of motherhood, of fertility, and the gentle hand of women and domesticity to flower their fields of settlement. In short, Pocahontas represents to these Florida settlers a perfectly Good Indian to juxtapose in a building physically adjacent to the doomed noble savage they represented through Osceola.

While contemporaneous narratives of the Seminole Wars focused on

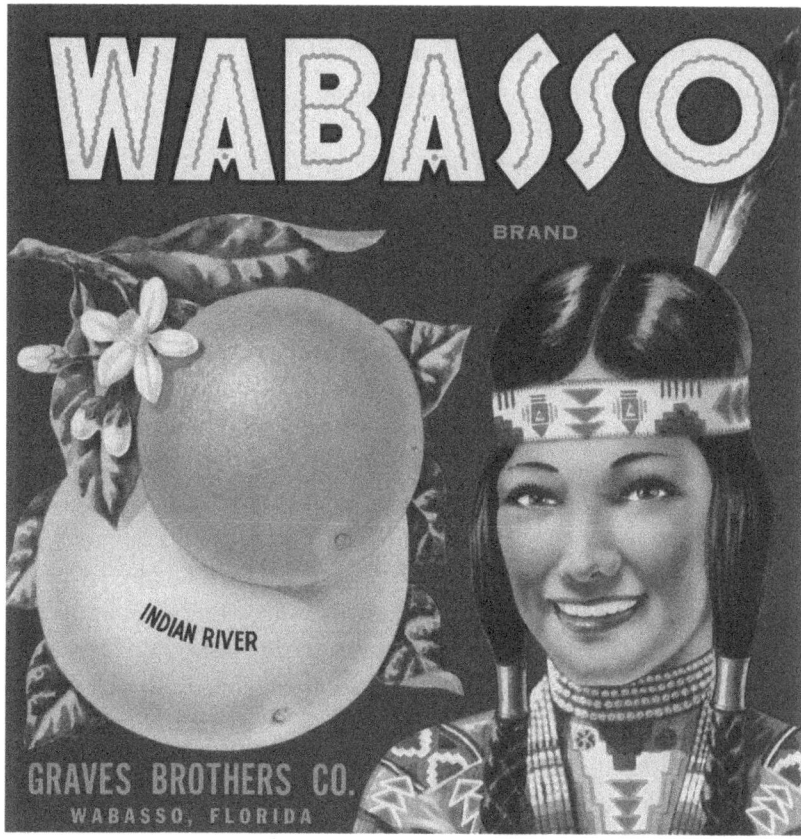

Wabasso Brand. Jerry Chicone Jr. Citrus Crate Label Collection, Special and Area Studies Collections, George A. Smathers Libraries, University of Florida.

Indian depredation, massacres, torture, and intense violence, by the time that settlers were building Vero Beach, Americans had transformed the legend of Osceola into the noble savage and he became rooted in American patriotism as settlers and authors cast the Seminole leader as an enduring hero and lover of freedom.[51] In contrast, Florida boosters marketed Seminole women as an opposite to the noble settler mother—they were sexualized as the "dusky maid" and the "Savages of Southern Sunshine."[52] All the while, Seminole men and women worked on Indian River Farms and for the white settlers of Vero Beach. Settlements around Vero had a robust trucking business specializing in the export of citrus, pineapples, tomatoes, sugar, and potatoes, as well as other vegetables. By the early twentieth century, these farms employed laborers that included Anglo settlers, recent Scandinavian immigrants, African Americans, and Seminole workers. One of the most profitable parcels of land was in the so-called Tiger Hammock, lands that Cow Creek Seminole women of the Tiger Clan once farmed.[53]

Other buildings and street names also reflect settler memory including streets named for Seminole, Osceola, Cherokee, Mohawk, Kickapoo, and Ute. The settlement of Vero had the Sleepy Eye Lodge across the street from the Pocahontas Building and the Seminole Building across from the Sleepy Lodge. Just down the street was the Pueblo Arcade. On July 20, 1917, the Vero News Bureau published in the *Fort Pierce News* an article entitled "Vigorous Vero" detailing the building plans under architect P. T. Burrows. The Seminole Building Corporation had capital funds totaling $70,000 divided into 700 shares. A. W. Young was the president, A. M. Hill the vice president, C. J. Gere the secretary, and Waldo Sexton was the treasurer. The original building was to be a two-story brick structure, with four business rooms on the first floor with at least one occupant determined before construction, the First National Bank of Vero. Included in the article were plans for the first movie theater in Vero.[54] One of the first businesses housed in the Seminole Building, in Room 15, was the Indian River Building Company who boasted "California Bungalows a Specialty."[55] At one point during its history, the Seminole Building housed a Piggly Wiggly and a dentist office as well as the Seminole Grocery owned by W. E. Riggs and the Simmons Dry Goods Store. When the city tore down the original building in 1968, a retrospective of the structure included some of its more salacious history, including during Prohibition when a portion of the section floor was reserved as a courthouse, "a back room facing the alley was full of imported Canadian and Scotch whiskey, as well as moonshine—some thousands of bottles." The article also noted some of the older street names and buildings in town including the Osceola building and the Pocahontas Building, both constructed in 1925, "now let us take a look at the Indian names which graced the old maps of the Original Town of Vero." Directly west of Seminole Avenue, "came Cherokee Avenue, then Mohawk Avenue, then Kickapoo Lane, then Shawnee Trail, then Apache Road, and what is today 20th Avenue in front of St. Helen's Catholic Church was Ute Pass. Today's 13th Avenue in front the downtown A&P was then called Pueblo Drive."[56] A newer building occupies this space now and is also called the Seminole Building.

The Pueblo Arcade highlights the Moorish, Spanish colonial–inspired trends found in the Pocahontas Building. Plans for the Pueblo Arcade began in 1925 for a new mixed-use building downtown. Investors included familiar subjects, A. M. Hill, Dr. LeRoy Hutchison, and A. W. Young along with William Atkin planned a two-story structure with "a ten foot arcade passage way which will give access to the store and offices which will occupy" the space.[57] Constructed by a local firm, Blackford and Davis, the Vero Finance and Improvement corporation planned to have the building ready for thirteen occupants by February 1926.[58] Like the Pocahontas Building, the second floor was reserved for apartments, "10 Murphy bed apartments with a living room, dining room, kitchenette and dressing rooms. They will be fitted up in the most modern manner throughout."[59] Complete with stucco walls and Mediterranean-inspired awnings, the Arcade underwent a massive restoration project in the 1990s that helped land it on the National Register of Historic Places on March 3, 1997.[60]

"Down this intriguing River, came restless souls, seeking new adventure and opportunity in a section of the United States that was as alluring as it was repelling," writes Anna Pearl Leonard Newman in her 1953 collection of settler narratives, *Stories of Early Life Along Beautiful Indian River*. These accounts are interesting, for starters, they encapsulate a settler perspective, but almost every time a settler is recalling any interaction with the Seminole, it is almost the exact same phrasing, "There were plenty of Indians, but they were friendly, and the children used to play together"; "Indians were plentiful but friendly"; "The Indians were so plentiful and so friendly, also curious, it was nothing unusual to see a circle of campfires at night near the house"; and only one woman who spoke disparagingly, "I didn't mind the critters so much but the Indians . . . they were troublesome. The women would walk right into the cabin, pick up my sewing and start sewing. I never did know why they like so much to sew."[61] Of these settler narratives, the most well-known work is by Dorothy Fitch Peniston, *An Island in Time*, a 1985 recollection and memoir of the wealth and prestige of a settler life on Orchid Island, "a Shangri-La where all unpleasantness ceased to exist." Peniston recalls fondly the budding commerce of Vero Beach and a Vanishing Indian motif, becoming increasingly prevalent in settler musings, reflecting that, "On Saturdays the ranchers in their high leather boots and ten gallon hats came to town with their families to do their shopping, as did Indians in native dress, the last remnants of the great Seminole tribe."[62] In this settler narrative, Peniston imagines the

Seminoles fading before the sun like the land falling to the developers plows.

To the north and west of the Indian River Farms Company and Vero, lay Wabasso, Roseland, Sebastian, and Fellsmere. In a series of pioneer recollections, the memories of Clarence A. Vandiveer stand out for their details of early settler encounters and relationships with the Seminole. In an interview with *Miami Herald* journalist Nixon Smiley, Smiley describes Vandiveer's homestead, "its sagging porches and its shutters hanging awry gave the place an atmosphere of picturesque degeneration . . . it was the kind of place where you would expect ghosts to flit at midnight."[63] Vandiveer settled in Wabasso in 1908 and planted a citrus grove. Frequently encountering the Seminole in the region, Vandiveer regaled Smiley with a tale that buzzes with settler stereotypes and expectations of stories that people wanted to hear about—a tale of drunken Indians. On Christmas Day, 1910, Vandiveer recalled, a Seminole man came to his home looking for whiskey, finding that he had none, they went over to the home J. E. Dodge who shared a jug, "the Indian and his friends drank the wyomy and they got drunk. They did a lot of whooping and hollering and some fighting and then they laid down under some orange trees and went to sleep. It was quite a Christmas for them, I guess."[64] In this same article, Vandiveer allegedly told Smiley that the town name was originally Louanna but that the name Wabasso came from "Mr. Parrott, one of (Henry) Flagler's executives, (who) liked Indian names," and that it meant "white heron . . . You would expect a man with the name Parrott to name a town after a bird." However, in a local newsletter written by Vandiveer, he contradicts himself, pointing out that the name Wabasso came from the Henry Wadsworth Longfellow poem, *The Song of Hiawatha,* and the lines, "From the Kingdom of Wabasso, From the Land of the White Rabbit." Like the use of Sleepy Eye and Pocahontas as familiar names and figures to settlers moving into the region, the choice of Wabasso highlights this trend once again, importing a Native name for settler claiming of territory. Vandiveer wrote a series of pioneer tales in this 1950s newsletter called *Mimeo News* where he described early settlement families and the history of the region. This newsletter included little sketches that ranged from wagon trains and cowboys to sunbathers on a beach. In these missives, Vandiveer continued to play to settler tropes about Native peoples, including the theme of the Vanishing Indian, the last of their kind, "the Seminole is slowly but surely passing from the Florida scene, but he has left us a reminder of his former presence by the place names he had left strewn all the length of the peninsula."[65] The Wabasso region, however, was already a Native space, once Aís and now Seminole. Wrote Vandiveer, "the application was eminently appropriate to this village, once a prominent trading post for the Seminole Indians living about the headwaters of the St. Johns River."[66] Wabasso became the second largest shipping point in Indian River County for fruits and vegetables and was dotted with several high-producing groves. In another article, Vandiveer recalled the oyster shell mounds, "the location of some old time settlement of aborigines."[67]

North of Vero, in the interior west of Sebastian, the Fellsmere Farms Company sold their booster dreams in the Kissimmee Prairie, a "land proposition about which enthusiasm entails no regret." Booster sales literature regarding Fellsmere promised "there is no better land in the entire Southern portion of the United State for general field crops" with perfect drainage systems in place and promised that raising cattle would be immediately profitable, "due to the fine grass and forage crops."[68] Efforts to develop the Fellsmere region began in the 1880s when advertisements began to appear in English and Yankee newspapers, promising paradise and commercial opportunity in Florida. Nelson Fell initially sought opportunity in Narcoosee before taking time away from Florida to pursue riches in central Asia at a copper mine and refinery he purchased with his brother, Arthur.[69] Fell returned to Florida at the heart of the Progressive Era that saw reclamation projects booming throughout South Florida. As the state experienced a significant population boom between 1900 and 1910, the need for new farmlands intensified and recently elected Governor Napoleon Bonaparte Broward was a champion of the cause. Broward had plans "to mobilize the state's resources to reclaim the Everglades" by constructing a series of canals across the state that would "allow surplus water to drain off into the Atlantic Ocean and Gulf of Mexico."[70] W. W. Russell created a company called Cincinnatus Farms to direct the reclamation project of 115,000 acres of hammocks and wetlands west of Sebastian, Florida, in 1895. By September 1910, engineers associated with the J. G. White Company had proposals ready for Nelson Fell. These proposals amounted to two plans: a levee or land drainage. Fell chose to drain the land using a series of five lateral canals and a series of sublateral canals that would drain water to the east toward Sebastian, "excess water from the entire tract would eventually flow into the middle fork of the Sebastian River."[71] Advertisements for Fellsmere appeared in the *Saturday Evening*

Post and other national venues, enthusiastically boasting claims of wealth to be had. A trade publication by the Fellsmere Farms Company, the *Fellsmere Farmer,* wrote on February 21, 1912, "Fellsmere Farms are located in the famous Indian River country, where the choicest fruit and vegetables are grown to perfection without the possibility of damaging frosts . . . Fellsmere Farms are ideally located, the soil is rich muck and prairie, and the drainage will be thorough and permanent."[72]

While the investors of Fellsmere and Vero both worked toward reclamation, other Florida land companies were far less scrupulous. That is in part why the Indian River Farms Company of Vero insisted that buyers see the land first and the Fellsmere Farms Company also had two demonstration farms for interested buyers. In February 1912, however, scandal broke out about land investments further south into the Everglades where thousands of buyers arrived at their plots of land only to find them still under water. Congress began an investigation of the Everglades drainage project and public confidence and interest in investing in Florida began to lose steam. The Fellsmere Farms Company sustained a loss that year of $8,105.95.[73] Fell put together a mitigation plan to readjust to the conditions by incorporating the town of Fellsmere, expanding the drainage plans, and increasing sales in 1915. He raised capital for the company by working with the Columbia Trustee Company on mortgage bonds and his colleague, Vans Agnew, wrote up the Fellsmere town charter, which the state assembly approved on April 29, 1915. Fell then met with Arthur Crane, hydraulic engineer representing the J. G. White Company, to figure out what to do about reclaiming the land by drainage canals.[74] While the company worked toward draining a smaller plot of land than initially considered, at least one history remembers that "prospective buyers who asked for directions to Fellsmere as they traveled down the Dixie Highway were often told that they would know they were in Fellsmere 'when they were knee deep in water.'"[75]

With company reserves depleted and a failure to meet their interest payment, a natural disaster struck the final blow for the first Fellsmere project. Unfortunately, a hurricane and subsequent flooding on July 31, 1915, wiped out the confidence the Fellsmere Land Company had in its project. Fellsmere defaulted on its bonds and went into receivership. On January 1, 1917, the remaining assets of the Fellsmere Farms Company were sold at auction on the courthouse steps in Fort Pierce.[76] Fellsmere would later experiment with growing sugar cane thanks to Frank Heiser's leadership in creating the Fellsmere Sugar Association in 1918, which an anonymous booster celebrated by saying, "I am in my opinion, that in cane Fellsmere is destined to greatness."[77] This dream would not immediately come to fruition as trying economic times hit Fellsmere again and again over the next decade. Heiser soldiered on "to go for broke," against the odds. He eagerly improved the drainage system, cleared an additional 1,000 acres west of Fellsmere for production, and hired workers to diligently plant cane, paying ten cents an hour to clear fields and twenty-five cents an hour for skilled laborers. By the summer of 1932, the *Vero Beach Press Journal* noted that "there is no unemployed labor in Fellsmere," as Heiser's efforts boasted a $4000 a month payroll.[78] Their efforts proved successful as demand for their sugar grew and even a hurricane and a devastating freeze did not dampen Heiser's enthusiasm for the project. While sugar production would eventually end in Fellsmere, during Heiser's lifetime it provided steady employment for the community for over thirty-five years.[79]

As Edenic as the boosters claimed, success in the lower Indian River Lagoon depended on arduous work and a stroke of luck. The Indian River Farmer championed hard work in its booster articles, including one entitled, "Put Your Shoulder to the Wheel," in its April 1914 edition: "Remember every dollar you put into your land will double and treble in the crop you take out, and while we live in this God-given country of flowers and birds, water and sunshine . . . we are planting our crops and enjoying the blessed privileges of an ideal climate."[80] That same edition included another editorial just a few pages later, "You Must Run The Gauntlet," which included the advice, "Before you can begin the big fight that will win or lose success for you—you must fight many smaller battles, battles that will give you strength and experience for the real and inevitable struggle."[81] A later edition, that same year, in an editorial by Moses Folsom, he opined, "You have met Couldahad. Everybody knows Couldahad," and invited his readers to "picture vegetables and flowers in every month growing in the open air . . . Grasp it now and independence is yours."[82] The Indian River Farms Company began drainage on approximately 45,000 acres of land beginning in January 1913, in a 1920 report made by the Indian River Farms Drainage District the board of supervisors estimated a total 2.5 million cubic yards of excavation with plans for an additional more than 1.5 million cubic yards to go.[83] A 1921 report prepared by the Indian River Farms Drainage District (incorporated on May 6, 1919) provides insight into the successes of the Indian River Farms Company to reclaim the wetlands for profitable agricultural production. Officers of the district included T. L. Hausmann as president, A. W. Young as secretary, and entrepreneur Waldo Sexton. Hausmann was also the president of the Vero Indian River Producers' Association and owned several groves. Sexton by this time was the president of the Florida East Coast Groves Association. Soil in the reclaimed land was "principally a fertile sandy loam, underlaid with good clay or marl subsoil . . . particularly adapted to the culture of citrus fruit and general farming in the heart of the famous Indian River citrus belt."[84]

Work on the original drainage plan completed in 1917 created a main canal that was 6.5 miles in length with lateral canals totaling 36 miles, sublateral canals measuring 120 miles and 26 miles of dikes. Smart fiscal stewardship left the district with zero debt and the value of the land "with improvements in the District, is not less than seven million dollars." Broken down, unimproved lands had values that ranged from $100–$250 per acre while improved grove lands had values as high as $2000 per acre, dependent on the age of the trees. Farm and trucking lands had values that ranged from $250–$400 an acre. Improvements also included more than 150 "flowing artesian wells . . . affording irrigation when necessary which in conjunction with good drainage, permits of perfect control of moisture conditions in the soils." Drainage district lands hosted 3,500 acres of citrus groves and 4,500 acres for general farming that included sugar cane and vegetables. Farms in the district also included three dairies. Two large fruit-packing houses "with a capacity of 2,000 boxes, or six carloads," prepped oranges and grapefruit for distribution daily. Five smaller packing houses handled the vegetable distribution, and a cane syrup mill had the capacity to produce eighty tons of sugar cane each day.[85]

As Vero developed, the founding settlers picked out choice tracts of land for their groves and pastures. Indian River Farms founder Herman J. Zeuch reserved a portion of the Tiger Hammock for himself. The Tiger Hammock was an important part of the region, a plot of soil the Seminole used for their own gardens. The settlers called it Tiger Hammock because members of Seminole leader Tom Tiger's family traditionally farmed there. As general manager for the Indian River Farms Company, it is no surprise that Zeuch would save this plot for himself, planning to plant beans there in the fall of 1914.[86] By May 1922, Waldo Sexton was in charge of developing Zeuch's tract in the Tiger Hammock two miles west of what became known as Oslo Road in a section called Lateral B near what would become the Viking settlement in south Vero for a grove, with plans that the entire 160 acres would be a grove by the end of the year.[87] Later in 1925 a settler named Newton R. Frost chose another tract of land near Oslo Road, "on a pretty knoll in the edge of Tiger Hammock he and his daughter selected the site for their Florida home." There they planted bananas, coconuts, and berry bushes, as well as planning sixty acres of cultivation. An "intimate friend and business associate of Herman J. Zeuch," Frost died in St. Paul, Minnesota, in 1926.[88] The Minnesota connection to the lands south of Oslo and the Atlantic Ridge that dots the Tiger Hammock did not dissipate, however. Nor did the desire for citrus and large groves. J. M. Knight and W. R. Duncan undertook the largest grove to date in 1926 by planting citrus on 160 acres, including 80 acres owned by A. W. Young and associates. The planting included 12,000 trees: grapefruit, oranges, and tangerines.[89]

While citrus was certainly the top crop for the Indian River region, tomatoes, potatoes, and other staple fruits and vegetables were also in demand. *The Indian River Farmer* booster publication regularly included individual articles touting the many crops that could be grown in the Vero region such as the mango, "without question the best of all tropical fruits," and a poem ostensibly written to a northern observer, "Our fruit sells well, truck the same, Lots of money coming. No walking hordes of workless men, Swarm our cities, bumming."[90] A 1927 article from the *Vero Beach Press* compared "enormous shipments from Mexico, Puerto Rico, and other outside producing sections [that] have filled the market with the lower quality. Fancy and choice grades from Indian River County find ready demand in the best market at a premium over shipments from other producing section."[91] In 1929, Fellsmere produced more than one hundred acres of potatoes with other acreage set aside for "tomatoes, white beans, peas, and salad crops, lettuce, escarol, and spinach," grown in "commercial quantities." Lateral A district had plantings of tomatoes, peas, broccoli, lima beans, strawberries, onions, and cauliflower. Lateral B and the Tiger Hammock had 400 acres of tomatoes, 100 acres of "Irish" potatoes and "considerable acreage in English peas, cabbage, celery, lettuce and other vegetables" alongside at least two hundred acres of citrus.[92] Potatoes held a special role in booster literature with one publication reminding readers that "of all the crops of the truck farmer, the Potato is the one which is always salable at more or less remunerative prices."[93] A fifteen-page pamphlet created by the Indian River Farms Company included effusive praise for the potato as well as practical advice as to how to grow, harvest, and take to market the best crop including an opinion from Mr. George T. Tippin, the president of the Vero Indian River Growers' Association, "I believe this will become the largest potato point in the state."[94] "Indian River Farms are not an experimental proposition," the boosters claimed, "potatoes as well as other crops are being produced on these rich soils."[95] The advent of the Flagler railroad made taking Indian River County produce to market so much easier than it had been in the late nineteenth century, when New York journalist, Amos J. Cummings lamented that, "Peas, beans, cauliflowers, asparagus, turnips, beets, radishes, cabbages, strawberries, and innumerable other vegetables ripen along the Indian River in December, January, and February, but they might as well ripen in the moon so far as a market is concerned. I believe that the Indian River hammocks contain the richest land in the United States."[96] When the Gifford family arrived in Vero in 1887 they found a banana plantation near the Oslo settlement, which had once been called Crawford's Point, "a company by the name of Baugh & Barnes Co. had started the plantation but it did not make a success of it, so had abandoned it."[97] The Florida East Coast Railroad and Dixie Highway changed all of that. An April 1914 edition of the *Indian River Farmer* highlighted the new Vero train depot on the first page, "the Florida East Coast Railway recently enlarged the station facilities at Vero made necessary by the increase of the traffic and freight business in this growing town."[98]

Included in the settler memories are some of the Gifford family "tall stories":

> Once I took a picture of our grapefruit stand. The mosquitoes were as thick as could be. I sent the picture to friends and asked them if they could see the grapefruit on the trees, as the fruit was still green. The reply was: "Couldn't see the fruit, but there was sure a nice flock of turkeys under the trees."

*

> I had the first fruit stand. It had a palmetto roof. Pelicans would fly north and would light on the fruit stand and call to the young mosquitoes, thinking there were her babies, to fly north with her.

*

Indian River Publishing Company. (1914). *Indian River Farmer,* 2(8–9). Accessed via https://ufdc.ufl.edu/ufo0091446/00004.

We used to sit around and watch the mosquitoes play games under the trees. The one that got the most oranges on its ball, won the game.

*

The business kept growing and it was a task to squeeze the orange juice, so I thought of boring a hole in the tree, and drawing out the juice before it got to the oranges. It didn't work too well, so a Texas man suggested we saw off the tree and cap it, as they do the oil wells in Texas, to get the juice. That worked just grand.[99]

Wabasso settler George Sears also had a sense of humor, "he had a cigar box and would tell you, if you would pay for the tax, that you have it. When it was opened there were no cigars, but some tacks in it."[100]

Settler erasure of Native history and presence took on many forms from the narrative presented by boosters to the transformation of the land by groups such as Indian River Farms. All throughout the United States, settlers found agricultural success in established Native spaces. Thus, the lands of the Seminole known as the Tiger Hammock presented an ideal opportunity for farmers, like Indian River Farms founder Herman Zeuch and the topic of the next chapter, newcomer Axel Hallstrom. Physically reshaping the land to Euro-American ideals is another form of removal, erasing the presence of Native spaces and changing the landscape of Florida to a settler space.

4

Citrus and Pineapple Dreams

Settler Memory and History

A poem is running through my mind from somewhere out of the past, and I think it would be a good thing to remember by those who are easily inclined to be discouraged:

> Smile and the world smiles with you,
> Knock and you knock alone,
> For the cheerful grin will let you in,
> Where the kicker was never known.
> Groan and the way looks dreary,
> Laugh and the path looks bright,
> For the welcome smile brings sunshine while—
> A frown shuts out the light.
> Kick and there will be trouble brewing,
> Whistle and life will be gay.
> And the world's in tune like a day in June,
> And the clouds roll away.[1]

As discussed in chapter 3, while settlers streamed into Jacksonville and St. Augustine in the postbellum era, the Indian River Lagoon was late in the settlement game, as few daring settlers and boosters came there to build orange groves, "with the hope that in the future, when a railway tapped this section, the Indian River orange would become famous. The foresight of the old settlers has been amply justified, as Indian River oranges now command the highest market price of any grown in Florida." Oranges were not the only cash crop, by the late nineteenth century, "the pineapple industry, although not a dozen years old, has now a more valuable crop than even the orange."[2] In one instance at Melbourne, north of Vero, a settler history recalled a strip of "large pineapple patches" near East Melbourne, "there is nothing particularly inviting about this beach-strip in its natural state but it certainly does grow pineapples to perfection." Speaking to the bounty to be found in pineapples, "one settler the other day sold his place for 10,000 dollars. He bought it six years ago for 50 dollars an acre. At the end of three years, he had spent 900 dollars on it, and taken 1,350 dollars out of it, besides getting the crops of the past two years." Pineapple patches in this era could be found as far south as Jupiter.[3] Alfred Michael, a settler whose parents arrived in spring 1887, described settlement patterns thusly, the "northeast section of this part of Florida was settled around the 60's and 70's, and down here in the 80's." Original settlement of the lower Indian River Lagoon focused on the barrier island, John's Island, which allowed for ease of shipment for fruits and vegetables, "for it was rich and being nearly free from frosts was a mecca for vegetable growing farmers." First the vegetables and crops were shipped by boat until Flagler's railroad arrived (1893–94) and then "brought over to the railroad by boat [across the Indian River Lagoon] to be shipped North. This grew to be quite a chore and gradually was abandoned, but nearly all the early settlers landed there first."[4]

Another wave of immigration to the lower Indian River Lagoon was not Anglo Northerners but recent Scandinavian immigrants often moving south from their first wave of migration into the Upper Midwest: Minnesota, Iowa, and Wisconsin. To the south of Vero just north of Fort Pierce a few small settlements emerged with Scandinavian immigrants in the late nineteenth century. John Helseth, a Norwegian, settled and named Viking. In a testimonial by the daughter of O. O. Helseth, another early Viking settler who first emigrated to Minnesota before making his way south, Dr. Inga Olla Helseth recalled the challenging times they had in the unfamiliar terrain as they sought to build their homesteads and find profitable commerce and livelihoods. He arrived in Fort Pierce in 1896 by train and moved north toward Vero by boat where the Helseth family befriended the Hughes family who were already there and shared persimmons and mulberries that grew at their home, a marvel to Inga. Inga's father named the settlement of Oslo and "started a post office, freight, express and passenger stop. We had a store, church and school, and he had the first Dodge agency. He owned the second Ford in these parts; Nate Penny had the first one."[5] Hunting and fishing were the most common means of providing food in the early days, as she remembers, "we had a garden in the hammock, and the deers were so troublesome we mounted a gun and stretched a string from the trigger so when the deer hit it, the gun would kill the animal. There was so much wild life."[6] They would then keep the meat for later use by grinding it and making "meat balls, cover it with lard and it would keep." Other foodstuffs included raccoon that they parboiled and fried as well as "sweet potatoes, cow-peas, honey and mulberries."[7] Early descriptions of the Edenic Indian River Lagoon by these settlers also included tales of abundant marine life and a wealth of flora and fauna.

Of the nearby Seminole, Inga wrote about seeing Seminole encampments near the Helseth homestead, "it was nothing unusual to see a circle of campfires at night near the house," and Inga remembered their visitors as "plentiful and so friendly, also curious." The Seminole would bring the Helseths meat and Inga had a specific memory involving persimmons that her mother had lying in the kitchen to ripen, "a horde of Indians crowded into the kitchen and insisted on having the persimmons. They were not ready to eat and they spattered them all over mother's cleanly scrubbed floor." This did not distress her mother, however, as she noticed a child that she thought looked "neglected" and so "she cleaned up the baby and put clothes on it." They later found the clothes discarded in the bushes but according to Inga, "Mother was a wonderful helper to others. She helped those who were sick, brought babies into the world, in fact, did anything which was needed in the lives of the pioneers." From this exchange, we can see that her kindness and sense of community extended to her Seminole neighbors as well.[8]

One of the most well known of the settlers was Axel Hallstrom, a Swedish émigré and botanist who moved to south Vero near the Viking settlement due to the illness of his wife, Emily. He created a forty-acre pineapple plantation on the Florida Ridge in the area near sections of the Tiger Hammock, once the agricultural lands of the Tiger clan of the Cow Creek Seminole, south of lands farmed by Indian River Farms founder Herman Zeuch. Lost in the narrative, however, is that settlers claimed land that Seminoles actively cultivated. The paradise they found, the land rich for agriculture, was land that Seminole created, a controlled environment of agriculture and cattle ranching that generations of Seminole shaped into their own landscape. Axel eventually expanded to the citrus business and was a charter member of the Florida Citrus Exchange, serving as president in 1927. His daughter, Ruth, carried on the citrus business at the Hallstrom farm well into the 1980s after a brief stint as a schoolteacher on Orchid Island. As a case study, this chapter highlights the dynamics of settler memory and colonialism through the lens of a successful citrus and pineapple grove and the personal cost of settling in the nascent community of Vero while reshaping the land and the narrative. This becomes increasingly evident when one considers the story of Axel's sister, Johanna, who paid for her brother's success by selling a successful restaurant in north Chicago to finance her brother's ambitions and even came south to help raise Ruth when Emily succumbed to her illness. Within these settler records are narratives of Eden and paradise lost, of the vanishing Native presence, and of the progress narrative of settler expansion, themes of the paradise to be found by the hardworking settler.

Born November 10, 1870, in Skåne, Sweden, Axel Hallstrom was the youngest of ten children who originally apprenticed as a landscaper in Denmark and then later in Berlin, Germany, before emigrating to Chicago in 1898 where he joined his sister Johanna and his brothers, Nels and John. The next year Axel accepted a position as the head gardener for James Jerome Hill, a railroad magnate who had an estate in St. Paul, Minnesota. Hill, the chief executive officer of the Great Northern Railway, a set of lines under the control of the Canadian-American Railroad, was known as the "Empire Builder" because of the lines he built through Minnesota, Wisconsin, and across North Dakota into Montana, bringing industry and settlement with him wherever his lines crossed. During Axel's time at the Hill estate, he met and married Emily Bjorkelund and had a daughter, Ruth Christina, born on January 5, 1904. Emily, however, was severely ill and Axel thought a change of climate might help her recover. With the building of the Flagler Florida East Railroad as well as the successes of booster literature from parties, like the Indian River Farms Company, many settlers flocked to Florida, and in 1904 Axel went south to examine lands near the Viking settlement between south Vero and Fort Pierce.

The Hallstrom family moved to a plot of land (near what is now Indrio Road in Fort Pierce) late in the summer of 1904. Renting a house, Axel hired a Norwegian settler, John Helseth, to build a home for the Hallstrom family in the Viking settlement as Axel set forth to build a farm and a pineapple plantation.[9] Unfortunately, on May 18, 1908, Emily died and Axel moved north of the Viking settlement to the Oslo settlement adjacent to the Tiger Hammock in south Vero, where Axel purchased forty acres along the Dixie Highway in 1909. For almost ten years the Hallstroms lived in a small two room, two-story wooden house on the east side of Dixie Highway but in 1915 they began construction on a new home on the west side of the road.[10]

When Emily died, Axel convinced his sister Johanna to move to Florida to help him raise Ruth and assist him in the management of the farm. The Hallstrom family records highlight the complicated family dynamics that accompanied this decision and how the loss of Emily affected young Ruth. An extensive collection of letters about business and family affairs highlights a vibrant and dynamic cast of characters in the Hallstrom story. Axel Hallstrom and his daughter Ruth maintained a transatlantic lifestyle afforded by his pineapple crops and later his citrus groves as Axel became a prominent member of early Vero and Fort Pierce commercial enterprises.

As an artifact of settler Florida itself, the house certainly tells a story about Ruth, who was an accomplished seamstress and very fashion forward and cosmopolitan, the house includes images of Ruth in Germany in front of the Reichstag in 1931 with a fox stole as well as of Ruth in a black 1947 Dior-style taffeta dress that she wore in an advertisement for the citrus grove. The house collections include many of her items acquired during trips abroad with her father as well as evidence of her other hobbies, including a card table where she played bridge, canasta, pinochle, and cribbage. Ruth was an amateur painter; local lore claims that A. E. "Beanie" Backus (the son of another pineapple farmer) taught Ruth how to paint. Backus himself was largely self-taught but his lasting inspiration and occasional instruction to the generation of twenty-six African American artists known as the Highwaymen (or Indian River School of Artists) has left a large catalog of vibrantly beautiful Florida landscape paintings. Backus created a community at his home in nearby Fort Pierce that included the various Highwaymen artists as well as jazz musicians and famed novelist and anthropologist, Zora Neale Hurston. Waldo Sexton of the Indian River Farms Company counted Beanie Backus as a close friend.[11] Ruth worked on her paintings during her spare time from running the citrus business after her father died in 1966. Ruth was fond of the Highwaymen style of painting and owned five landscape paintings, all created by Alfred Hair, one of the original Highwaymen.

Examining the rest of the house, one can witness the story of changing eras in Florida history and the lives of recent immigrants as they brought with them cherished possessions from their home country and adapted to their new surroundings. The story of the Hallstrom house is certainly one of financial prosperity and consumption of goods. While Axel packed all his belongings in a single steamer trunk (now housed in the foyer) when he emigrated from Sweden, he managed to bring with him a Flow Blue

Milk Pitcher, inscribed with a family note on the inside. The Hallstroms decorated their home with an eclectic taste in furnishings, including an Egyptian Gothic revival-style bronze chandelier, Hayasi fine china from Japan with "ghost geisha" visible in the bottom of the teacups, a reindeer candelabra from Lappland, a Delft pitcher from the Netherlands, and a Hoosier Cabinet from Indiana.[12] The Hallstroms were no longer "roughing" it in the Florida wilds.

Hallstrom's former employer, J. J. Hill, made an appearance in a May 1914 edition of the *Indian River Farmer* advertising journal who quoted him on their front page, "Farms are producing far more substantial wealth than gold mines, and men who are now seeking gold mines should turn to the soil to make their fortunes."[13] Hill emerged again in a June 1914 edition where they reported, "He emphasizes that the only thing that endures is the soil and this, too, to be preserved at its highest fertility must be treated right."[14] In the Oslo settlement, that gold mine came by way of pineapples. The Atlantic Ridge afforded soil particularly conducive to the cultivation of pineapples. Pineapples grown in Vero are quite unlike any other, their flesh is light in color but deeply fragrant, sweet and delicate to taste. In one settler history of Florida, Robert Goodbread recalled, "Pineapples, beans, and fishing, that's all we had. Plant the pineapple about 18 inches apart, almost on top of the ground. Put cottonsead meal and tobacco dust in the furrows. They'd get ripe in June. Put 'em on the boat to Titusville or ship 'em out on the railroad."[15] Successful commercial pineapple cultivation began in the Florida Keys by settler Benjamin Baker who brought in pineapples from Havana and started to plant them at Plantation Key. The shallow soil of the Keys, however, soon became depleted of nutrients and settlers throughout Florida experimented in other regions, including Orange, Volusia, and other interior counties of central Florida. Success would be found along the Atlantic Ridge extending from Fort Pierce south to Miami and in a few spots north of Vero. As the booster journal the *Indian River Farmer* describes it, "the west bank of the Indian River is a high narrow strip of sandy soil about twenty-five miles in extent, and this is the far-famed Indian River pineapple belt through which the Florida East Coast railroad passes."[16] By 1910 there were more than 5,000 acres of pineapples with an annual crop exceeding 1,000,000 crates. Varieties included the Red Spanish, "the most widespread pineapple planted . . . used for their hardiness, and ability to maintain freshness during shipping and harvesting." Other types included the second favorite, the Smooth Cayenne and the Abbaka.[17] At one point 83 percent of the pineapples grown in the United States were harvested from the Atlantic Ridge, citing one farmer whose "eight and one-half acres cleared the owner $9,000 in one year. Grapefruit was grown. Twenty-five acres of land brought $15,000 for a crop of pineapples."[18] Describing the "attractive bungalows and handsome residences on the river bank" whose backyard held "pineapple fields far over the ridge," Joseph Hill in an article about "automobiling" through the county, shared, "Here on the purest white sand," they produce 600,000 boxes of pineapples on average, netting a profit of $750,000.[19]

In a 1914 article in the *Indian River Farmer*, a writer calling himself "An East Coast Optimist," offered a reflection of expectations that northerners had about coming to Florida, "When he gets to Florida he expects to find cantaloupes, watermelons, pineapples, corn, cassava, oranges, and alligator pears, and running around among the vines, alligators, snakes, mosquitoes—all this in the family garden in any place and at any time." Calling these visitors, "Northerner skeptics" the author surmises that they might wonder "just how dangerous the Florida crackers are," fearing "razor-back hogs at every station along the road, and would not be surprised to see some long-haired son of a gun who totes a pistol jump from the side of the road to start a circus just to see a sick Yank run like the blazes." Bemused, the "Optimist" recalling a conversation he had with a friend who asked why the grower did not plant sweet potatoes along with his pineapple fields, spoke of abundant opportunity, "My friend, that piece of ground produces five times as much profit in pineapples and I can afford to buy my sweet potatoes and have money enough left over to pay for gasoline to run to town in the motor or automobile after them." His advice to the skeptics was to come and see the land, but, not limiting themselves to best time of year where they might see "flowery stories about the land of perpetual sunshine, of beds of ease and the charms of earthly paradise," no, his suggestion was come to the pineapple section from June to October when the mosquitoes were at their worst, when the heat was highest, and the hurricane season and wind storms were "as strong as the ones along the New England states." Why would he advise this? Because the harvests were so plentiful they made up for the bad times, his own crop requiring labor "as much as ten hours a day, six days a week for six weeks," leaving no time to go fishing but a mighty surplus when it was all done.[20] In another article in the May edition, Superintendent Adams of the Southern Utilities Company opined, "Every northern man, before he

Workers harvesting pineapples in the Indian River region, 1909. State Archives of Florida, Florida Memory, https://www.floridamemory.com/items/show/99, accessed 30 March 2023.

comes to this state, is certain that it is all sand and mosquitoes, or all water and alligators, while most also have a childish vision of oranges growing everywhere and waiting to be picked."[21]

For families along the Atlantic Ridge, prosperity came from pineapples and patience as clearing out the hammocks was an exhausting and time-consuming endeavor. The July and August 1914 double edition of the *Indian River Farmer* highlighted pineapple production as its cover story, reprinting R. L. Godwin's column, "How Pineapples are grown on East Coast of Florida," from the *Florida Grower*. This editorial relates that the "largest acreage of pines will be found at Vero, Oslo, Viking, St. Lucie, Fort Pierce, Eldred, Walton, Eden, Jensen, Ankona, Rio, Stuart, Delray, Boynton, Deerfield, Pompano, Little River, and Miami," all astride the bountiful soils of the Atlantic Ridge. To clear the land and prepare the field for planting it cost on average between $70 to $150 an acre, "flatwoods pine land, or prairie, may be cleared at much less expense." The average life of a field without re-cropping was about fifteen years until the old plants needed to be removed and new ones planted, although some fields near Fort Pierce yielded crops for twenty-one years. By 1914, however, "the Smooth Cayenne, Porto Rico and Queen," varieties went out of favor in "the Indian River Section, as the fields are shorter lived than the Red Spanish."[22]

A good crop of 300–350 crates, average weight of about 80 pounds, containing roughly 16–24 Abakka or 18–48 Red Spanish pineapples was "a good output for the first two years. After that around 250 crates per acre per year for a period of the next 12 or 14 years" was an admirable crop, costing about 85 cents per crate to "grow the fruit, pack it and get it on the cars ready to move." Netting on average about $1.60 a crate in 1913, this left growers with a profit of nearly 75 cents per crate. The author also provided detailed instructions on the use of fertilizer including such advice as "drop in the heart of the plant about heaping tablespoonful of fertilizer that will not burn, to prevent sand from entering the heart during a beating rain." Goodwin advised on a proper mixture for fertilizers, whose "results with me have proven satisfactory in using a 5 per cent ammonia, 6 per cent potash, 2 per cent phosphoric acid formula from the budding of the young plants to old age, and the fact that I have some fields that have borne consecutive crops for 21 years tends to prove that I am right."[23] Reports for the spring harvest that ended June 30, 1914, included 2,119 carloads of miscellaneous fruit; 300 carloads of lettuce; 1,634 carloads of celery; 4,194 miscellaneous vegetables; 5,434 carloads of tomatoes; 210 carloads of strawberries; 2,138 carloads of potatoes; 979 carloads of pineapples; 3,667 carloads of watermelons; and 329 carloads of cantaloupes. All told this represented three months of "six trainloads every day of the week . . . when one considers that this was a very poor season—on account of the drought—the figures are stupendous."[24] Booster literature tells a story of abundant sunshine and growth:

> Down here in Florida the bright sun will shine and the farmer will sweat and the crops will smile, just tear themselves up by the roots growing so fast, and the genial, salt-laden sea breezes will sweep over the state and fill the lungs with the bracing air, the temperature will

rule warm and even, about 10 degrees lower than up there... And the happy farmer will wear a deep path to the bank, where he will drop in a few more dollars of surplus earnings to help swell the pile already looking pleasing to the eye.[25]

Abundance came in time but an examination of the letters from the Hallstrom homestead tell quite the story of the realities of farming in the region and what settlers faced in Oslo and along the Atlantic Ridge, from heartbreak to success in the bright sun laden fields of South Florida. To this one can add the intrigue of family scandals, in this the Hallstrom's are uncharacteristically open in their letters about their concerns and feelings, providing a unique window into their experiences. Axel Hallstrom was one of ten children from Skåne in southernmost Sweden, thusly his correspondence involved many of his extended kin and family across the world. Axel's family moved from Skåne when he was six a little inland to Bonderup, later even further inland and to the north to Ostra Sallerup where he "finished grammar school and then worked on the parental farm until he was eighteen." A 1955 profile of Axel in *American Swedish Historical Foundation: The Chronicle* described him as "a true *skåning* he was attached to the soil, but not destined to become a father in the old sense of his native province."[26] Fruit trees such as apple, cherry, pear, and plum are common in the region of Skåne as well as other fruits like strawberries, blackberries, loganberries, and blueberries and Axel worked for several estates in Skåne.[27] In memoriam following his death in 1966, fellow Swede and friend, Walter G. Nord, President of the American Swedish Historical Foundation, opined on Axel's history and interest in horticulture, "he worked with flowers, vegetables, berries and later citrus fruits... We both had keen interest in developing and producing products that would not only save the customer money, but could be sold a price that would yield a fair profit." Continuing with his praise over his departed friend and colleague, "His broad experience in growing things in many places prior to coming to Florida had a great deal to do with giving him confidence that he could go into an undeveloped Florida."[28] Axel was contacted by the Lunds Botanical Garden in Sweden on February 25, 1910, asking if he was "willing to gather and send seed from some interesting and rare plants that grow wild in Florida."[29]

Family dynamics played a keen role in Axel's life, an 18 January 1895 letter from Kerstin/Kirsti Sodeberg (Axel's sister) in Dalby, Sweden, included some details of the exploits of her son, Nils, "You have now, as you say, told the truth about our brothers and we appreciate it much, because to hide things is not a good characteristic." Speaking plainly, she continued, "it is better to have it said, as with the criminal things that Nils has been involved in for many years. It clears up what is going on with him, yes, drunkenness, lying, pride, betrayal, and cheating are on his list and I have long known how it will end for him and have said that before."[30] A 8 May 1904 letter from Kirsti to Johanna Hallstrom, shared, that "Now it is so many years since I have seen you so that I can barely recognize you . . . You are fat but I am now old and thin . . . But dear sister, we have been separated for such a long time so we may never meet again." In this same letter, Kirsti opined on Nils, "I wonder so much about Nils, who has married such a young girl and why she would want someone who is as old as Nils."[31] The issues relating the Hallstrom siblings and their children connected to Axel's farm as the Hallstrom plantation was a family investment as related in an August 1904 family letter, "you and our brothers Nils and John bought a large part of Florida to raise fine fruit in order to become billionaires or maybe only a millionaire. Good luck as for that I would rather wish to see you in a sparkling luxury yacht in Malmos harbor where I would get to hug the lucky Yankee to show my faithfull brotherly love."[32]

A 21 June 1904 letter from Emily and Axel to his sister Johanna began to detail their life in Fort Pierce and the young settlement at Viking, "Home life is totally different than up there but we like it very much . . . Where we live is very comfortable. When we came we had no screens on the windows or doors. We put on cheese cloth around the patio and on the windows and it became so cool on the patio so we sleep out there."[33] Family drama popped up again in this letter which otherwise discussed the cost of living, "Butter is 34 cents and eggs 15, Milk is 10 cents a quart. Everything is more expensive than Chicago," when the Hallstroms related to Johanna, "We heard that Nils has decided to move here this fall . . . it will be allright [sic], even though Betty allways [sic] has lied and carried on and it surely will not be any different when she comes her [sic] and must live in the country."[34] More intrigue on Nils's relationship with Betty, his aforementioned young wife, emerged in a 13 October 1904 letter from Emily to Johanna, "We are wondering about Nils and Betty's happiness is in jeopardy," Emily wrote to Johanna, speculating, "I am attempted to think it is the best would be to see a doctor and examine the head."[35]

What can be seen here are the ways in which families, separated by long distances, maintained kin networks across the Atlantic world. Many of the letters from this period relate to the death of Axel and Johanna's mother and the subsequent death of their sister, Karna/Carna, who died of a lung disease in May 1904. Anna Hallstrom confided to her sister, Johanna, in a 12 November 1904 letter about settling Carna's estate, sending her a picture of the grave site, "I thought it would make you happy to see the place where your dear parents lie . . . and you can see how beautiful and well kept their resting place is . . . you are the only one of all their children that has thanked us for all we did for them." Carna's long illness and the division of Carna's estate proved quite contentious, especially with Per/Par (Axel's brother) according to Anna, who lamented the bitterness it created, "I was at her home the day before she (Carna) died and I had then as always bought some good things to eat that I thought would taste good to her and make her happy. Even so she laid there filled with hate and bitterness to the last day. Isn't that sadness that can bring down a person and I wasn't well either."[36] Per/Par asked to borrow money from Axel, "400–500 Kr, which he wanted to borrow from me, the same as my share of the inheritance from Karna. I disliked that and I did not respond and now he reads my silence." In that same letter, John and Nils came up in Axel's commentary and the translator of the 8 December 1904, letter from Axel to Johanna noted in the margin about Par/Per and Nils's problems, "My translation of this is: drinking problems."[37] Yet even more emerges about Par/Per in a letter from Kersti on January 24, 1905, "But what you do Axel, keep your money and don't pay attention to what Par needs." She repeats this advice in a postscript, "Don't forget my warning. Let Par take care of himself."[38]

In the midst of this family turmoil, one sees the hardships that Axel and Emily faced before her untimely death as farming along the Atlantic Ridge involved extensive reclamation as well as plant acquisition, in a letter to Johanna on August 25, 1904, Emily explained that they could only manage about four acres so far, "that is about all Axel can get planted as we thought that we couldn't get any plants but Axel advertised in 3 different newspapers, so now he has gotten enough for the area that he is going to plant orange trees on . . ."[39] Axel found the time to report on his progress to Johanna on December 8, 1904, "I am walking up to the land every day almost . . . Next week I will get the timber moved up to the house and after two weeks it will be up. The plants are growing well, the orange and grapefruit trees are planted and the fence is done and all is done." He also shared about his daughter, "Ruth is so big now you would not recognize her. She has four teeth and she eats oranges, eggs, porridge, bread, etc., she is starting to walk a little now."[40] In a long letter from Axel to Johanna on March 11, 1905, Axel reported on the conditions, "We have very fine weather now although it is a little dry but that doesn't hurt the pineapples and they are growing just fine. On Monday we should put fertilizer on them so long as everything goes as intended." Axel wrote that he intended to "farm about four acres . . . about 125,000 plantings which would be really good. Our orange trees are growing now and one of them is blooming very well but we don't expect any fruit this year." Axel continued in his description of the farm and his laying hens, whose eggs provided a much-needed source of income, "This week we have sold seven dozen eggs at 25 cents a dozen and it should be pretty good for next week too. Just today we got 17 eggs. They are expensive here and so one can earn an enormous amount on the hens, because with good care they lay all year long down here."[41]

Aside from his work tending the farm, Axel found time to hunt as well, describing an alligator hunt, "caught one about 2 feet 10 inches down by the railroad. I took the rascal home today. I laid a trap and trapped in a corner and led him home. And now he is sleeping in a box. Tomorrow I will kill the rascal and skin him because it can be great to have." Axel hoped to catch a larger alligator later in the summer, "when the water is higher," and to "have a rattlesnake hunt also because if I am not mistaken there are many of them on our land and about 5 feet from the house I could possible kill some, and if you would like a fine skin of one I will get one for you."[42]

As mentioned earlier, Axel also asked his sister Johanna, who had her own successful restaurant in Chicago, to invest her money in his farm, offering that once she had the funds, he could place them in the bank at Fort Pierce.[43] Later that month, on March 26, he repeated his request, "When you have a thousand dollars in the bank or I mean invested in the plantation, you can if everything goes well, which we hope, and I am going to do all I can to make our wishes come through. The money you are sending I am using to buy fertilizer and to pay for workers, etc." It is telling of their relationship that Axel felt the need for transparency and to account for Johanna's investment as he catalogued that he utilized the funds to not only purchase fertilizer but to clear more lands, delighting in the progress, "the plants grow and so do the orange trees, especially as we got wonderful rain last Friday evening, they will grow even better." Exuberant in his hopes, Axel also shared that he had plans for building a packing house and that his hens were quite productive with a personal note on his daughter, Ruth, "she is able to work where ever she wants. She helps Mom to carry woods and she takes a rug and cleans up after herself when she drops something on the floor."[44]

The content of the letters from Axel to Johanna illustrate the trust present between the two siblings as Axel diligently reported details of the farm to Johanna to justify her investment in his enterprise. From these details we learn that Johanna continued to invest, giving her brother $350 in April 1905, which he reported back to her, "I am going to use them the best way, you can be sure of that." To that end, Axel made good on his plans to expand the farm, building a packing house and shared that once the house was completed, then he could "concentrate on the fields, the different trees and plants are doing good and if we just could get some rain now it would be even better."[45]

The farm continued to be a family affair and Johanna continued to invest, sending an additional $50 in July 1905, which Axel appreciated greatly, however, he related the difficulties he faced, as he related, "It is very thoughtful of you to send some money unexpectedly... But as I said everything costs money and as we do not have a fixed income we do need income from other sources to keep a balance on the account." To that end Axel expected to receive at least $200 from Nils and an additional $200 from John which he planned to utilize immediately, ordering "25,000 plants down in Dade eventually for $6.50 per 1000, freight not included. I have also ordered some here in Viking for $500 and some from north of here. Totally I will plant 35–36,000 or 3 acres this year and possibly double it next year."[46] Axel included with this letter a clipping from a local newspaper so that Johanna could read the news of successes from Viking and determine the impact of her investment, although Axel admitted that "these are overdone, but journalists are not always so reliable, just as long as it sounds good," he confided that he continued to plant citrus and added a few watermelons "in between the orange trees, which was very successful." Returning to personal matters, their correspondence touched upon some ongoing family issues with John and Kjersti before closing on an offer of help for Johanna, should she need it, "Ruth is very capable, if you need help we can send her up to you. She can scrub, do dishes, serve, cook, and make beds. She eats watermelon, drinks coffee, takes sugar and looks in the mirror when she has the time."[47] Ruth was less than two years old at the time this letter was written. By September 1905, Axel was addressing letters on his own stationery that included a sketch of a pineapple, soon to be the best crop of the Atlantic Ridge.

While we know that Emily's time in Florida was brief, the remaining Hallstrom letters illustrate her remarkable family as well as their insight into the Florida project and their views on the idea of Florida. In Book 3 of the Hallstrom letters, Gottfrid Bjorkelund, Emily's eccentric and colorful brother starts to make his presence known, "It is almost unbelievable that you could hold out so long without much income . . . Setbacks are almost impossible to avoid. Florida is a paradise and the man that discovered Florida surely gave it the name 'Tera Florida' for a reason . . . I would rather see your plantation in Florida than New York, Chicago, or all the states in the U.S.A."[48] After these initial pleasantries regarding the Hallstrom farm, Gottfrid related some personal and family details, "My health is getting better and I should be able to begin to work in September, but the hope to be totally well escapes me. My stomach is sometimes out of order, but overall I feel pretty good . . . Everyone is healthy and doing well here. Mother has a bad cough. Johanna works too much, but nobody is really sick." Gottfrid also had some personal advice for health, "Chew your food well, don't eat too much, eat easily digested food, don't drink with food and avoid coffee, tea, etc. Sour milk or water are good drinks. Mix water with orange or lemmon [sic] juice. Bath two times a week." He ended his letter with a comment on his niece and showed his imagination of Florida and the prevailing ideas about the Florida frontier when he said, "I hope Ruth is well and is a good girl and soon can help mamma a little. She is certainly brown as an Indian, that sweet little girl."[49]

Gottfrid's advice was of a personal nature but also intended as a way of addressing some of the health issues that Emily was facing. In a letter that begins with comments on various doctors of the era, Gottfrid opined, "But neither Ottosson, Kellogg, or Readen could cure peoples sickness if the sick didn't take the task in their own hands and with dedication." Regarding Emely specifically, "a basic for her is to always keep her blood clean. This is done by 1) a good diet 2) keep the organs such as the kidneys working."[50] Continuing with his advice, "for a good diet, don't eat too often, and don't gain weight. A sick person can not digest food to hold weight up." From personal experience, Gottfrid lost "14 kilo in a year," he suggested that people should eat two "main" meals a day with a smaller meal, allowing six hours in between meals, "never eat so you are full and eat easily digested food, mainly grain, milk, butter, eggs, and fish. Avoid beans, cabbage, fat pork, spices and cucumbers etc." Breakfast should be consumed at six or seven in the morning, "a bowl of cooked milk with bread, and butter and bananas." Lunch at noon, "meat with porridge and apples, rice pudding, oatmeal, fruit, pumpkin and spinach steamed." Dinner at six in the evening, "bread, butter, one egg, porridge with fruit, two bananas, and an orange."[51]

Gottfrid's health plan was inspired by the physical culture movement and a Danish man named Jorgen Peter Müller, a gymnastics educator and author, whose 1904 book *Mit System,* included a guideline of eighteen exercises that became the basis of many modern physical exercise plans. Franz Kafka was a fervent follower of the protocol. Gottfrid modified the Müller system, "so that it is not too difficult for a sick person," and included detailed instructions in his letter to Axel and Emily. The exercise began with twenty-five deep side bends on each side, with hands placed on the hips, slowly moving with deep breaths. Next was "bend your body back and forth ten times," followed by wide leg side bends, twenty-five on each side, with two to three deep breaths on each repetition, advising that "if you are tired, you can now rest a little as the following exercise demands a lot of energy, but it is very good for you." The next exercise was core work, lying on the back making slow leg circles, two to three times on each side, slowly with breath followed by crunches, "lay on the floor with the toes under a sofa that is heavy, put your hands on your hips lift upper body from the floor, let it down slowly, two to eight times depending on your strength."[52]

After these physical exercises, Gottfrid recommended to "wash your whole body in cold water, carefully dry off your body with a coarse towel," then begin the process of rubbing the body with the towel beginning with the stomach on the right side, "in circles toward the breast and the left side as the food goes that way. After one to two months these exercises should cure all possible sickness." Gottfrid advised that the side bends were good for the liver and kidneys and the rest were good for the joints, and that "this message is my thought for Emely's only salvation and if she will follow that advice, she will be well." He suggested she take twenty-five minutes each morning and evening "for the sake of her health."[53] Gottfrid liked to use "ice cold water and rinse off in a room with open windows," but thought this was not necessary for Emily. This practice, Gottfrid believed, was "worth 100 times more than the doctors compounds and syrup." Along with the physical practice Gottfrid combined suggestions to keep the intestines healthy with a "balanced diet and exercise and use a hot water bottle after supper," plus drinking plenty of water, buttermilk, and juices to flush the kidneys while avoiding "too much meat, peas, beans, etc.," and daily excursions outside to breathe in fresh air and sunbathing. "I admire that you live in sunny Florida," Gottfrid wrote before closing his letter, ". . . you need energy and desire to start and continue the program. You need months for the first program, weeks for the second, and days for the third. And fourth and lastly, you will be better for every hour and don't pay any attention to the doctors, just your devoted brother, Gottfrid."[54] Evidence that Axel was financially stable and beginning to have some discretionary income is present in a letter from Hosegerod on February 6, 1908, regarding transatlantic shipping and the fruit of their labors in a shipment of their goods to Sweden:

> I want to express thanks for the beautiful and wonderful fruit that you sent us. It was not a small cost for you, with such a long way. I am sure Gottfrid has told what happened to the fruit. It was too bad that the wonderful fruit should be damaged, but you can be sure that they do not handle them carefully, especially when it is something special. Mother has used them another way as inside they are not ruined. Better oranges we have never tasted. The juice runs when we eat them and oranges like this we never could think of getting. Something that good we never get here as it would freeze.[55]

Despite Gottfrid's predictions and plans, Emily's health concerns grew worse. Writing to his sister Johanna on February 8, 1908, Axel began to describe in grave detail Emily's failing health, "she cannot leave the bed, and probably she never will be able to do so, because her illness has made her so weak and she has no strength left at all. Her entire right side is impacted even the lung which gives us no hope." Emely had been in better physical health prior to Christmas and sought to give their daughter Ruth a small birthday party, "she worked two days in a row with baking bread and cookies late in the evening. That was too much for her and after that she got worse."[56] In this letter, Axel asked Johanna to come and help with Ruth, suggesting that Johanna come quickly, "could you sell to someone or do an auction so you could get rid of everything and come immediately and it doesn't matter if you lose a bit since I can pay you back for that after some time."⁵⁷ Axel promised he would pay Johanna back for her efforts. Johanna made plans to come, and Axel wrote to her again on February 20, 1908, asking if she had "preserved things like fish meat or vegetables" to bring it with her, "because we used some during the summer of these things and we can share it and reimburse you for the value."⁵⁸ Emily died on May 18, 1908.

Emily's death complicated and strained the relationship that Axel and Ruth had with Johanna. The situation remains unclear, however remaining evidence and letters indicate that Axel took a return trip to Sweden after Emily's death and considered remarrying. Due to this, his relationship with his sister became tense and Johanna's frustration and sense of betrayal over her brothers' actions is abundantly clear. This engagement surprised Johanna and she corresponded with their brother Par, who wrote in the margins, "I was sure that you knew about the engagement or at least before traveling . . . You have always had a mild and forgiving heart. Have you changed in the American atmosphere and could it be true that even the best people there get to be selfish and lose?"⁵⁹ This letter included effusive praise of the woman in question but also hinted at duplicity on the part of Axel, "It is so strange that Axel didn't say anything about it to any of us even though his fiancee [sic] said that he had promised her that he would tell us before he left Sweden as she has asked him to do that."⁶⁰ Continuing with his opinion of Karolina, the fiancé in question, "I do not say that she is an angel, as there are none found on this earth, but to be honest, I will say that I have hardly ever met a young servant girl with such intelligence, together with a supportive conduct and moderate, sincere and mild temperament." The rest of the letter was no less effusive in praise of Karolina before declaring, "Don't leave Axel and turn on him, but stay quietly with him and take care of his house and his little Ruth as they need you and don't demand too much. If any of your brother have done you any good, it is him."⁶¹

Par's notes in the margin and his entreaties on the part of Axel received a stark response from Johanna when she wrote him a long and scathing letter on June 3, 1910. She began the letter with a thank you for the praise of their brother, "but you know those words were a farce." She continued with her assessment of Karolina, "one thing is certain, that woman and I can never meet." She references several arguments with Axel regarding the matter, "I have told him what I think and the poor man is so afraid that I will leave." She counters that she would certainly "back away but then he and I must settle our affairs first." To this she is of course referencing the money he owed her for selling her restaurant, her deep investment in the farm, and likely for her time spent in Florida, "if he didn't have my money and it wasn't tied up till next year, I would have a way out of this situation." Money was not the only issue, as she lamented, "after all that has happened, all my adoration for him is gone," writing to Par, "If you were here, you could realize the feeling. You can't believe how my hands grip and my blood boils, when you beg me to stay here." Calling it the "height of audacity" she accused her brothers of wanting her to play servant to Karolina, "you want me to spend my best years here so a lazy woman can be taken care of." She then admonished Par for money that he owed her as well, asking that he repay her plus interest, "I get five percent in the bank, we can call it the same, 111 crowns with 5 percent interest. You know yourself the time."[62]

Johanna's letter paints a clear picture of her frustrations with her brothers; however, the details also describe the realities she faced in Florida, "you should not believe it is a paradise, or that here is a good place to be." Her letter details the sale of the first Hallstrom farm and how in 1910 Axel sold the Viking property and moved his farming and household three miles to the north on a plot of land that he purchased from a Mr. Kroegel for $50 an acre. There he would begin planting fields of pineapples.[63] To Johanna, "it was a high price, and I said he wouldn't get any help from me." The situation she described was a farm on the brink, "if we don't get rain soon, there will be nothing. What is he thinking to bring a woman over under these circumstances that exist here, I don't know."[64] Florida, she wrote, "never gives much as farming and everything else like that is just a gamble. Everything is unknown and at a loss as everything has to be sent so far to market, so when all is subtracted, there isn't much left for the farmer." But it was not just the financial considerations that had Johanna worried, she was lonely. The only nearby settlers were recent Norwegian émigrés who she could barely understand, "they are nice and kind but very one sided." That coupled with the weather, where the "sun burns so warm, the sand gets hot, and no grass grows," and nearly impassable vegetation, "bushes or palmettoes," made a person "as good as a prisoner in his own house." When she did venture out, "in the heat and sand and full of mosquitoes and in between I had to carry Ruth on my back," they returned to a home where they always had to have a stout fire blazing to keep the bugs away with smoke. Johanna insisted that she invested so much of her money and then suffered in Florida for her brother, Emily, and Ruth because "he had my blind trust." She had come to the realization though that the "Hallstrom men surely thought that sisters were good as servants . . . It was a disgrace. What is sown will in time bear fruit."[65] In the end, Johanna remained at the Hallstrom farm in Florida and Axel never remarried. In a letter from Kjersti, she remarked to Johanna, that Axel "must have fled to the fields after such a storm."[66]

Another perspective on the Oslo settlement is presented by Matilda Miller Marshal, nickname Mrs. Goody, in an oral history collected by Pearl McKenzie in 2008. Born in Madison, Florida, in 1916 and moved with her grandparents to Oslo in 1925, she described the bustling community thusly:

> Once a month Oslo residents would sell their food at the Oslo Citrus Packing House (old house). All the food and vegetables that didn't sell were put aboard the train to be sold. (Henry Flagler train). They grew sugar cane, collards, mustard greens; raised chickens, geese turkey and hunted squirrels. They fished at the south east end of Oslo Road, the Old fish house, owned by the Judah family stood there south east of the Indian River Lagoon. The Judah family were commercial fisherman, but the old fish house disappeared around 1969. Mr. Knight, owner of a small boat with oars would leave his boat attached to the boat house and Oslo residents would use the boat to fish, clam and harvest oyster. William Merchant had a horse and would hunt with a gun for wild hogs, in the area now known as McKee Botanical Gardens. Mosquitoes were very bad in Oslo, residents used large metal tub with Saw Palmetto soaked in kerosene. These were burned to smoke the mosquitos out of the house . . . The Helseth family, farmers who grew pineapples and citrus, hired many Oslo residents. Axel Hallstrom and Daughter Ruth Hallstrom, farmers and flower growers, bankers. Many Oslo residents work for the family. Waldo Sexton, a business man, brought Bahamian workers to Oslo to work in Citrus. The Bahamian area was called Bahamian Quarters, present-day Vista Royal area. He built a church in the Bahamian Quarters.[67]

By 1915, unfortunately, harvesting pineapples was no longer a feasible growth plan for farmers as soil depletion led to decreasing yields, and within two years many growers abandoned their fields. In February 1917 a hard freeze hit the region and destroyed any remaining crops, and by 1920 only a few hundred acres of crops remained in growth.[68] One of the reasons for the decline of pineapples were changes to the soil in the Atlantic Ridge alongside competition from Cuba, blight caused by red spider infestations. Drainage affected the ridge, which ". . . had served as a dam for back waters. There was a break in the ridge at the Jungle Gardens where Willsey Creek runs through, and when water was high it would seep through a low gap at Oslo, but it acted as a reservoir and made the ridge very fertile." That fertility was not to last.[69]

For Axel and his daughter Ruth, Florida became paradise found as the Hallstrom farm continued to thrive, adapting to the changing nature of the region. Axel's business flourished and he becomes one of the region's foremost businessmen and leaders. By 1914 Axel was active in the St. Lucie County Bank in Fort Pierce where he invested the funds his family had entrusted to him for the development of the Hallstrom plantation, later he became one of the bank's directors. Intriguingly, this bank was one of very few that "successfully weathered the depression, which laid so many others low, and never closed its doors to its depositors in the frantic years of the early 30's." By 1948, Axel was Chairman of the Board and then by 1950, president of the bank.[70] As a charter member of the Florida Citrus Exchange and as the president of the cooperative Growers' Association, Axel was deeply invested in the citrus business and the archives of the Hallstrom House attest to his and later his daughter Ruth's keen understanding of the ups and downs of the business. "The only way to live is one day at a time without fret," Ruth Hallstrom.[71] The Indian River Historical Society purchased an additional 115 acres of the original Hallstrom holdings from the descendant family and maintains the area as a conservation region for gopher tortoises, Florida scrub jays, and Lakela's Mint, "a small flowering plant which only grows on the Atlantic Ridge from Indian River to St. Lucie Counties."[72] To each subsequent population, it is a garden that then delivers forbidden fruit or challenges. Transformed entirely, the Tiger Hammock became Hallstrom space, a testament to settler memory, but this is also a form of Native erasure and further research is necessary to understand the longer history of the landscape, the story of the Seminole peoples whose original cultivation of the land likely made success for the Viking settlement possible.

5
Memory and the Built Environment

T. D. Allman, in a recent popular history, *Finding Florida,* posits that "for five hundred years successive waves of conquerors, ignoring the reality of Florida, have tried to re-create, in Florida's alien clime, a more perfect—sometimes outright hallucinatory—version of the society they left behind."[1] Thinking about symbolic landscapes, "the symbol only is a symbol on the basis that an interpretant takes it as such; otherwise there is no connection . . . a symbol once in being, spreads among peoples," images become symbolic in context, "perception allows us to take something as something, but whatever *the something* is that is perceived, requires conceptions/ideas." The question then becomes, what does the Indigenous and colonial past of the region symbolize to the settlers of Vero Beach and the surrounding spaces? The historically and socially layered landscapes is one that settlers alter and utilize to create their visions of the colonial and Indigenous past.[2] One must then consider the root of memory and nostalgia for Old Florida, as one 1960s historian lamented, "the new Florida has largely drained the Everglades, built a highway from Tampa to Miami and turned the coasts, both the Atlantic and the Gulf, into a series of glittering resorts. The new Florida may be beautiful (indeed it is!) but to the few of us who are left, who remember the older, wilder Florida, there is something lacking."[3] Famed journalist Al Burt wrote about the Old Florida phenomenon, "Out there is the fabled La Florida, exotic enough for the careless to call it paradise, beautiful enough for almost all to love, but too complex and changeable for easy understanding."[4]

As a bicentennial history offers, "Florida's utterly enchanting paradoxes is that it is at once un-American and super-American: where else does the weary pilgrim find feudal farming, huge live oaks hung dreamily with thick strands of Spanish moss, and—not far away—the launching pads of moon rockets?"[5] Often, however, the colonial Spanish Southeast and the impact of that Spanish history is relegated to what Charles Hudson refers to as the "forgotten centuries," yet new scholarship seeks to counter this as Juliana Barr has argued, "what might we get if we leave the nineteenth-century approach behind and try to unite the narratives of the seventeenth- and eighteenth-century Southeast and Southwest into a new colonial South—a colonial Sun Belt—sweeping from the Atlantic to the Pacific?"[6] When doing so, "we see far more clearly the Indians who could manipulate colonial ventures to their own advantage and not merely benefit from but dictate to their European neighbors."[7] While farmers and boosters further transformed the lower Indian River Lagoon for settler agricultural interests, several parties also sought to capitalize on Florida's potential for tourist revenue. National interest in Vero, the Pleistocene era, and the Vero Man controversy led to at least one tourist attraction that played to the idea of the Garden of Eden while situating the Vero Man as part of a paleontological past, where the Indigenous people of Florida were extinct alongside the mastodon and saber-toothed tiger. Capitalizing on the ancient Eden and jungle past of the Vero region, John H. Chase, from Youngstown, Ohio, opened a roadside museum in December 1932 called *Tarzan Park*. Chase described the park to an interviewer from *American Motor Traveler* in January 1934, opining, "Can we picture the life they [the mammals] led, why this life reached a climax, and disappeared as completely as a fairy story . . ."[8] Harkening to California attractions, the local reporters wrote that, "Vero should be proud of the distinction this undertaking is sure to bring. No place in the country is as full of strange prehistoric mammals as this county, except the tar pits of California and in this latter place no human beings have ever been found."[9] The site included five stations for tourists to view the past. At Station No. 1, Howdy House was a thatched hut with an artist rendering of a saber-toothed tiger charging at an Indigenous man. Following a trail to Station No. 2, visitors would view "quicksand" where they could dig and find artifacts of their own to take with them as souvenirs. Moving on to Station No. 3 was a partial skeleton of a saber-toothed tiger designed to look like a recent discovery. Continuing along the path, visitors would encounter a mega sloth in a jungle river scene. In the sand at Station No. 4 the park creators carefully placed mastodon and mammoth fossils in the sand. Finishing the trek at Station No. 5, a large live oak, the creators envisioned the Garden of Eden, where the "first man was found among the animals . . . We have dreamed of Florida as a beautiful country, but we have never bragged of it as the real

American Garden of Eden . . . Station No. 5 is an exact replica of the find that stirred up this interest. Spectators can make up their own minds as to whether they are looking at the 'Adam of America.'"[10] Like western boosters before them, the boosters of Vero presented Eden, not as a cautionary tale, but akin to western towns who focused instead on "Edens before the fall from grace, before the snake had entered the garden, before the forbidden fruit had been tasted."[11]

Vero had few visitors during the Great Depression and the park shut down by 1935. However, settler and tourist fascination with an Indigenous and Edenic past would be the key for success for two important Vero boosters, both with vivid imaginations, Arthur McKee and Waldo Sexton.[12] Arthur Glenn McKee (1871–1956) was originally from the Pittsburgh region but made his mark in the steel industry in Cleveland before a doctor advised him to go to Florida for its restorative properties and to rest and recuperate from the stresses of being an industrialist. There he would meet and collaborate with a self-made man, Waldo Emmerson Sexton.[13]

While it was Zeuch's initial imagination that began the project of conceptualizing the Indigenous and Spanish colonial past with the Indian River Farms Company, it was an employee of the company that masterfully transformed the narrative to the Vero Beach mythos that is well known today. Capitalizing on settler fascination with a mythical colonial and Indigenous past in the semitropical lagoons and hammocks, industrialist Arthur McKee and Indian River Farms Company employee, Waldo Sexton, were the settler men most responsible for the vision of "Old Florida" that the city of Vero Beach lays claim to. McKee worked with Sexton to build an extensive eighty-acre jungle garden where a Seminole man named Lewis Tucker came to live and build a traditional Seminole house, the palmetto-thatched chickee, becoming a part of the entertainment complex, even living on site from time to time.

Seminole camps and laborers were a major component of Florida history and the tourist industry. According to Andrew Frank, the Seminole of Florida recognized the potential for utilizing the stereotypes of Native peoples tied to natural history, "In essence, Indians and non-Indians have sold their history by playing on the long-standing beliefs that they are unconquered peoples and that the Everglades are an equally untamed environment."[14] Popular Florida roadside attractions that featured the Seminole and Miccosukee included Musa Isle, Miami's Tropical Hobbyland, and Silver Springs' Seminole Indian Village.[15] Seminole assistance with the

Jungle Garden mystique worked perfectly with the tourist attraction that McKee and Sexton sought to create.

While Arthur McKee and his cousin Charles certainly provided financial assistance, it was Waldo who was the driving force and visionary of the development of the Vero Beach region. Waldo Sexton is remembered in Vero as an "eccentric pioneer" and one of the foremost "founding fathers" of the community, "he played many roles at different times in his life, and among those were: salesman, builder, developer, rancher, dairyman, antique collector, 'pack-rat,' thrifty, scavenger (today known as a 'recycler'), nature lover, and many other titles, depending on what business he was pursuing."[16] Sexton, as one collection of pioneer/settler stories records explained, "grew up with the place, so to speak."[17] Sexton came from central Indiana and initially matriculated to Indiana University to study medicine before switching over to Purdue University in September 1908. He self-financed his education by working a variety of jobs including "waiting tables and tending furnaces" as well as selling aluminum cooking utensils. Another side gig he pursued was to purchase discarded fraternity jewelry from pawn shops that he would later resell "at high prices to fraternity men at whatever school he could visit."[18]

A creative and boisterous man, after graduating from Purdue in 1911, with a degree that he referred to as "hog feed engineer," Sexton went to Barberton, Ohio, to work as a farm manager before moving to Cleveland to work as a traveling salesman and demonstrator for an agricultural tillage equipment supplier financed by Charles McKee (cousin to Arthur) that worked closely with the Indian River Farms Company. While in Barberton his interest in pawn shops and collecting discarded eccentric antiques and materials grew.[19]

Timeline of *Waldo's Business Ventures:*

1911–1913: Manager, Barber Farms, Barberton, Ohio
1913: Salesman, Spaulding Deep Tilling Machines
1914: Cleveland District Agricultural Representative, Indian River Farms Company; Establishes Vero Beach Realty Company; Purchases 160 Acre Homeplace Tract of Land
1915: Waldo and Davis form Indian River Fruit and Vegetable Company
1917: Establishes citrus grove on his land

1920: Waldo and McKee form Indian River Products Company; Waldo and McKee form the McKee–Sexton Land Company; Waldo and McKee form Oslo Hammock Corporation; Waldo and McKee form Oslo Packing Company

1923: Waldo, McKee, and others form Royal Park Development Corporation

1924: Waldo establishes Vero Beach Dairy

1925: McKee and Waldo form Royal Park Exotic Nurseries, the precursor to McKee Jungle Gardens

1934–35: Waldo builds the Driftwood

1935: Waldo builds the Patio

1940s: Waldo purchases land northwest of town to develop the Treasure Hammock Ranch

1941: Waldo opens the Ocean Grill Restaurant

1955: Waldo builds his mountain

1960s: Waldo builds Turf Club, which becomes the Szechuan Palace Chinese Restaurant[20]

In 1913, he was demonstrating equipment in Vero and stayed several days at the Sleepy Eye Lodge because of a failure with the Spaulding Deep Tilling Machine. A double disk plow that had "the revolutionary result of bringing up to the surface the soil which had never been disturbed before," typically held Waldo "in his element," except, in the sandy Indian River soil, it failed. A few tales emerged as to why his demonstration failed, however, the incident allowed him to stay at Sleepy Eye Lodge, where he saw firsthand the enchanting potential of the newly reclaimed marshlands. Waldo quickly bought 120 acres of land from the Indian River Farms Company within just a few days.[21] According to Waldo's cousin and later partner, Walter Buckingham, "Doc Leroy Hutchison said, young man, how much money do you have? And he said, $500. He said, well, you have bought enough land for the time being. So, Waldo did not buy any more land for a little while. [Laughter] But, he knew good land. Waldo knew good land."[22] Sexton took on a position with the company to act as a sales agent and bring in prospects from Ohio, convincing Charles McKee to buy 1,000 acres of land from the company.[23] As mentioned earlier, they would soon be joined by Arthur McKee, who on doctors' orders, became a seasonal resident of Rio Mar on the ocean side of Vero in 1922 joining in business with Waldo to form the McKee–Sexton Land Company and the Oslo Hammock Corporation.[24]

The remaining letters of Waldo Sexto to his soon-to-be wife, Elsebeth, detail many of his efforts to build Vero and his enterprises. In a letter scribbled in pencil on a Western Union telegram dated May 4, 1918, Waldo Sexton wrote from the train, "I never knew how exhausted I was until I got safely housed away in a pullman and away from care and trouble." Within these missives, one can see that Sexton has a characteristic flair for the dramatic as he declares that he has "no pep, sparkle or interest in life other than to sleep I have lost my imagination, focus point and whip that drives me on." Despite this alleged exhaustion, he goes on to describe the scene, a beautiful young actress across the way, "who keeps looking me over like I was someone escaping with a little sparkle of interest in her eye but so far I have not weakened," while two crying babies to the front and back of him "keep the air blue with yelps," as the train rocked past Savanna and Charleston on the way to Washington. Although he had a lower compartment the night before, this evening he was stuck with an upper berth, lamenting his sleeping arrangements, he told Elsebeth he was "wishing I were going to bed in a real bed instead of a makeshift. I never used to care just so I could find a place to perch. I could not sleep last night until I had turned a crank in the car which resembled cranking a Ford after I worked up a glow such as I generally have at Vero I could sleep with ease."[25] Sexton's letters set the stage of a hero's quest or journey with Vero as his paradise found.

A letter from this same journey, written on "The New Ebbitt" stationery from Washington, DC, dated Monday 1918, described his travels through Pittsburgh and his procurement of items for the Indian River Farms Company, "have gotten several new creations of Fla and some which will be of worth to our growers I think." He also got a present for Elsebeth from Martha Washington's kitchen, as he decided that Elsebeth could use "a small quantity of her special brand of sweets," which he sent in a two-pound box via parcel post, "I hope it arrives in good condition," he writes, "and proves equal to anything you can get in Vero."[26] Setting the scene of his time in DC, Waldo told Elsebeth, "this is no place for a girl like you. You would never withstand the military atmosphere existing here." He described a "100 of the Blue Devils from France" passing by his hotel as he "took at peep at this," proclaiming that "our men are twice as large and a 100% better looking but do not have the same kind of determination in their faces as the Frenchmen." He also commented on the fashions of the day, "I paid special attention to the well-dressed women in the dining room and full 50% of them were dressed in Black." He related that it was a thin type of material, "showing their *meat* in the arms . . . hats were of many shape but the ones I could imagine you in were of the same shape as your hat. I imagine you would look very snappy and show a lot of sparkle in such a make up" (emphasis in original). Nonetheless, Sexton was insistent that she would not do well in the city, to Elsebeth he related, "I can see you losing your heart every day. You would be a war bride within two weeks. The board and room are not to be had."

Within these letters, Waldo is seeking his Eden and is filled with booster dreams, establishing himself as the hero, an inheritor of dreams, with pitfalls along the way to overcome. Looking forward to his return to Vero, he admonished that Elsebeth should keep her calendar free, "you had better not have an engagement the night I arrive for it will cause me to whip the man who has it and I would hate to start off my second coming to Vero with such a record so I am telling you in advance." Thinking ahead to his duties he related, "I guess I will have plenty to do when I arrive. I can see again now the things to be done which have not been done and which are suffering to be done." Admitting that he was feeling "bossy" he closed his letter, "enough for the time so goodnight."[27] His trip to Washington proved a success as he held meetings with "what is supposed to be hard men to see and very important men," with whom he claimed to "have gotten along beautifully seeing every man I set out to see and accomplishing as far as possible what I hoped to do." This included a meeting with E. Percy Miller, the man in charge of the distribution of potatoes in the US Food Administration. Proud of his accomplishments, he opined, "everything looks so easy when you get it at close range excepting a woman. I still maintain that they are the largest and most difficult problem man has got to contend with." Why did Waldo include this opinion? Well, he proclaims, "the world is run in 'Bull' pardon the expression, but it is a very effective word to use after having spent a day getting by in Washington." From this correspondence we also learn that Elsebeth does not tolerate a load of malarkey as Waldo jokes to her, "you are so far away I cannot hear your complaints so you make a very good audience." Playfully continuing,

Waldo shares "I would always rather play to the people in the galleries because I never could see the expressions in their faces or hear their hisses so you are in the boards now and at my mercy."[28]

Once home to Vero, he described his work ethic to Elsebeth thusly, "working my hand at hard work during the day and my mind at night trying to get this old imagination of mine to turn some trick which will help me do the things I want and it has never failed me so I am hopeful," and to Elsebeth he reminds her, "outside of you I like my imagination more than anything I know for it gives me more pleasure and thrills than anything else . . . I miss you very much, more than I expected I would and I thought I would miss you more than anyone who has ever come into my life." Continuing with information about their community and neighbors, including commenting once again on the war, Waldo returned to describing his work once again, "I am right at home with that hoe and you should have seen me today I am making some flower beds and I was so hot when I quit that my clothes looked as if I had been in the river but a bath and a ride to Gifford to take the men home healed all my wounds."[29] In other news of home, Waldo related that the Anderson household suffered a grievous loss when their home burned down, including a white dress that Elsebeth had gifted to Dora. Waldo asked Elsebeth to be "the queen angel of my flock" and send another dress down, "one you have discarded and Anderson a shirt and tie and you will be the finest woman in St. Lucie county and Fla. [sic] for that matter."[30]

Waldo's labor and efforts to secure their future in Vero are the subject of the next letter, dated June 16, 1918, as Waldo wondered how to procure the right ring for Elsebeth, "I had fully thought all the time that I would have a chance to come north and I could take off after coming up where I would have a chance to make a selection . . ." Finding himself at a loss, Waldo takes time to paint the scene with literary flair, "believe me living in the woods is great until you have to begin doing the same things that the customes [sic] and old mother convention have educated the people to do and then you need stores and pajamas and a lot of things you hate." Waldo claims to be able to "clear land and sell land" and handle his workers but was frazzled about Elsebeth being away and the matter of her ring.[31] By July, Waldo was writing letters on July 2 addressing Elsebeth as "Hello Wife," that included his plans for the development of Vero and its farms, its progress and future paradise, "Leave it to me tho [sic] for I have always been able to do the things I want to do when I want to do them bad enough and I sure have my mind set on this proposition so I am planning just the same as if I knew it was going to happen." He advised Elsebeth to be prepared, "don't let any of my letters take the starch out of you completely for you may have to stiffen up at any moment . . . when the real time comes for action you will not be asleep at the switch."[32] Excited about his prospects, Waldo promised to write soon to "set forth the sad story or good news which ever it happens to be." His letter does not stop there, however, as Waldo related, "I had some very good news today I tried to sell a tract of land last week by mail and today I have a wire asking for me to wire more particulars by wire if it goes through it will make me about $300.00 and I will get the job of setting the trees and selling them which will make me a few hundred more so I feel that the fates are with me."[33] On a more personal note, Waldo shared that he was "eating three square meals a day again and can face the world," before beginning to tease Elsebeth about their courtship, "I decided I would marry you before you had time to get a wooden leg or glass eye and take no chances in what I might do."[34] "I went to sleep on the porch swing during a heavy rain," he closes the letter, ". . . since early childhood, a rain meant rest from the usual routine of work and this day I kid myself in thinking I am a small boy at home and do not have to get up on a rainy morning . . ."[35]

In the summer of 1918, Waldo described the heat of Florida, his dreams for Vero, his farm, and the issues he faced, as he wrote:

> This has been one of those soft mushy days in which one seems to rub up against the weather and get it all over one's clothes and as a result I have been on the urge of dashing across the pessimistic line for there seems to be more people on that side and I think they will win. I rather like to climb up on the fence and see the old world and her actors pass once in a while and take a squint at myself and see whether I have been a fool or whether I have been using the wrong measuring stick for I am always back to the old money stick when I take my measure of past work and altho [sic] I have done what I think is a lot of hard work, yet I feel from a financial standpoint that I have been a miserable failure. Happiness and money either go hand in hand or travel in sight of each other don't you think? I have been looking all my life to see them separated but so far they are in hailing distance and while people try to rush in-between them I don't believe they have ever been able to keep them apart.[36]

One can visualize the hammock he's working in, the idea of toiling in the sun on a very hot and humid day, pausing for dusk as the mosquitoes buzz around, watching the moon rise, thinking about conquistadors of the past, if his name would be on the scroll of those remembered, wondering if the labor is worthwhile and whether the gamble is worth its weight in gold. Plotting a future while swinging from ambitious dreams to the depths of despair. We learn a bit more about Waldo's mercurial moods as he describes a terrible day to Elsebeth, "Well how did you feel about 8 A.M. this morning? Did you have a feeling that you were about to lose the biggest thing that has ever come into your life?" Waldo lost control of his car and almost drove headlong into "lateral A near Dr. Stones farm and if the fates had not been with us, the fish would have been getting ready a lobster supper tonight." In a particularly sour mood, Waldo relates, "Everything I touched today went wrong." He "cussed Mrs. Roach" and "rsed [sic] hell in general" and blamed this turn of events on the late arrival of a letter from Elsebeth, "then the dogs of hell were turned loose on us today in the form of a million mosquitos of each individual and as I represent two now they sent your proportional share to me." He left a squished mosquito on the letter, with a circle drawn about its body with an annotation, "Lest you forget, Here is where he died."[37] After ranting a bit, his tone turned toward more affectionate, "I never lived before as I have lived since you came into my life and places and I am hoping that this is only a start and will look small besides the big reality." On the bottom of the page, he wrote one more humorous annotation about the mosquitoes, "Do you recognize the smell of B. B. Brand of Insect powder?"[38]

By late July, Waldo's mood had changed for the better, with grand plans and dreams for the future with Elsebeth. He purchased the "shanty" that carpenters used as they built a new bank building in front of the Sleepy Eye Lodge, with plans that Elsebeth could run a commissary, "in this house I am going to build you a storeroom and in it you can carry a stock of snuff, tobacco cigarettes, meats, peas etc.," for the Black workers that Waldo employed. To Elsebeth, he proclaimed, "you are the goat and general dispenser of sundrys . . . You are now in competition with Sears Robuck [sic] and Montgomery Ward so you will have to be a good buyer and collector. Do you like this idea?"[39] By August Waldo was sharing that in preparation for Elsebeth's return to Vero he worked "like a dog but have never gotten more pleasure out of anything in my life . . . I walk around the farm with a paint brush in my hands and I dob everything that looks dull.

I need someone to dob me for I sure feel dull even if I don't look it . . ." His plans for their homestead were not only commercial but ornamental as he planned for gardens, including a rose bush that he simply could not resist, "the finest white roses on it I ever saw . . . I couldn't miss the chance to get it so I bought it from the lady and have been petting it like a child . . ."[40] In an undated letter of five handwritten pages to Elsebeth noted as Wednesday he writes, "Before I forget it, go out and look at the moon and see if it is as bright or as romantic as a Florida moon and then tell me in your reply. I have forgotten how a northern moon looks."[41] These personal missives continue with a letter dated August 18, 1918, where Waldo teased, "Dear Heart can you fry chicken and make milk gravy. If not, begin immediately to learn for I stole 30 young chickens today for you to practice on and only paid 20 cents each for them so we are sure of chicken dinner for 30 Sundays if we have nothing else." He also related an update about the garden, "By the way your rose(bush) is trying its best to have a rose for you when come."[42] His optimism faded however, within the same day, writing in a different letter:

> I need you very much tonight for I am tired mentally & physically and am discouraged and blue and I have always found you true at these times in the past and I am betting you would be still. It seems that everything I do here of late is wrong. I have just about lost my pep and nerve and the whip that drives me cannot be found tonight at all. I haven't ambition enough to use this typewriter but am dragging this pen along instead. I made hay all day and that is real labor possibly when I recuperate from the exertion that I will not feel as less inspired as I do now but I will still want you just the same.[43]

As devoted as he was to Elsebeth, he was still quite industrious, planting flower beds with plans for roses and enjoying the fruit of his past labors, "eating fresh figs every day from my own fig tree which I set myself two years ago and they are delicious and it gives me a lot of pleasure to eat fruit of your own planting." His plans extended well past their homestead, "I am going to form a company and take over the L&W holdings put them in at a price that will give me a profit and sell the stock to people in the north." With plans to set 40 acres to "grove" this winter and 30 more each year for three years, "Michael sold $27,000 worth of fruit from a ten acre grove and it cost less than $6,000 to produce it and market it leaving a net of $21,000 can we starve for ten years until we can do that? He has only been on that farm 12 years. My farm will do the same thing . . . I have a gold mine if I can hang in until it begins to pay but sometimes I think I will starve until that day comes."[44] Industrious and determined, hopeful, come hell or high water, Waldo had big dreams for his paradise and the future.

Another undated letter in their correspondence, noted as Sunday 3:30 p.m., "I am constant and when I start to do a thing which I want to do and think is right, all hell cannot stop me so I am hopeful yet I am blue for I cannot see my way clear at this time, for the dogs of hell were certainly loosed on me in a financial way this year as far as my crops were concerned." Waldo noted to Elsebeth that he only sold his car of potatoes for $0.75 per barrel, "not enough to pay for freight let alone digging and all other expense." In his characteristic fashion, Waldo skips from financial planning and his aspirations for the crop to his plans for Elsebeth, albeit in a jovial and teasing tone, "What progress are you making in your quest of information and experiences in house hold economics and domestic science as it treats with the house and the feeding of a hungry bear such as you have encountered in your experiences in the wilderness?"[45] Following this theme, in a letter dated as Saturday night on Indian River Fruit and Vegetable company letterhead, Waldo reminds Elsebeth of the commitment they are both making, in marriage, and in their businesses:

> Yes I think a lot and wonder a lot many times if our lives will be as pleasant as we expect and as much of a success as we hope. I think they will, yet at times I have a nervous chill when I think of how much it means and for how long a time we are signing up for it is no two or three year war we are enlisting in but a life struggle.[46]

Waldo would have many careers in the Vero region and acted as its greatest salesman, convincing many from his graduating class at Purdue University to join him as well as selling to influential industrialists from the Cleveland and Cincinnati region. Sexton filled his family beach home turned resort, the Driftwood (opened to the public in 1935), and other buildings with his eclectic collections of wood, wrought iron, tiles, and bells. Sexton pillaged, salvaged, and saved many of these items sight unseen by the truckload from razed mansions in Palm Beach or in his travels around former Spanish colonial territories. In an important act of preservation, many of the pieces came from demolished Spanish-inspired mansions in Palm Beach, designed by Addison Mizner. Once Waldo saved items from the demolished Edward T. Stotesbury estate in Palm Beach, proud of his actions, he placed a sign on the accumulated goods in a lot in Vero Beach, "It may be junk to you, but not to Mr. Stotesbury. He picked up the three million dollar check and thought he was smart and knew values . . . 'Neath these relics General Douglas MacArthur was married; Paderewski played his last concert, and Waldo spent his last dime."[47]

Mizner and Sexton had a lot of design inspiration in common, harkening to the Spanish colonial past of the Florida coast but combining it with a love for the natural environment. Mizner once opined, "You need not ruin the environment of Florida by development. You could preserve it all, enhance it even, if you only knew how."[48] Mizner's influence on Waldo can be seen in his architecture, the breezeway at the Driftwood "could easily have been influenced by Mizner who designed a house where, upon entering, straight ahead, framed in a tunnel straight through the house, was an unobstructed view of the ocean."[49] Images of Waldo with exotic animals are very similar to a photo of Mizner with his monkeys, suggesting a familiarity in tastes in their personal styles as well as the oft-repeated theme of the jungle and the exotic.

South Florida was in the throes of the land boom when Waldo and McKee began their plans for the Jungle Garden and Waldo began building the Driftwood. As many as seventy-five Pullman cars made their way into Miami each day, "full of would-be millionaires" adding to a population boom that rose from 29,000 in 1920 to 175,000 by summer 1925. Many thousands more streamed into South Florida along the Dixie Highway, "with wads of cash and letters of credit, and they were eager to buy land—any land anywhere, even if it was soaking wet."[50] And as mentioned earlier, in this, Vero was different, Indian River Farms advertised that would-be buyers should not buy sight unseen. As Vero grew and thrived, its prosperity lent it enough cache to petition the state legislature to develop a new county, Indian River, and in June 1925, William Jennings Bryan, on a tour of South Florida, spoke at Pocahontas Park, "This year I am going to every tourist city in which they will let me speak and tell the tourists who are there that Florida is the greatest opportunity of this generation." One can imagine that would-be investors heard the speech from the deep porch at the Sleepy Eye Lodge where just a few years prior, Waldo first arrived as a salesman before deciding this was his Eden. Bryan continued in his praise, "When will Florida's prosperity fail? My answer is, Not until the sunshine fails and the ocean breezes cease to carry healing in their wings."[51] The

Driftwood Hotel, circa 1900. State Archives of Florida, Florida Memory, https://www.floridamemory.com/items/show/165119, accessed 30 March 2023.

land boom in Florida would indeed fail. Vero however, would continue to thrive as would Waldo.

John Dean, a local Vero Beach architect, described Waldo's style of construction and decorating as "Waldo-tecture." By this he meant, "a less rigid, less angular rustic style made of old parts that didn't come in uniform pieces from assembly lines."[52] Waldo's wife, Elsebeth recalls, "We used to go somewhere and he'd disappear. Pretty soon he'd be back with a big truckload of stuff. It worried me because we didn't have very much money then. I was always having a fit, because I thought it would be better to buy shoes for the children."[53] Among these acquisitions were a pair of cannons in the courtyard of the Driftwood that Waldo claimed were Spanish in origin, telling resort guests, "You know, the Spanish hid their gold in cannons, they plugged 'em, like these. No, don't intend to tamper with 'em. Who knows they might be full of gold." On more than one occasion, it appears that Waldo believed he was the inheritor to the long tradition of gold seekers, a conquistador of Florida reborn in the modern era. On one of many trips to Europe, he picked up a pair of statues of St. Peter and St. Paul in Barcelona. According to family lore, his best buy was an offer from a woman at a party to sell heirlooms that had been in storage some thirty-five years; she offered to sell them to him, sight unseen, for $100.

He took on the gamble and found a motherlode of oriental rugs wrapped around ornate twin beds, festooned in green and gold, "the like of which probably graced Chapultepec Palace, the showplace home of Maximillian and Charlotte." Whatever their provenance, they soon found a home in the Spanish colonial and maritime kitsch the Driftwood was quickly becoming famous for. Lore of some of the items included a reading lamp allegedly once owned by William Jennings Bryan, John D. Rockefeller's favorite chair, bells from Henry Flagler's Key West train and bells from Harriet Beecher Stowe's home, a sofa that Flo Ziegfield gave to Billy Burke and many more.[54] A 1971 *New York Times* article on Vero Beach described Sexton as a "man who was not afraid to render an opinion and who never hesitated to embroider a story. He loved martinis and women, bells and things from the sea, and he possessed a compelling urge to create."

Determining the exact origin of many of the relics at his various buildings remains quite a task as Sexton did not keep records of their provenance and loved to change his story, as his son Ralph recalled:

> One day my father was taking some women through the Driftwood Inn and he was telling them how he had acquired each item they came across. He was really laying it on, and the women were fascinated. One of them was so interested she came back that afternoon while he was taking another group around. To her surprise, some of the stories he was telling didn't jibe with what she had heard earlier. "Mr. Sexton," she remonstrated, "that's not what you said this morning!" "Madam," he replied frostily, "I'd rather be a liar than a bore."[55]

Regardless of their specific origin, the items that he spread all over town had a story to tell. What story was that? When Waldo was nineteen years old, he visited the Louisiana Purchase World's Fair Exposition in St. Louis and was enchanted by the grandeur of the exhibit halls and grounds. As settler constructions of the colonial past, one can find within Waldo's later work the deep influence of the exposition and carnival cultures. Imagining himself to have a little bit of P. T. Barnum in him, Waldo was a great showman, storyteller, and salesman. Waldo liked to be surrounded by objects that he loved and wanted to share that aesthetic, "visual excitement, not in the manner of a museum—staged and symmetrical—but haphazard, wherever the eye may rest."[56] Inspired by the sea, Spanish colonialism, Vero's Indigenous past, and the ancient past of the Pleistocene era, one can find captain's wheels, tiles depicting Cervantes's Don Quixote, mission bells with the Virgin of Guadalupe, landscape paintings of Seminoles in the hammocks and rivers, and mammoth bones jutting from the pillars of the Driftwood.

On land owned by Charles and Arthur McKee, Arthur and Waldo Sexton dabbled in amateur horticulture and tropical plants inspired by McKee's travels to Brazil where he built steel plants. Originally, the eighty acres was part of the Oslo Packing Company site, but Arthur McKee deemed it too beautiful to plow under.[57] In 1925, Arthur and Waldo formed Royal Park Exotic Nurseries to develop the McKee Jungle Gardens from lands north of the Indian River Farms Company south relief canal.[58] Both avid amateur horticulturalists, Arthur McKee and Sexton originally opened a nursery together in the 1920s, decided to expand their investment into the tourist attraction in 1932, and invested over $100,000 in their gardens. For over forty years, McKee Jungle Gardens operated along US-1 as one of the original roadside attractions seeking tourist dollars as they flocked south for the winter. An Eden of eighty acres, it was the dream of Arthur and Waldo, brought to life by tropical landscape architect, William Lyman Phillips. Student and protégé of famed landscape architect, Frederick Law Olmsted, Phillips is considered by many to be the Dean of Florida Landscape. He also worked on Mountain Lake Colony-Lake Wales, Bok Tower Gardens-Lake Wales, and Fairchild Tropical Gardens-Miami as well as numerous private gardens.[59]

Envisioning a little bit of the World's Fair at Vero, the original gardens included a bird aviary, several small animal displays, and a vast collection of water lilies throughout the park.[60] Jens Hansen was the first botanist on site and worked with Arthur McKee's original collection of orchids and exotic plants that Arthur collected from throughout South America. The jungle trails eventually also contained three hundred Royal Palms that became the showpiece, "Cathedral of Palms." Waldo salvaged the original iron gates at the entrance to the garden from the demolition of Henry Flagler's estate, Whitehall, in Palm Beach, another reinvention of the Florida landscape.[61]

Waldo found in the McKee Jungle Gardens a place to build his grand fairgrounds. This included collections of global artifacts and sites to dazzle the tourist. One must consider the influence the 1904 Louisiana Purchase Exposition in St. Louis had on Waldo, particularly the Native American exhibits which one newspaper opined, "the historian and the student of world's history can see in the aboriginal Indians the remnants of the peo-

Bird's-eye view of parking lot at McKee Jungle Gardens, circa 1940. State Archives of Florida, Florida Memory, https://www.floridamemory.com/items/show/156282, accessed 30 March 2023.

ple who lived on earth when the world was yet in its youth."[62] According to local legend, staff at the Jungle Gardens found a Seminole man sleeping in the kitchen one day. While this was likely a story concocted for tourists and to inspire visions of a Edenic jungle untouched by civilization, a Seminole man named Lewis Tucker did work for Waldo, tying tags to bumpers on cars to advertise the Jungle Gardens.[63]

Lewis Tucker was born in the late nineteenth century, around 1876, and his mother was a Black Seminole woman named Old Nancy (Nagey Nancy). His father was a Seminole man named Charlie Peacock. Nancy, although a slave, had been adopted into the Snake Clan (Muskogee-speaking Seminoles). Some Seminole, including Betty Mae Tiger Jumper, referred to Tucker's clan as Little Black Snake Clan, a modification of the Snake Clan, possibly for racial reasons. Tucker's extended family included a sister named Lucy who married the Seminole man, John Pearce, and his half brother, Billy Bowlegs III, the son of Nancy and Billy Fewell. There is no indication in the census that Lewis himself ever married.[64] It was

Tucker who brought with him some members of the Seminole to build chickees in the gardens and in one collection of Sexton memories, he is mentioned as a "medicine man," who left seasonally for the Green Corn Dance. Human zoos, or ethnological expositions, were a popular feature in late nineteenth and early twentieth century attractions, part of global trends on race science and colonization. At the St. Louis Exposition, "Native American and the Filipino exhibits were located across each other at the Arrowhead Lake, which symbolized the Pacific Ocean, connecting, not separating them. The motive was to show the connection between America's imperial past and its imperial future."[65]

By 1940, they built an entire Seminole Indian village, a construction that can be linked to the earlier Jungle Park and themes of Florida and Vero as a bucolic and Edenic space. Waldo's son, Ralph, frequently spoke about Tucker, telling a more realistic version of how he came to work at McKee, "Waldo went out and talked the Indians into coming to McKee Jungle Gardens to live there to attract tourists." Ralph remembered a time when Waldo brought Tucker home to visit while Elsebeth was away, "He said, 'How'd you boys like to have an Indian spend the night?'" Ralph and his brother Randy then took turns peeking through the windows from their kitchen to check on Tucker, who was sleeping in the enclosed porch. Why did the Seminole come to work for Waldo in the first place? Financial opportunities. That Tucker would spend the night at Sexton's home shows a bit about their relationship as Waldo was an incredibly generous man and patron.[66] Outside of his work with Waldo, we can surmise some of the economic motivations for Tucker by his response to regulations and circumstances pressing down on the Seminole. For example, in a 1932 survey by the Office of Indian Affairs on the Seminole, one finds a note that in 1915 Tucker was producing gallons of sugar cane for sale on diminishing lands as the author notes a "half century of disintegration," and that "their economic position has become increasingly insecure."[67] Later, in that same survey, Tucker shows up again regarding hunting rights and government promises to protect Seminole land and interests, Tucker remarked "Guess hunting season come, same old thing." The author noted, "What is needed is a feeling among the Indians that they will be defended in their rights to these lands."[68] These factors contributed to Tucker seeking work with Waldo in developing the Jungle Gardens.

In keeping with the theme of an Edenic jungle, Waldo and his associates also assembled a menagerie of animals, including several hundred

Founder Arthur McKee stands at McKee Jungle Gardens, circa 1920. State Archives of Florida, Florida Memory. https://www.floridamemory.com/items/show/156292, accessed 30 March 2023.

monkeys collected by naturalist Lucile Anderson from Africa. A 1941 park flier included a section entitled "Africa in America," which explained that "the thrills of a trip to the heart of darkest Africa may be had in safety and comfort, and in a matter of minutes." With 80 acres of "wild, exotic jungle," the park advertised its many attractions including varieties of plants that Central American Natives might use to make musical instruments or to "the Dumb Cane from which they draw poison for their arrows." At play throughout the park and their advertising are settler themes of pan-Indigenous "wild" spaces intersected with the modern and settler memory and interconnecting the theme of paradise, the flier also includes a quote from Sam. J. Schlappich, a woodcarver from Lake Worth, Florida who opines

> In the Jungle dwells a spirit, a beautiful, brooding, quiet spirit which fascinates and draws on. Deeper and ever deeper it enmeshes the soul with its wild, riotous growth and glorious colorings. Its harmony, flowing from the heartsprings of Nature, swells into perfect symphony, overpowering and submerging within itself the fortunate soul who loves its matchless beauty and understands.[69]

The exotic zoo eventually had around three hundred animals: macaws, toucans, flamingoes, a Mynah bird called Joe, a brown bear called Doc Dolittle that featured in wrestling bouts, native Florida birds, rhesus monkeys from India, Malayan gibbon apes, ringtail and spider monkeys from Central and South America, and finally the chimps named Napoleon and Josephine. Famed for eating with knives and forks, as well as chain-smoking cigarettes, Waldo took Napoleon and Josephine on tour with him to the New York World Fair where "they gave a press party and served hors d'oeuvres."[70] During the Second World War, the site closed briefly but became a training site for the military and rare orchids housed there for safekeeping from the European theater of the war.[71] The Seminole camp at McKee ended with the war as Ralph Sexton reflected, "The Indians moved out when the war started and businesses went to nothing because people couldn't go up and down U.S. 1 (because of gas rationing)."[72] Lewis Tucker died in 1948. At its height, the gardens entertained 120,000 visitors per year.[73]

Waldo traveled extensively, ever keen to gather new materials for his sites and to advertise to would-be tourists about Vero and to expand on his desire to re-create a bit of the World's Fair and a carnival in the gardens. On his various travels, Waldo acquired at one point, well over 250 antique bells, acting as supplier for many churches in Indian River County and a 750-pound bell to a Haitian mission. At the Driftwood, Waldo had, "Swiss bells, cow bells, camel bells, school bells, fire bells, church bells, locomotive bells, bells from cathedrals, farms and ships—all hung in convenient places so guests could ring them at will." The bells became a way for guests to express joy, for example, if they liked a particular guest, like Marjorie Kinnan Rawlings or Leopold Stokowski, "every guest and employee on the premise turns out to whang him on his way." On the other hand, deafening silence accompanied a guest departing that they did not want to return.[74] In a June 15, 1960, *Boston Traveler* article about his bell collection, Waldo remarked, "I'll make a bell out of anything. I like to collect them and give them away to friends and churches. 'Course when I give them to a church, I ask the people to pray for me. I'm a sinner."[75] As was often the case with Waldo, his personal feelings on the items he collected reflected insight into Waldo's personality, "The most beautiful music I've ever hear was the clanging of the dinner bell on my father's farm in Indiana. It peeled out across the field I was plowing, and it meant rest and food."[76]

For his palatial Hall of Giants building at the gardens, Waldo had his eye on a table that he had first seen at the 1904 Exposition. Holding it long in his memory, he bought it from the American Museum of Natural history and had it shipped to Fort Pierce, Florida. It was a whopping thirty-five-foot slab of mahogany that he intended as the centerpiece of the Hall, bragging in advertisements that "It was so huge that ten mounted horsemen once stood on it side by side, accompanied by a couple of small boys, a dog, three kittens and a string of catfish." Waldo was a fan of large communal-style table settings at all his sites and for the Hall, he set his large table with lamps and an entrance door from Spain. Outside the hall he built an outdoor kitchen.[77] It was a direct replica of a kitchen Waldo had seen in Mexico, covered in brightly colored ceramic tiles with six open grills. The first meal prepped in the kitchen was 100 steaks complimented by swamp cabbage and potatoes.[78]

Another dining adventure that left a lasting impact was the Ocean Grill. Waldo acquired a piece of oceanfront property north of the Driftwood late in 1925 and for a time leased to a resident named Bert Scent who ran a hot dog and hamburger stand, "but the business was poor and the lease was allowed to lapse." Waldo then built the Ocean Grill with a "patio-dance floor having a view of the ocean." Promising "dancing under the stars," the open-air patio lasted only one night of business as the mosquitoes and biting no-see-ums proved intolerable. Like the Driftwood before it, the Ocean Grill was a structure that was "not so much designed-and-built, but collected and assembled." To this day, the building appears like a shack made of scraps of wood and inside one can find the odd assortments of fine Tiffany lamps, marine artifacts, massive wrought iron grill works, and original Highwaymen paintings. Like the McKee Hall of Giants table, the Ocean Grill features a round mahogany table taken from the palace of the Philippine President during the Spanish American War, said to be the second largest round cut.[79] Like settlers before him, Waldo constructed his Florida, but going beyond naming streets or buildings with vaguely Spanish and Native inspiration, Waldo created and archived spaces all over the region that continue to shape settler memory about the concept of "Old Florida."

The Patio originally started out as a fruit stand near downtown Vero in 1930 under the operation of Waldo's sister, known to everyone as "Aunt Lulu." Originally conceived as a real estate office, gift shop, and produce stand, the Royal Park Development Corporation never occupied the allotted space, opting to continue real estate sales from Waldo's office on 14th Avenue instead. Aunt Lulu worked alongside her housemate, Mrs. Jones, who operated the gift shop. They lived nearby at a home south of the Patio on the corner of 20th Place and 11th Avenue in a frame house that Waldo affectionately called his "Flea Market" as he used the space to store and stage many of his collected "treasures." The fruit stand ceased operations during WWII, and the space went through several businesses, including a dress shop and an ice cream and hamburger stand before it became a full-time open-air restaurant in the 1950s. Like all of Waldo's spaces, collected goods from around the world and South Florida adorned the space. Wrought iron grillwork as well as tiles that Addison Mizner originally salvaged from France and Spain for the estates of Palm Beach, saved from the trash heap by Waldo. Tiles in the bar of the main dining room included a coat of arms of the Spanish royal family, hand carved wooden panels in the bar and cocktail lounge from bridal chests of the Druze people in Lebanon, and lighting fixture throughout include items salvaged from Mizner, Rockefeller, Dodge, and Stotesbury estates. A portion of the walls in the bar and lounge were made from the garage doors of the Stotesbury estate, El Mirasol.[80]

Late in his life, Waldo decided to build a mountain, his last major public works art project, "it would incorporate his two principal loves; a fierce respect for the land and its harmonies coupled with a desire to enhance that land with the majestic beauty of art."[81] Another motivating factor of course was to create an enticing space, as Waldo told the Vero Beach Planning and Zoning Board, "I want to build you a tourist attrac-

Waldo Sexton with monkeys at McKee Jungle Gardens, circa 1950. State Archives of Florida, Florida Memory, https://www.floridamemory.com/items/show/156291, accessed 30 March 2023.

tion worthy of this A-1-A, which will be one of the best traveled highways in all of Florida. I want to harvest the 'Tourist Crop.'"[82] Waldo's Mountain was the inspiration for a pictorial book authored by his grandson, Sean Sexton, who included detailed images and personal details on every page as he told the "brief history of a small elevation." As a result of the dredging out of Bethel Creek, Waldo gathered the fill from the bottom of the creek on an empty lot he owned adjacent to the creek. He hired a crane to place large slabs of rock and concrete as stairs to the top. Recalls Sean, "Waldo's sense of grandeur and powers of promotion were always at play, regarding any of his creations." To this end, Waldo brought an elephant to the Driftwood Inn at one point to pose for pictures in the dining room and borrowed a pair of llamas from a visiting circus to pose at the top of the mountain with a picture captioned, "These llamas prefer Sexton's Mountain."[83] In this case, Sexton's creation is the Eden, conquering the land and its people, reshaping the landscape. At first the mountain only had a large pole atop and two birdlike statues flanking the bottom of the stairs, but Waldo was far from finished. Waldo sketched out a design plan for completing the mountain with tiles up the stairs and ornate details. The actual height of the mountain remains unknown with reports varying from anywhere as low as 25 feet to as high as 100 feet. Waldo set to work in his outdoor workshop where he housed his as yet unplaced collected pieces of wood, ironworks, bells, discarded windows and doors, and other architectural relics salvaged over the years from South Florida and Europe, "full of possibility and available for reintegration into places, that only Waldo could see."[84] Many of the tiles that made their way to Waldo's Mountain came from the demolished Palm Beach Stotesbury estate, "El Mirasol" that Waldo haggled over with Big Chief Salvage before purchasing the entire lot for $15,000 and used his own dairy vehicles to transport the tile, which he stacked in the pastures of the dairy lots. The mountain had at least forty steps going to the top that Waldo meticulously decorated with inlaid antique tiles, some harvested from Palm Beach and others he had collected in his worldwide travels, "including the Holy Land."[85] By physically reshaping the land to exhibit Euro-American life and culture, Waldo claims the territory for himself and future generations, creating a concept of Florida based on his own beliefs of paradise and Eden.

Envisioning the steps as "'Santa Scala' or Holy Stairs," Waldo at first viewed the mountain top "as a vantage point for the purpose of seeing out, but in its metamorphosis, became introspective, a place for reflection, 'a meditation grotto,' as Waldo once called it." He installed a set of thrones at the summit, "with a king and queen's regal chair, 'in the manner of ancient Babylonian ziggurats,'" and a plaque at the base of the steps that read, "Let this stand for man to enjoy. Please leave the beauty and do not destroy."[86] A fifteen-foot cypress spire, "Waldo's Needle," stood atop the mount with a four-sided balustrade reclaimed from a balcony at the Windsor Hotel in Jacksonville along with preserved giant seagrapes, live oaks, and cabbage palms, "to show future generations what Florida's ocean dunes looked like before man, the despoiler, and his bulldozers and draglines came in."[87] Ever the patron of all types of artists and creatives, Waldo "perceived the mountain as a spiritual center of artistic activity and the beginning of an art colony that might grow and flourish," and collaborated with a local artist, Elena Mead, who taught classes to local children to "sketch and paint its interesting features."[88] Lost in his description of the space is that the mountain is another construction of a settler viewpoint of Eden, in a town where Native-constructed shell middens lie bulldozed beneath the streets and beach architecture.

One should note that the mountain was the result of settler dredging from Bethel Creek, located near to what had once been the principal townsite of the Aís, building a mountain out of the remains of what had once been the spiritual and economic center of the Native polity, out of Native shell middens and town sites that settlers leveled to pave roads, and build up parks and construct houses along the Atlantic coastline. The mountain, to Waldo, held his own deeply symbolic and religious expectations, "You've heard of Mt. Hebron? The Ten Commandments were delivered on a mountain. How about the Sermon on the Mount? Great things have come from mountains, it could happen again." Reflecting on his grandfather's legacy, Sean Sexton shared:

> Perhaps the Mountain was at least a kind of monument to the unattainable horizon, visible from its heights, that always lies just beyond the grasp of a human life. He'd always felt a kinship with Ponce de León, the Spanish Explorer who came to "La Florida," reaching for that horizon in search of a Fountain of Youth, discovering in the process a new place where he'd never been, and in his own mortality.[89]

Styled as the "Hanging Gardens of Vero Beach," Waldo intended the space to be a traveler's shrine, "where weary travelers could pause and feast their souls on the beautiful sunrise over the ocean and sunsets over Bethel Creek and the Indian River." Unfortunately, the structure instead became a target for "vandals and culprits who work at night," Waldo lamented, "cowards as they are, tear down faster than I can build." Waldo even offered a reward for the arrest and conviction of the vandals, "there is a weed for every flower and blood where poppies grow, and in order to handicap their work I will pay $100 reward to anyone giving information."[90] His efforts to preserve the space failed, and as "the mountain fell into disrepair Waldo fell into a depression from which he never fully recovered." The diminished mountain remained in ruin until a tropical storm ravaged the coast in the 1970s and "it was decided to dismantle the mountain and use its 'sacred' components to restore the beach" in front of the Driftwood, restoring the landscape to a "natural" developed state and controlling the natural world for future commercial development.[91]

The destruction of Waldo's Mountain intersects with his mental and physical decline late in his life. Waldo's health was a consistent point of concern for his family, according to his son, Ralph Sexton, "several times in Waldo's life, he had different levels of depression, which normally occurred near the end of a specific business venture that had created too much pressure, too much responsibility and having borrowed too much money." While developing the McKee Jungle Gardens, Waldo and "Pop" Hansen went to Cuba to gather plants and allegedly the Cuban government called Waldo's wife, Elsebeth, to "come get him." She did, bringing him "back in a straight jacket." In February 1933, Waldo agreed to go to North Carolina to rest at friend Alfred Michael's home. Michael grew citrus in the Deerfield Groves at Wabasso and in north Orchid Island, and was a close personal friend to the Sexton family. His time in the mountains would not be the first time he had to take a rest, and Waldo began to regularly summer in the mountains with his family.[92] At the height of expanding the Driftwood from a family home to a resort, Waldo experienced a nervous breakdown in 1936–37 due to the pressures of financing the project. Allegedly a bank refused to lend him money to complete the project but his friend, Purdue classmate Walter Sheil, a contractor, completed the project for him. Waldo later got his revenge, according to local legend that several years later the bank went bankrupt and Waldo "'got even' by buying the bank's fixtures and strewing them around the Driftwood as reminders that 'unorthodox hotel methods' can support a wife and family as well as profit him with a lot of fun."[93] By 1947, Waldo's mental health concerns worsened as he fell into a continued depression that his family felt required medical intervention. Utilizing the help of Waldo's local physician, Dr. Carter Robinson, they brought in Dr. Sullivan Bedell, a psychiatric specialist from Jacksonville. Robinson believed that Waldo needed shock treatments and so Waldo's sons, Ralph and Randy, as well as family friend "Big John" Tripson got Waldo "loaded in the car" for a trip to Jacksonville, where Waldo would receive treatments for "almost the entire summer before he was brought back to reality.'"[94] Within two years, Waldo experienced another bout of depression, "showing increased irritability, depression, confusion, and restlessness." It took two days to convince him, but Waldo's sons brought him back to Jacksonville for treatment. Undeterred, Waldo "convinced the doctor that nothing was wrong, and returned home by train, beating his sons home by several hours." In another story, Waldo brought a friend named Bert to Dr. Bedell for treatment related to dementia but when they arrived, "the doctor kept Waldo and sent Bert home."[95] Later Waldo received treatment by Dr. Selinsky who felt that Waldo should receive inpatient treatment at the Menninger Clinic in Topeka, Kansas.

Ralph Sexton allotted $500 to take Waldo by train, stopping over briefly in St. Louis before taking another train to Kansas City and then to Topeka, Kansas. Waldo, characteristically, had a different plan, in St. Louis, "Waldo convinced Ralph they should stay overnight and see the sights, which turned out to be 'every bar and antique store in town.'" In a restaurant that specialized in exotic dishes, like elephant and bear meat, "Waldo was bragging how famous he was and showing brochures of the Driftwood, Ocean Grill and McKee Jungle gardens." For their part, Waldo and Ralph dined on rattlesnake sandwiches and local beer.[96] Waldo would frequently carry pictures and brochures with him all over the country, writing personal notes such as "Give the man a free room when he visits Vero Beach," on Driftwood adverts. Once arriving at the Menninger clinic, "Ralph remembered that it looked exactly like the Haunted House at Disney World." They admitted Waldo and Ralph found a hotel for the night before returning midmorning the next day to check on his father who had an orderly with him, "This is Igor, my keeper." Ralph stayed in town for three days before returning to Vero for two weeks, coming back again to check in on his father one more time. All told, Waldo spent close to three months at the clinic, Elsebeth eventually brought Waldo home opining, "the whole thing was a waste of money—all Waldo needed was a little rest." That being said, Waldo went back to the Menninger clinic twice more before eventually seeking treatment closer to home at the newly established Jackson Memorial Clinic in Miami and hiring private nurses at his home as his condition deteriorated later in life, "but even with around the clock nurses, his occasional unpredictable actions created a lot of uneasiness in the house." Eventually Waldo lived out his days in the care of the Royal Palm Nursing home.[97]

Waldo's Jungle Garden would eventually lose its luster as a tourist attraction as did many other sites along US-1. The vast majority of Florida roadside attractions between 1929 and 1971 "included a focus on Florida's natural resources," and most failed in the aftermath of the Florida Turnpike and Disney World.[98] Research conducted by the 3M corporation in the mid-1960s, designed to convince businesses of the important of roadside signage using their reflective paint, found that "29 percent of tourists traveling through Florida by automobile had no plans at the beginning of the day; they simply drove and stopped wherever their fancy took them. Another 49 percent had no definite itinerary or stops planned other than trying to get to a certain town by nightfall."[99] Dozens of attractions throughout Florida sought to provide "visitors with a brief diversion while they were on the tiresome, hot drive through the state." This included Gatorland near Orlando who hired Seminole to construct their gift shop to provide "an authentic Florida experience, the gift shop was made of cypress poles, a palm-thatched roof, and a sawdust floor."[100] High-speed interstates and the development of Disney and Orlando drastically changed Florida. While extremely popular throughout the 1950s, the opening of the Florida Turnpike and the distance from US-1 to I-95 routed travelers far away from the city of Vero Beach and many of Florida's roadside attractions struggled to compete with the opening of Disney World in Orlando.[101] By June 1976, McKee Jungle Gardens closed and fell into disrepair. Richard Treadway, co-owner and manager of the Royal Park Inn (1937–1960), talked about his memories of Vero Beach for an oral history in 1988, commenting on the community as it developed into a resort destination and changed over the twentieth century. "I must say that, for the record, that I am very disappointed that McKee Jungle Gardens could not continue. They were really quite good." The interviewer interjects, "Oh, it was beautiful," and Treadway continues, "You remember them?" Opining on the sale of most of acreage to a developer, the interviewer said, "I did have a chance to go through that, yes, before they built in there, and that is really a sin. It was so beautiful."[102] Arthur McKee Latta, grandson of founder Arthur McKee, told a local newspaper about the closure, "I'm somewhat disgusted with humanity, I guess, people no longer want to feel like Thoreau. They want things thrown at them. They want to be mind-boggled ... They don't want to walk the Appalachian Trail, they want to ride it."[103] Eventually development firm Vista Properties purchased the eighty acres and developed sixty-two into a golf course and condominiums. A local preservation organization called the Indian River Land Trust eventually bought the last eighteen acres. McKee Botanical Gardens opened in 2001, incorporating the outdoor Spanish kitchen, the Hall of Giants with its thirty-five-foot-long mahogany table (from the Louisiana Purchase Exposition of 1904), William Lyman Phillips's Cathedral of Palms, and many of the other hallmarks of the original site in the diminished park.[104]

More recently, historically minded preservationists rallied the community to save another Sexton space, an old building that once housed the Szechuan Palace restaurant on the corner of SR 60 and 43rd Avenue.[105] Once a country store on 43rd between 12th and 16th streets in the 1930s, the widening of SR60 necessitated a move for the rambling structure in 1950. With characteristic flair for embellishment and drama, Waldo Sexton got involved in the building's move. According to his son Ralph, Waldo Sexton saw Grover Fletcher driving the building south and suggested that Fletcher place the building on one of Waldo's lots. At first, the spacious building held an art colony that included artists Jim and Joan Hutchison who painted frescoes along the walls of what would become the dining room of the Turf Club and Grill. In a feature for *Vero Beach Magazine*, former chef and proprietor Eddie McGuire shared, "Waldo loved to build restaurants without parking lots or kitchens. That was his specialty. When I took over, I had to buy the lot next door so we could have parking." Several restaurants attempted to make a go of the space, including German, French, and Greek cuisines, before it became the Szechuan Palace. Ralph Sexton "wanted to make it like Waldo would have, using pecky cypress where he could," and cedars of Lebanon from trees planted near St. Helen's church.[106]

Jim Hutchison, along with his wife Joan, spent time on Seminole reservations studying for a series of portraits and landscape paintings. In 1962, the Arthur Vining Davis Foundation awarded Hutchison with a grant to produce fifty paintings depicting the lives of the Seminole at Brighton Reservation. With this privileged insight to Seminole life, Hutchison "produced the first paintings of tribal elders and their families at then-remote camps in the Everglades." He and his wife would live there for six years, and he exhibited many of these paintings at the 1965 World's Fair in New York City as well as throughout Florida's museums and cultural centers. Later for the Florida bicentennial, he would produce portraits of Osceola, Alligator, Wild Cat, and Billy Bowlegs II.[107]

Lillian Tutcik and possibly A. E. "Beanie" Backus painted many of the murals throughout the interior of the old Szechuan Palace restaurant that depict settler memory of Florida's history. Lillian came up from Palm Beach and Waldo let her stay at the Driftwood, Ralph recalled that the mural painting "seemed to take months and months... my Momma could hardly wait to move her out and finally did." Waldo took Lillian out to the Seminole reservation. Details of Lillian's time come from the notes of writer Willi Miller who conducted a 2005 interview for *Vero Beach Magazine* with Lillian's daughter, Merilee Tutcik. Merilee recalls, "she met the (I believe it was) great granddaughter of Tommy Tigertail." Commenting on the details in the murals, the Seminole presented Merilee with a traditional Seminole ribbon dress, "the dress is the same one in the painting of the Seminole woman on the water in the storm. My mother called it 'The Goddess of the Storm.' She also used her own face as the Seminole woman's face."[108] Another mural features "soldiers on white horses, which might have represented the Wars of Removal in the 19th century," and yet another details the Green Corn Ceremony or busk, with a bonfire that many believe Backus painted. For that same article, Miller interviewed Joan Hutchison who shared, "As we painted, Waldo would often come and watch, entertaining us with tall tales. The mural was finished just before Vero Beach's first Waldo Sexton Day." Waldo himself is immortalized in one of the murals, a scene of Waldo sitting in front a fire with a particular pair of boots that Waldo wanted to include, as Merilee detailed, "Waldo brought the boots in one day . . . He then proceeded to tell her that the boots were from the same manufacturer that manufactured the boots worn by the troops of Field Marshall Rommel in North Africa and would she be sure to paint them in such a way that the label would be visible."[109]

Comparing California and Florida, "as remote and distinctive states, California and Florida suited new formative narratives for white Americans that were constructed around ideas of labor and leisure in fertile surroundings," and Waldo Sexton certainly capitalized on this.[110] Around the world resorts present a postcolonial gaze, centering on the "myth of the uncivilized, with a wild nature and untamed people . . . [and] tours around heritage districts . . . spaces that celebrate colonial luxury and elegance." At Waldo's spaces, the idea of creating an authentic old world meets a shipwreck fantasy that hearkens to a type of colonial and maritime nostalgia, akin to resorts in former plantation regions where, "luxurious graciousness of colonial existence" focuses on the manor hours, yet, tourists "are not invited to imagine the lives of the plantation workers."[111] At Vero and with the idea of Old Florida, the Seminole and African American artists are featured and represented, however, the lower Indian River Lagoon has a far more complicated history regarding Indigenous peoples and African Americans.

6

Guinea Cows, Landscape Paintings, Waldo, and Zora

There's a tradition in the Florida mythology that connects cattle firmly to white settlers, known as Crackers, perhaps because of the sound of a cracking whip on a cattle drive. Some scholarship attributes the origin of the term to refer to "backwoodsmen," although it may have originated to describe a "braggart or talker," by the 1770s and 1780s, the term came to refer to "notorious braggarts, shiftless, sadistic in temperament, and brutish in behavior." Cracker and criminal became synonymous in some of the colonial literature as is the case in Spanish colonial Florida, in a 1790 letter from then governor of East Florida Don Vicente Manuel de Zéspedes y Velasco, who feared that if the Spanish did not populate the region to "impede the influx of rootless people called *Crackers*," then "their presence will cause further embarrassments" and problems for the crown.[1]

While in these aforementioned cases and certainly in other parts of the country the term has a derogatory meaning, for many Floridians, Crackers represent "a state of mind, a self-sufficiency, an attitude of independence," with "Crackerisms," like "when you ain't got no education, you got to use your brain."[2] Florida journalist Al Burt believes that negative connotations came from "exploitative big-city writers who saw the state as an exotically backward place and felt compelled to emphasize the grotesque side of reality for the amusement of the readers back home in 'civilization,' where much the same problems went unrecognized or undetailed."[3] This is similar to how boosters presented Florida history at times, another side of the coin of the exotic wild space, a place to "tame" with northern settlement.

Gilded Age New York journalist Amos Jay Cummings wrote about settler scavengers and wreckers along the Treasure Coast after a ship had gone aground. Settler methods of plundering a wreck included the use of "winged-wagon, or cat-rigged sailboat," and that "within twenty-four hours Indian River is dotted with winged phaetons, all striving for the nearest point to the ship." Some wreckers would barter for cattle or for water, for example a mare for "125 pairs of brogans, a peck of buttons, a half bushel of spool thread, and a pint of fish hooks." Fresh water being scarce near the wreck, the advantageous would offer water to the wreckers, accepting payment for "the most valuable thing he sees."[4] In a description of the character of the Florida Cracker he wrote, "the people are honest and passably industrious, but they will go for a wreck like gulls after dead fish. They reason like philosophers." The reasoning being, once a ship went aground, "before the authorities can take any action, everything will be ruined. The people declare that they might better secure what comes ashore than leave it upon the beach to rot. So they take what they can find. They look upon it as a gift of Providence." In that same passage, Cummings also referenced a history of Native peoples as wreckers, a practice they undertook from first encounters with European shipwrecks.[5]

One guidebook for northern travelers, George Barbour's *Florida for Tourists, Invalids, and Settlers* (1882) described Crackers thusly, "soft-voiced, easy-going, childlike kind of folk," that nonetheless were "quick to anger, vindictive when their rage is protracted," while prone to feuds, yet, "generous and noble in their rough hospitality." Living the "most undesirable of lives," yet surrounded by Edenic conditions, "every facility for a luxurious existence," this writer lamented that Crackers, "subsist on 'hog and hominy,' and drink the meanest whiskey."[6] Another of these northern writers was none other than Harriet Beecher Stowe who made North Florida her winter home from 1867 through 1884, becoming a tourist attraction herself as she wrote on her porch. Like many writers of the postbellum period, treatises of this era "followed a stylized literary path as predictable as the Grand Tour, with three motifs—the *Edenic*, the *exotic*, and the *exaggerated*." These writers, male and female alike, "generally portrayed Florida as an earthly Eden whose luxuriant landscape was scattered with exotic characters: Crackers—poor, rural white Floridians; Seminole Indians; and newly emancipated slaves."[7] As northern writers participated in a colonial discourse about the residents of Florida, they created caricatures of poor whites, newly emancipated African Americans, and Native peoples, basing their "local color" literary treatises more on legend than experience.

Romanticizing the Florida Cracker story and the origins of the settler cattle industry also involves deconstructing the impact of Patrick D. Smith's wildly popular 1984 novel, *A Land Remembered*. Smith, born in Mississippi, wrote several historical novels about the American Southeast but his most famous is the fictional founding fathers' story of the MacIvey clan, a group of settlers who moved south from Georgia into Florida in 1858. Following the family from Tobias and Emma MacIvey through their son, Zecheriah, and his sons, Sol and Toby, the book is celebrated as authentic Florida history, at one point included in the state K-12 curriculum, covering the rugged individualism necessary to survive for early white settlers. Faced with swarms of insects and dangerous animals, the novel is an adventure story that champions the theme of the hardy pioneer up against the elements. Central to the story is the roundup of wild cattle that the family drive from the interior to the coast to ship to Cuba. These drives allow the family over the generations to become wealthy as they witness the changes wrought to the Florida landscape by development and civilization, in the end, saddened by the changes in the land and the "vanishing" presence of the Seminole people as South Florida grows.

The story of cattle interconnects settler memory, race, identity, and myth. And Vero has a remarkably intriguing connection to the history of cattle and literature. Anthropologist, folklorist, and African American literary powerhouse Zora Neale Hurston came to know Waldo Sexton late in both of their lives as he sought to be her patron on an article about his Spanish guinea cows, a breed that he raised out at his ranch, Treasure Hammock, whom he claimed had origins in Spanish colonization. They developed a relationship of mutual respect and admiration as they spoke candidly about their own issues with mental health.

Hurston was a writer whose focus on the truth led to censure of her works for the Works Progress Administration as she detailed Florida and the impact of its history in hyper realistic prose. Born in Notasulga, Alabama, on January 15, 1891, she and her family migrated to the prosperous all-Black town of Eatonville, Florida, when she was a young child. She and her family thrived there (her father, a Baptist minister, was later mayor of the town) and she completed high school at Morgan College before matriculating to Howard University where she earned an associate degree before receiving a scholarship to Barnard College where she graduated with a BA degree in anthropology. Hurston studied under famous anthro-

Portrait of Zora Neale Hurston, circa 1930. State Archives of Florida, Florida Memory. https://www.floridamemory.com/items/show/17243, accessed 30 March 2023.

pologist Franz Boas whose methods defined the field of anthropology for generations. As a student in New York City, Hurston had the chance to befriend Harlem Renaissance writers and artists such as Langston Hughes and Countee Cullen. Utilizing her training in anthropology, Hurston traveled around the Americas studying Black culture in the African diaspora, spending time conducting field research between 1927 and 1932 in Florida, Alabama, Louisiana, and the Bahamas. She not only published her findings as nonfiction essays in American newspapers but also used her research as the framework of a series of fictional stories like *Mules and Men* (1935) which was a collection of music, games, oral histories, and religious practices that she collected over the years with a similar collection of folktales that she published in *Tell My Horse* (1938). She also had a collaboration with Langston Hughes, the play *Mule Bone*. Her work in her self-proclaimed home state of Florida led to the novel about the Lake Okeechobee Hurricane, *Their Eyes Were Watching God* (1937).

Unflinchingly honest and earnestly poignant, Hurston had a deep commitment to sharing the stories and the culture of the African diaspora but often found herself unappreciated and underfunded during her life. Though she established a dramatic arts school at Bethune-Cookman College and worked as a drama teacher at the North Carolina College for Negroes at Durham, she found herself frequently sinking in debt and poverty.[8] Hurston chose to live in the South because of what she called "the pet Negro System," whereby Black intellectuals stayed in the South, despite its problems. They did so because they faced challenging circumstances in the North, where they faced "segregation and discrimination . . . with none of the human touches of the South," while those that remained in the South were "afforded special privileges to blacks who met standards set by their white benefactors." While this system "reinforced the white southerner's sense of superiority," and "was not a desirable substitute for social, economic, and political equality," in an essay on the topic, Hurston showcases an "affirmative attitude toward the region, despite its dubious customs."[9] It was in her final years of her life, as she lived in Fort Pierce, Florida, that she encountered Waldo Sexton. Impressed by one of her nonfiction essays, he endeavored to hire her to write an essay on his cattle as well as encourage her to write about other local business and human-interest stories in and around the Treasure Coast that she could sell to support herself.

At least one of the letters between Waldo and Zora is now digitized at the University of Florida in the Hurston papers.[10] The remaining letters were discovered in the desk of Waldo's son, Ralph, after his death. His wife Chris was cleaning and found "a thin file containing a small cache of correspondence," in his desk, Chris was "bowled over" by the discovery, "I read and reread them. I just couldn't believe it." Local reaction to the letters to date have produced a 2017 production, "Jazz in America" by the

Vero Beach, Indian River Charter High School (IRCHS) theater and discussion within the community about the relationship between Hurston and Sexton. As the assistant director of IRCHS Jeremy Mezzina told the *TCPalm* in 2017, they are "kindred spirits: both adventurers and you can't put a single label on either of them. They were also fearless, creating their identities out of nothing."[11]

Unpacking the relationship between the two involves an acknowledgment that all letters have an intended audience, and the careful dance between patron and artist in a paternalistic and racially charged atmosphere cannot be ignored. The lower Indian River Lagoon had many "sundown" communities and while it is unknown exactly how these two came to know one another, it is likely that at the very least they knew of one another from their mutual friend, Albert Ernest "Beanie" Backus. The artists community in Fort Pierce was a vibrant and thriving scene, centered around the group of landscape painters, The Highwaymen. Throughout the 1950s and '60s, these daring African American artists produced vibrant and expressive landscape scenes of Florida that they sold to tourists along Highway 1. Some trained with Backus at his studio. In a recent *New York Times* remembrance of overlooked African Americans, they published an obituary of Alfred Hair, the "star of the group," who received formal training with Backus alongside his contemporary artist, Harold Newton. "More than anything," Gordon K. Hurd writes, "what distinguished the Highwaymen artists were their colorful landscapes, eschewing any formal color theory and relying on instinct and intuition to depict their steady stream of beaches, palm trees and Everglade scenes."[12] Newton and Hair invited anyone interested in painting to join in with them, all told, twenty-six artists (one woman, Mary Ann Carroll) are identified as a part of the Highwaymen movement, selling their landscape paintings along the roads of southeastern coastal Florida and as far north as Georgia for prices far cheaper than Backus's originals commanded in galleries. At the Backus studio, one might find artists and entrepreneurs of all kinds, Hurston as well as the Hallstrom and Sexton family all had connections to Backus and the Black community in Fort Pierce.

Zora first published a story about Waldo Sexton and the Tripson Dairy in the Fort Pierce newspaper, *The Chronicle*, on February 6, 1959, with a tagline of "Milk of Human Kindness," that describes, "When the white truck marked Tripson's dairy tumbles slowly down the street dispensing its wares, you have witnessed material evidence of marvelous dreams." Dreams, that she proclaims, were made possible by "a fabulous maker of dreams—Sexton—yes, Sexton of Vero Beach." This article was the result of several years of correspondence that led Zora to opine, "Out of this mind full of both imagination and daring . . . a fine and enduring experiment in race relations which is welcome news in this hour of racial stress over the entire nation."[13] From Sexton family records, it appears that their correspondence began in the early 1950s, around 1953, after Waldo was impressed by an essay Hurston penned for the *Saturday Evening Post* entitled "The Conscience of the Court."[14]

Their correspondence begins as typical expressions of patronage but reflects a desire for understanding about the nature of writing and, on Zora's part, her desire to make sure she was writing her best. In a letter from Hurston dated May 22, 1953, she references the article on "Ginny cows" and began their discussion of her mental health and circumstances, "I did not lose my enthusiasm for the piece about Ginny cows. But life has been very unkind to me for a long time. I have known the depths of despair since I talked with you. I feel that I have been in Hell's kitchen and licked out all the pots."[15] At this point one can see that this is a continuation of a discussion, perhaps a conversation started at one of Backus's many gatherings, or merely another letter in a written correspondence, regardless, it is very clear that Ms. Hurston felt that she could be quite forthright with Waldo about her mental, financial, and physical health. "First I lost some assets," she writes, which caused issues with her gallbladder and kidneys, "it is a horrible thing to find yourself stony broke. So I was sick because I was broke and then again broke because I was too sick to produce any work." She continued, "you know there is no such thing as a well mind in a sick body . . . so nothing for me to do but to wait."[16]

Turning her attention to her project with Waldo, "Now I am back among the living, as it were," and asked him to send her a "refresher" on his biographical story and some more details on his cows, relating, "I had all of this in my mind clearly when I first came away from you, but now, I fear that I might be fuzzy, and I have a passion for exactness about things." She asked for Waldo to tell her about his home, the Treasure Hammock Ranch, as she hoped to "mention the rare objects about your extraordinary home and your wife too, if I may." Please, she wrote, "please help me out on these things and as fast as you can. I am burning with inspiration now.

Creative moods are spotty and I want to do it at white heat." Importantly and indicative of their relationship, she ended her letter with the line, "Being creative yourself, I know that you will appreciate my feelings."[17]

Waldo responded the next day, May 23, 1953, kindly and supportively telling her, "I have been sick in mind and body and I know it is no fun. You don't want to get back into your work too fast but I will give you something to chew on and then will send you more information from time to time as I can pick it up."[18] Describing his origins and history, he wrote, "First, I will say I came from a place eight miles from a dirt road in Indiana," and working his way through college and after, he saved about $500 in silver dollars, counting it one night with his father, "this money in front of us looked as though it covered a forty acre piece of land." It was with this accumulated wealth that he came to Florida, "bought 120 acres of land, a business lot and 100 acres of ocean front, making down payments on all of it, and I have been in debt ever since. I have had a lot of fun ... I went through the Florida boom and bust. I developed the McKee Jungle Gardens, the Driftwood Hotel, the Ocean Grill, a lot of orange groves and my guinea cow ranch."[19]

Affectionately turning his attention to the guinea cow, "she doesn't ask for much," Waldo writes, "can make a living in the back yard and gives enough milk for a family. I wanted animals that would 250# in 120 days so I could sell them for veal and let the mother breed back and have a calf every year." With that information out of the way, Waldo begins weaving his origin story for the Treasure Hammock Ranch concocting a plausible background for the history of the land before he acquired it, interconnecting older colonial dreams of gold with a veil of Florida settler authenticity, as "an old cracker lived on it. He was an old hermit and used nothing but gold. He had cows and raised vegetables. I am not saying he made liquor but he could have and all the folks thought the house would be filled with gold when he died, but they didn't find a thing." The name, he explained, came from rumors that the former owner buried his gold somewhere on the land, "occasionally the 4H and Boy Scouts go out," Waldo explains, "and have a picnic and they dig around for treasure."[20]

Waldo is a storyteller, and his yarns interconnect with his worldview and his aim to construct his own reality and the places he inhabits. "My philosophy of life has been to play with nature—tickle her and watch her respond," Waldo told Hurston as he described his menagerie of acquired goods, including his two massive Philippine mahogany tables, one at the

Driftwood and one at the Ocean Grill, that he included pictures of for reference. He closes with a promise, "I am going to send you a bundle of literature while you are hot—some about the guinea cow and also some about the Driftwood Hotel." Hoping that this would give her enough to "chew on for a few days," he continued that he would send more as she asked for it, with the hope that if "you can sell it to one of your magazines that hongry [sic] for a little of your 'writin' and you can get some money that you can exchange for bread and other things that you want I will be happy."[21]

Two letters remain from May 28, 1953, one from Zora to Waldo, and Waldo's immediate response. Delighted with the materials that Waldo sent, Zora wrote back about Waldo's bull, Double Muscle, with glee, "I am just as active on it as Double Muscle in a pasture of heifers."[22] Within these letters, we can see that Zora also held anthropological interests but expressed anxiety about delving too far and facing rebuke. Referencing famous Floridian writer, Marjorie Kinnan Rawlins, Hurston asked Waldo if she had anything to fear of retribution that someone might sue for "invasion of his privacy," for naming people involved in the story she was writing about Waldo's various enterprises, "as that terrible Cracker woman did my friend." Using a story of an unnamed Black worker of Waldo's, Hurston hoped for permission to tell the story, "in connection with that killing you got him out of? I think that it is very amusing, his defense, and it would afford what is known as comic relief to keep the article from being too heavy . . . Perhaps if I do not use your man's name, he might not mind. But that 'soft kind of a head' is a killer-diller to me." In praise of Waldo, she mentioned an article she wrote previously on Senator Taft that needed comic relief, though she did not want Waldo to think he was "as stiff as Taft. No, you fairly drip with human juices, and that is where the other interviewers have failed to properly evaluate you." As an added touch she wrote in her postscript that her agent at Scribner's advised her that MacMillan's was interested in her next book, "I am going to offer two themes for a choice, a biography of you as one."[23] It is within these small comments that one can see Zora's interest beyond the surface, to continue her incisive ethnographic research of a topic, in this case, her patron and his constructions of Old Florida.

Assuaging her fears of rebuke, Waldo encouraged more personal details and in response to Hurston's letter, Waldo shared some stories that reflect his views on race relations and settler memory about the Native past.

"I could give you another story about colored men who worked for me," he writes, "one was named Crip and the other Kid. Crip stutters. They are both old bachelors." Employing the last of their kind and the Vanishing Indian trope he continued, "They lived in an orange grove down in the Tiger Hammock section where old Tom Tiger made his last stand against white invasion."[24] When Crip and Kid decided to ask Waldo for a raise on their wages, he decided "I would raise them but I didn't want to do that without having a little fun and kidding them a bit so I started out to give them a little hard mouth." Kid, for his part, decided to talk back, "Mr. Sechion [sic] do you know what I think of you?" Kid continued, "I think you is the tightest white man I ever is know. You know what I see you doing? I see you following behind the car-pinters [sic] picking up crooked nails and putting them in your pock-it [sic] so you can straighten 'em later." Waldo found this story amusing, "I have told it on myself numerous times."[25]

This letter also details some of Waldo's showmanship as Waldo related Eddie, an African American man that worked for him as "cohort and curator, chef, etc, etc," at the Driftwood. Waldo explains that Eddie was most instrumental for Waldo's enterprise, as "coming from Georgia and having trapped coons and possums he knows that what I was trying to catch was winter tourists and Yankees."[26] As Eddie was the first cook for the Driftwood and a longtime employee, Waldo trusted his assessment of people and would sometimes ask him, "Eddie, what kind of people do you have in the Driftwood," when Waldo was thinking about selling a piece of land. Eddie would "shake his head and say, 'I wouldn't fool with them. They are not our kind of people,' or, conversely, 'We have our kind of people there now,'" Waldo informed Hurston, "I don't mind telling you that Eddie's appraisal of folks is just about one hundred percent correct." Continuing with some more details of the business of operating the Driftwood and some of his plans to get in the Duncan Hines "Adventures in Good Eating" List, Sexton continues his letter with a little more humor, "I will be delighted to see what you knock out about me and will also start a private investigation to see whether I want to sue you myself after you write the article. I might be able to sue you or the Saturday Evening Post." Continuing with his joke he referenced an unflattering image of himself in the *Lincoln-Mercury Times Magazine* that he and a friend considered grounds for a joint suit for "misrepresentation in the picture they show of me." On a more serious note, Sexton concluded, "I think I told you that I thought you did a swell job on Senator Taft."[27]

It is clear from the remaining letters that Hurston sent Sexton drafts of her story in progress in installments as his June 2, 1953, letter provides notes, corrections, and miscellaneous comments on her draft. Waldo's reflections continue to touch on the matter of race, "When I first saw you were carrying a bag and I wondered what you had in it. Now I know that is what you carry your vocabulary in, and with that I am going to tell you a colored story that I think is tops." Related to the discussion of vocabulary, Waldo related a story about a laborer named Dave at the McKee Jungle Gardens digging ditches and artificial lakes, "all the time he was working the guides were going through and telling people about the trees and unusual plants." Dave asked Waldo, "Capt'n, I wish you would go down to the maze with me . . . what is the name of that plant?" Waldo replied that it was "Monstera Deliciosa," to which Dave exclaimed, "God, what a name! I am going to Okeechobee Saturday to see my gal and wants to get that word in my vocabulary."[28]

Waldo had another story about a cook named Sally and an encounter with Herman Zeuch, of the Indian River Farms Company. Sally, according to Waldo, had an affinity for pork chops, for a visit with Zeuch at the Driftwood, Waldo writes, "we had pork chops, fried potatoes grits and gravy for supper. The next morning we had pork chops, grits and gravy for breakfast." Apparently, this was not to Zeuch's liking as he told Waldo, "You can't eat pork chops three times a day, and grits and bacon and fried potatoes in this tropical climate—it will kill you." Sally, for her part, had a retort which she told Waldo privately, "You know who dies eating pork chops? The folks who don't get enough of 'em." For another visit by his partner Arthur McKee's wife, Sally was to prepare her traditional Sunday morning breakfast, which consisted of waffles with creamed onions. Waldo told Sally, "I want you to make them so that she will ask for a second helping," which Mrs. McKee did. Waldo spoke with Sally and informed her, "Mrs. McKee said those were the finest waffles she ever ate in her life," to which Sally replied, "Well, what does she expect?" Waldo responded, "Sally, you don't hate yourself at all, do you?" to which Sally had the quick retort, "It is a poor frog that won't praise its own pond."[29]

It is in this letter that we learn a bit more about the story involving Eddie referenced in earlier letters, for Waldo is offering the previous two stories as a substitute for the one "about Eddie and the man with the soft head because no one saw Eddie hit this man and the supposition that maybe he dies by accident and I don't believe, when I think about it appearing in print, that we had better bring that subject up. Maybe these stories will be good and maybe not but I believe we had better delete the soft skull story." He related one last incident about an unnamed preacher who worked at the Driftwood, whose job it was "to kindle the fires in the rooms in the morning." This man would announce his arrival to the guests by knocking on their doors and saying, "to whom it may concern! I is the boy who light the fires!" which, according to Waldo, the guests found "rather interesting" and he thought it interesting enough to share for inclusion in the article.[30] There is a tentative balance in these letters between artist and patron, Waldo is constructing a vision of himself to present to Zora just as much as Zora is carefully crafting her narrative to fit Waldo's needs.

The rest of the letter deals with Waldo's comments on her story as it relates to his origins and on his cattle. On cuts of beef, Waldo added to Zora's draft, "In defense of smaller cuts Sexton says he has never seen anyone who wanted to divide a T-bone steak. I think the day of big steaks that resemble washboards is a thing of the past. In my opinion, these big steaks are vulgar and they passed out with the robber barons." Throughout this letter we see some hint of Waldo's opinions on modernity, for the steaks, "they can't get these steaks through the doors in modernistic homes and in the second place, they couldn't cook these on these production line stoves," and as reminisced about his country childhood in Indiana, "I long for the horse and buggy days and the covered bridges."[31] Waldo is a man between generations, responsible for the rapid growth of Vero and its environs, yet nostalgic for an Edenic past, constantly aware of how he presents himself.

Waldo included several photos in his letter to Hurston, some of which tell the provenance and story of items Waldo collected over the years.[32] Describing his collection and his furnishing aesthetic, Waldo shared, "Someone asked what period my furniture that I designed fell in and I told them that it was earlier than early American. I hate chrome and plastic." This letter provides an important insight into Waldo's activities and his collection, while we know the provenance of some pieces, salvaged from West Palm Beach, others have dubious origin as Waldo's various stories change, depending on the audience. These pictures include Double Muscle "standing behind wrought iron that Addison Mizner brought from Spain and never used" and an image of the entrance to the Driftwood, "On either side are lights made out of buoys. I cut the bottoms out of them and designed church windows and use them for gate lights. On the right-hand side is a pirate chest which takes 5 keys to open it and a bell out of colored church that burned in Ocala, Fla. On the other side is a bell that came out of a church in Miami and another pirate chest." Waldo asked that Hurston return the photos and offered that he would procure 5 × 7 copies for her of any image that she might like to use.[33]

Further correspondence between Hurston and Sexton on June 13, 1953, referenced the return of his photos and that she submitted the article, "Double Muscle and His Pappy, Too" for consideration to her literary agent, Jean Parker Waterbury. "This is the hardest part," she confided, "to sit and wait until an editor decides your fate. I would be sweating blood if I had any left to sweat. The success of the article means so much to me in everyway. If it does not click, I'll be following you and picking up the bent-up nails that you overlook. And eating them too." This sentiment continued with her closing thoughts for the letter, "I hope that my shaking and shivering will be over the next time I write you. I do thank you for your most generous cooperation in every way. I hope to be using my big-mouth laughter again soon."[34] One must wonder again how these two met and was this merely a relationship of letters?

It is within this letter that once again, the friendly comradery between Hurston and Sexton becomes evident as Hurston relates a bit of environmental history about Merritt Island that might "appeal to the nature-lover in you." Describing her interest in the island, Hurston includes the following, "they have Coquina, which is a sedimentary rock, and typical of Florida, on one side of this narrow strip, and a hard igneous rock on the other," this mattered to her because she argued, "perhaps geologists are going to have to revise the statement that Florida rose in the Quaternary about 40,000 years ago, and that as yet there has been no volcanic action. There can be no igneous rock without vulcanizing." Her friends, the Frank Stocktons, she writes, own the most southern half mile of the island, and "sunk a well 380 feet and struck such a strong stream that they use part of it to create electric power. And at 65 feet they had cut through the Coquina and brought up prehistoric relics of marine life. I mean shells of things no longer found." To Waldo she shared, "I know that you are going to want to explore some on the island some day."[35] Waldo, for his part, enjoyed the information Zora shared about Merritt Island, writing on June 23, 1953, "I have always found it interesting but was unaware that it had igneous rock under it." He commented vigorously, "I would like to have been here when these things were happening and then when the waves built up the big ridges down by Fort Pierce and I would like to have choked one of those prehistoric animals with my bare hands."[36] More importantly, in this letter we see Waldo again relate to Zora's feelings and describe anxiety, "I have chewed my finger nails until I have supplied my calcium shortage," he writes about the "anxious seat." Writing from personal experience, Sexton says, "I know that finger nails without a little bread is a dull diet. I always feel as rich as hell if I have a loaf of bread in the larder." For her effort "in behalf of Double Muscle," he sent Hurston a check for $25.00, "that will buy you a loaf of bread or a bottle of shine and you can quit chewing on your nails until you get the letter you are looking for."[37] Unfortunately, that letter never came and the article was never published.

Waldo remained undeterred and did not waiver in his support of Zora and the last two letters of their correspondence highlight his attempts to procure further patronage for her. On March 3, 1954, he wrote about Mr. Walter O'Malley, the president of the Brooklyn Dodgers, whose spring training facility was in Vero Beach at the time. Waldo writes, "when I saw those fine colored boys out there making such a good showing I thought about you and thought there might be a possibility of you writing an article about them." He took the liberty to tell Mr. O'Malley about Hurston and shared that O'Malley would be "tickled to death to cooperate with you if you saw fit to write an article." Waldo shared some contact information and closed with, "this is just a thought and if you want to follow it, very well."[38]

The last letter related to their correspondence that remains is from March 15, 1960, in a letter to John D. Pennekamp, then editor of the *Miami Herald*, after Zora's death. Replying to a March 11 letter from Pennekamp, Waldo references a clipping that received from Pennekamp, "my reason for wanting this goes back to 1953 when I was promoting the development of the Guinea cow. Everytime I stuck my hand out somebody gave me a ragging about promoting a little cow."[39] While he and Zora worked together to get a publication in the *Saturday Evening Post*, they rejected the article because they "had already carried a story about me written by Ted Pratt." Waldo found Hurston to be "a very interesting person," and was writing Pennekamp regarding an article on her, thinking "that you might know more about her than you revealed in the article . . . I tossed her some crumbs from time to time when she indicated she needed bread." He included a copy of the article Zora wrote in his letter to Pennekamp, writing, "I would appreciate any information you could give me about Zora Hurston. If her story about me and the Guinea cow could be marketed I would see that everything that was paid for it went toward erecting a suitable marker for her grave."[40]

The article, "Double Muscle and His Pappy, Too," can be found in the Appendix of this book and before considering it, one must ask about the history of cattle in Florida and how Waldo Sexton integrated his mythological origin story to it. Guinea cows/Cracker cattle/Florida Scrubs are all descendants of Spanish herds. Spanish conquistadors brought cattle with them from the first settlements in 1493, known as Criollo, less a breed than a "New World landrace" created by the few hundred cattle transported to Hispaniola in the early sixteenth century that spread across the greater Atlantic world, as a supply of food and hides, as well as plow drivers for Spanish agriculturalists. The Spanish Criollo were a new species that remained the only domesticated cattle in the western hemisphere for over a hundred years until English and French cattle appeared in the seventeenth century. However, scholars note that crossbreeding between northern and southern European cattle herds did not occur for another two centuries.[41] In Florida, the first mention of cattle occurs with the Ponce de León expedition into Charlotte Harbor on the southwest coast in 1521. De León's second voyage to La Florida included between 50 and 200 head of cattle, likely left behind when the Spanish departed, with one scholar commenting, "given the Spanish cow's propensity for survival, and the certainty that when an expedition failed, any remaining cattle would be abandoned, the possibility of a small herd of wild cattle establishing themselves on Florida soil cannot be denied."[42] The first breeding cattle arrived in St. Augustine, Florida, in 1565, brought from Cuba to support the fledgling Spanish settlement, however, feral cattle may have survived and flourished from those earlier attempts by de León and other Spanish expeditions in the Southeast. As the Spanish created their forts and missions, where the soldiers and friars went, so too did bulls and cows, all the way up to the Chesapeake Bay tidewater areas. While many of these missions failed, the abandoned cattle may have continued to roam the Southeast.[43] Florida scholar Jason Herbert contends that South Florida Native peoples, including the Seminoles, became the first cattle herders and drivers in Florida.[44] The Criollo was able to adapt to its different environments, from the Florida peninsula to the South American llannos and the Andean sierras. By 1600 there is evidence of Criollos herds in Texas and in Argentina.[45] The Florida scrubs are small by cattle standards. To survive in the Florida environments, feral cows dwindled in size, noticeably smaller than that of other Spanish varieties but the Criollo proved a remarkably hearty animal that could handle the humidity, the onslaught of mosquitoes, no-see-ums, ticks, and the ever-present heat.[46] Most modern-day herds in Florida consist of American Brahman with only a few small Criollo herds remaining by the 1970s.

Waldo Sexton favored the small guinea cow descended from the Criollo, which became a special project in 1942 when he discovered that the breed was "the foundation cow designed by nature to do a special job for South Florida and decided to salvage these rare animals." This is one of the major themes of Waldo's life, natural Florida, or rather, nature as Florida would have it in Waldo's mind, his Old Florida. He started a breeding program designed to produce herds for veal, "while the cow may not be tall, it is wide and can be bred to have heavier loins and hind quarters which produce the higher priced cuts."[47] Regarding their dairy production, Waldo, ever the braggart, claimed that he placed one guinea in his 170-head milking herd and "she produced 4,000 pounds of milk," in comparison the entire rest of the Holstein herd produced "up to 15,000 pounds of milk per year but the little Guinea made more money for Sexton than did the average of all of his cows." Commenting on the benefits, Sexton claimed, "She made more milk at less expense than the other cows . . . If we had used all Guineas we would have netted $24,000 more than we did."[48] Sexton marketed his experiments with Guineas and publicized his beliefs widely, in one agricultural article the reporter proclaimed, "she will respond to the slightest degree of kindness and will do more for you with less help than any other breed . . . Sexton says humorously that she is the 'poor man's cow.'"[49]

Embedded within each letter are not only the tensions of patron and artist but also the constraints of Waldo's vision, Old Florida and New. It is also the last decade of Zora's life, a time of frustration and repeated rejection, but also a time of hope, personified in her desire to write for Sexton and her other literary ambitions, most notably a biography of Herod. Waldo and Zora's interaction provides unique insight into a troubled era of Florida history, a transitory era as the state grew into its modern self, an era before interstates and corporate tourism. That the story of Waldo and Zora is garnering so much attention in recent years after the discovery of the letters is reminiscent of the nostalgia and art collector frenzy over the Highwaymen paintings in the 1990s. While it is estimated that the artists created between 50,000 to 200,000 of their landscape paintings, by the

1970s tastes in art changed and many of the paintings ended up in garages and attics, with some remaining in restaurants and offices. With a shift in tastes once again and a desire for "authentic" folk art, collectors of all kinds suddenly had a renewed interest in the paintings in the 1990s. Art scholar Kristin G. Congdon posits the question, "Why are the Highwaymen suddenly so popular again?" The answer may be found in frames of authenticity, and once again, a question of Old Florida's characters and heroes. One can also compare their popularity to the story of Waldo and Zora, as the story of Backus's studio is a great story, "We like the fact that Bean Backus crossed color lines; he reflects on who we want to be in terms of acceptance . . . We need to believe that people who are different in one way or another can celebrate each other's creativity and successes."[50] Examining Florida's past and the relationships between creators of its narrative, its artwork, its architecture, and its legacy is an act of collective memory by recognizing the role of individuals in positive and negative aspects of creating a narrative.

Conclusion

This Land
Having no literary past to speak of, no
ruin or olden scroll buried in this land
find the imprint of fallen leaves, news
shining in the grass, rumors cast
amid shimmering fronds.
With no forespoken hardness, no igneous
Heavenward reaches and bereft of precious
mineral and ore, look to swollen clouds
in the distance, or glassine, horizonless
underlands, empty as a widow's joy.
Heed *here today, gone tomorrow* whispers
in the air, fading voices in a shoaling river,
overtaken metes and bounds where tree-
telling ditches and nothing less recent amble
through headland and marsh to a murmuring sea.
Nothing happened here that isn't happening now.
Forsake all allusion and memory, doubt
any worth of this land, save the fervent mist,
half-hiding, half-revealing abandoned dreams
now consigned to the sky. Wonder anew if this day
or another begins your journey to a directionless
realm, a final embarkment into light.
Shall we fall from the world like a stone, fail time
as a weakening heart and be lost, one place to another?
Is life but a lapse upon a crust, set beside a dark
salvage where we've been ever flowing, *water-like*
to the end of the eye, gathering mindward
as we go, a barely remembered story.[1]

"Nothing happened here that isn't happening now" connects to the perceived ephemeral history of the region, yet Vero settlers present a specific type of story about their region, symbolic of their type of settler memories. The story presented here is both one of Florida and one that could be applied to any number of American towns. When we think of the past, we often forget the myriad elements that memory plays in our analysis of the events we choose to remember and how we tell the story of our communities. Settler memory refers to the ways in which individuals and communities with a history of settlement in a particular area remember and commemorate their past. This can include the stories, traditions, and cultural practices that settlers use to connect themselves to their past, as well as the physical spaces, monuments, and memorials that they create to commemorate their history. Settler memory often reflects the values, beliefs, and perspectives of the settler community, which can include a desire to celebrate their achievements, assert their ownership and control over the land, and preserve their cultural traditions. However, settler memory can also be contested and shaped by competing narratives and interpretations of the past, particularly those that challenge settler claims to the land or highlight the experiences and perspectives of Indigenous peoples or other marginalized groups. As such, the study of settler memory is central to exploring the complex and dynamic relationships between heritage and identity. This plays into the concept of "Old Florida," the romanticized and nostalgic vision of a simpler, more idyllic time in the state's history. However, it is important to remember that this vision is often selective and does not reflect the full complexity of Florida's past or present. Nor does it reflect upon how each generation captures their own quintessential vision of what Old Florida is, or what Florida should be. Indeed, there are some who mourn the removal of Australian pines, an invasive species brought in by citrus farmers in the early twentieth century, for to these individuals, the pines swaying on tropical afternoon is their Old Florida. Each generation defines its own vision of Florida and negotiates their version of the past.

The study of settler memory when we consider both local and national history is important for several reasons. First, it helps us understand how dominant groups in society construct their collective identity and historical narratives. The way that settlers remember and represent their past reflects their values, beliefs, and social norms, and it can reinforce or challenge power structures within society. By examining settler memory, we can gain insight into how these narratives are constructed and how they shape our understanding of the world. Second, the study of settler memory is essential for recognizing and reckoning with the legacy of colonialism and its ongoing impact on Indigenous communities. By understanding the ways in which settlers remember and represent their past, we can better understand how this past continues to inform present-day relationships between settlers and Indigenous peoples. This can inform efforts to address historical injustices and work toward reconciliation. Finally, the study of settler memory is important for understanding the broader dynamics of memory and history in society. The ways in which settlers remember their past are shaped by a complex interplay of factors, including political ideologies, cultural norms, and individual experiences. By examining these factors, we can gain a deeper understanding of how memory and history are constructed and contested in society more broadly.

The settler creation of Vero Beach typifies Florida's connection with its past as the naming of streets, the types of architecture, and the character of the town is reflective of a national phenomenon. Across the United States, settlers erased the memory and presence of Native Americans to allow settlers to be the first inhabitants or at least the most important developers of the land. Vero, and Florida more generally, has its own flair. Sexton and other white boosters used Spanish architecture without much detail of its people, imported Indigenous names from far and wide, and otherwise created a historical fantasy land for new settlers and developers alike. Native dispossession by settler words and memory preserves an inaccurate portrayal of settler innocence, just as settler movement from the colonial and national period sought to dispossess these groups of their physical land.

For scholars of American settlement, the long shadow of historian Frederick Jackson Turner's 1892 frontier thesis and its emphasis on settler expansion looms forebodingly as does his focus on the "way older European identities had been molded into a new 'composite nationality' by the force of settler colonialism."[2] In crafting their settler memory and history of the region, these US settlements justified westward expansion through the literary removal of the Native history of the region by venerating a false narrative that celebrates the historicizing and mythologizing of Native peoples. These settlers were echoing Turner's romantic nostalgia for an imagined past. Florida and other southern states provide New South examples of the West as a process—how the "westward" direction of settler colonialism sometimes looped back eastward and south, at the hands of northern capitalists wielding fictions about English America's founding moments. Manufacturers of white settler histories employ a common strategy, whereby they relegate Indigenous people to "anonymous savage denizens of the forest" to be "replaced by God-fearing farmers who have tamed the wilderness." In the process of crafting so-called American history, the "lengthy, complex, and contested history of Indian relations is dispensed with in a series of sweeping assertions that dismiss Indians as long gone, replaced by non-Indians who are making modernity."[3] When white settlers of the lower Indian River Lagoon deliberately and actively neglect the written history of the Aís throughout the hammocks and Indigenous use of the region after Spanish colonization, they contribute to a national narrative of extinction that continues to haunt Native peoples and polities to this day.

By the mid-twentieth century, the rise of the space age along the coast of Melbourne and the development of Disney in Orlando changed the nature of Florida, both figuratively and literally. With the advent of air conditioning, small sleepy hamlets like Vero and countless others became year-round destinations for vacationing families as well as snowbird retirees. While citrus was still a booming crop for Florida farmers, the world that the Indian River Farms Company and Waldo Sexton created was changing rapidly.

In 1958, the city of Vero Beach celebrated Waldo Sexton Day on November 6, a spectacle that even included "animated floats portraying various stages in Waldo's life," as well as the dedication of Sexton Plaza on the beach. Waldo kept a "Spanish treasure chest" filled to the brim with silver dollars that he would toss out to participants marching in the parade. Remarking on the event, a full-page advertisement in the *Press Journal* featured letters and messages to and from Waldo. Waldo opined, "FOLKS, I didn't deserve it, but I'm going to pretend I did . . . You folks really put me on a pedestal last Wednesday. You made me a blasted hero, but I'll tell you right now, you can't make me a Saint. I'm jealous of my position as chief sinner in my church."[4]

The stories remain so long as we remember them, as we allow voices from the past to be a part of our present, as we all construct our own ver-

VERO BEACH REALTY COMPANY
REALTORS
2046 14TH AVENUE
VERO BEACH, FLORIDA
"WHERE THE TROPICS BEGIN"
Mar. 3, 1954

Mrs. Zora Neale Hurston
Eau Gallie, Fla.

Dear M.rs. Hurston:

    This afternoon Mr. Walter O'Malley, President of the Brooklyn Dodgers who train here, asked me to come out and watch some of the boys practicing.

    When I saw these fine colored boys out there making such a good showing I thought about you and thought there might be a possibility of you writing an article about them.

    I told Mr. O'Malley about you and he said he would be tickled to death to cooperate with you if you saw fit to write an article. He told me to have you contact Frank Graham, in care of the Brooklyn Dodgers, Vero Beach. I assume that he is head of their publicity or public relations or advertising department. I have not met Mr. Graham.

    Mr. O'Malley said he was going to New York and would be back in a week or ten days.

    This is just a thought and if you want to follow it, very well.

    With kind regards,

                  Sincerely yours,

                    W. E. Sexton

WES:B

Signed typewritten letter from Waldo E. Sexton to Zora Neale Hurston. Zora Neale Hurston Collection, Special and Area Studies Collections, George A. Smathers Libraries, University of Florida.

sion of Florida's story for as Waldo reminds us, "I am going to be terribly disappointed if people ever stop talking about me, whether good or bad."[5] This volume has presented one variation of the story, but there are more to tell, and Waldo would want us to talk about it, to explore as he did the variations of the myths and legends that have been forgotten, but need to be told.

APPENDIX

From the Sexton Family Records, A Typewritten Rough Draft Copy of Hurston's Article "Double Muscle and His Pappy Too"

Double Muscle is a bull, and a bull in full, the sort he-king of the Guinea Cows. His "Pappy" is W. E. Sexton of Vero Beach and he is mighty proud of Double Muscle. He calls him his "Bragging Bull."

There is a long story behind Double Muscle and his Guinea cow kinfolks, more than 400 years to the Florida part. This little kind of cow was brought to Florida by the Spanish discoverers and has been here ever since. Sexton has not been successful as yet in finding out just what part of the World this midget cow came from, but being the kind of nosy man he is, he will keep on trying. He admires to know all he can about the little heifers. What is already known is that the Guinea cow is in the same class with the razorback hog. Both are residents of the southern piney woods, and that makes them first-class Crackers.

Waldo Emmerson Sexton is the champion of the despised Guinea cow. "I was attracted to her because everyone else was against her. I consider that foolish because she is the natural beef producer for Florida. She has at least 400 years of natural selection back of her, and has managed to live and thrive despite her sorry environment. She is one of the few animals that can make her own living in the woods. She has lived too, despite the constant effort to exterminate her. Her male off-spring has been killed off every time one of them is discovered. Yet, she has kept Florida Crackers well supplied with fresh meat—off unimproved pastures and conditions under which most other cattle would have died. And she has done this without the help of a mate of her own. Most ranchers are ashamed of her. But not me."

His enthusiasm aroused, Sexton went Guinea cow. He got this foundation for his herd from the wilderness in mid-Florida around Kenansville.

"'The work I have done is purely experimental, and for a time I too thought that the pygmy of cowdom wasn't worth salvaging. But the way she has de-

veloped crossed with the Brahman strain has convinced me that we've got a source of veal that can't be beat. They develop fast and cheaply."[1]

So now, Sexton has up and organized the American Guinea Breeders Association. Its officers are: Waldo E. Sexton, President; Waldo Emmerson Sexton, Treasurer, and W. E. Sexton, Esq., Secretary.

This is a natural with Sexton. He is one of the few men on earth who rate the title of "Gang." He has so many sides to him that if he were in the Army, an officer meeting him would feel like saying, "Company, halt!" He is a whole squadron by himself.

We had better get personal with this Hoosier right in here. Sexton is a Double Muscle among humans. Along with the Brooklyn Dodgers, he is Vero's bragging bull. Get all his sides together and you really have got yourself some Sexton. It is not extravagant to say that Waldo E. Sexton is a latter-day Leonardo da Vinci. He does many things and does them all well.

Sexton is a scholar without making a trade out of being one. He is an intellectual who speaks in the vernacular. There is nothing of the pedant about him. His language is very colorful and nail-head descriptive. He could talk for a living if he wanted to and that is a fact. And like all people full of ideas, he likes to talk, admits it with a laugh. He might yield the floor under certain circumstances, "but when I'm drinking, don't try to tell me anything. Just listen." However, Sexton's flow of words more than justified its existence. When he get to fabulousing around, the listener feels he is tromping over a garden of herbs. You get so many flavors. About as colorful and imageful as he talks, his doings are yet more full of bloom. Every task he projects bursts out into exclamation points. That indicates that the inside dream is greater than his talk about it. It shows you the inside of the man.

There is his incredible DRIFTWOOD HOTEL, which Theodore Pratt has already written about in the Saturday Evening Post, his ranch known as Treasure Hammock, because a Cracker recluse once lived on it. He had some cows and raised vegetables, and used nothing but gold for money. The neighboring folks thought the house would be crammed with gold, but when he died; they couldn't find a thing. The theory is that he buried his hoard of gold somewhere in the hammock. Even now, the Four-H and Boy Scouts go out to the ranch and have a picnic and dig around for treasure.[2]

W. E. Sexton developed the justly famous McKee Jungle Garden on US Highway No One four miles south of Vero Beach, The Ocean Grill, a number of orange groves, a flourishing dairy, a real estate firm in addition to his ranch and hotel.

How and when did Sexton come to Florida? He says this is the way it was: "I come from a place in Indiana called Tailholt, made famous by James Whitcomb Riley's poem, 'A Tail holt is better holt than none.' It was eight miles from even a dirt road, and that puts you in the country, I believe. I graduated from Purdue University, and worked my way through school.

"After I had paid off the debt accumulated by college expense, I worked and saved up $500.00. I had it changed into silver dollars and headed for Tailholt, arriving there about one o'clock in the morning. I hired a livery-stable man to drive me out to our house in the country. My father lit an oil lamp and we got down on our hands and knees in the center of the floor and counted the money. My father said that I was rich because I had $500 in cash money and didn't owe anybody. All that silver money in front of us looked as though it covered a forty-acre piece of land.

"I put the money in the bank and lit out for Florida, I came directly to Vero Beach where I bought 120 acres of land, a business lot and 100 feet of ocean front, making a down payment on all of it, and to tell you the truth, I have been in debt ever since, but I have had a lot of fun and excitement. I used to go out from Old Sleepy Eye Lodge, where I lived, to my acreage with an ox team. I plowed up all my grove land with this team of men. You see, Vero Beach was nothing like it is now. There were neither street nor electric lights in Vero Beach then.

"Well, I went through the Florida boom and bust and I have experienced many things during my Florida years. I could have been a millionaire if anyone had told me they were selling government bonds. I had never heard of them. The only thing I thought you could buy was more real estate.

"What is my philosophy of life? To observe nature and play with her. To tickle her and watch her respond. The Thanatopsis thumb, you might say. In my compelling love of nature to hold communion with her visible forms, and let her speak to me in her varied language."[3]

In such words Waldo E. Sexton puts a finger on the key to his life and doings. It explains his activities. The eternal asker of questions of nature around him, and the experimenter, the pragmatist. As he talks on, you become aware that Sexton is a man of much learning, evidently from much reading since his college days and observation of nature. An intellectual without making a profession of it, scholarly without being a pedant. He speaks in the vernacular as a rule. This is sort of protective coloration. Evidently, Sexton is convinced about pearls and pig-pens. He will not open up fully until he is certain that he will be understood and interesting to his listener. With seem-

ing casualness he will drop a word or a phrase and wait for the response. If it fails, he keeps on the surface of things. He will leave with the impression that he is only interested, for instance, in the financial angle of the Guinea cow. But when he finds that you know something about genetics and the laws of heredity, his eye gleams and fairly glow. You begin to hear about animal ecology, pangenesis, gemmules and genes.

"What I am doing with the Guinea cow goes beyond my personal interest. She means something vital to the beef-dairy business in Florida. I call the Guinea cow the poor man's cow. She doesn't ask for much. She can make a living in the backyard, and give enough milk for a family. I wanted animals that would weigh 250 pounds in 120 days so that I could sell the calf for veal and let the mother breed back and have a calf every year. These guinea have not disappointed me. Often that have over-shot the mark, weighting more than I expected them to. I am crossing the guinea cow with Brahman bulls. This cross produces calves that are much shorter than the Brahman, but they average 464 pounds at weaning age. And they made these gains on Florida pastures and their mammy's milk. That is the chief merit of the guinea cow.

"I do not want an animal that keeps me working for it. What I am after is an animal that works for me. Don't get the idea that a guinea cow is a substitute for feed, however. She just makes better use of it than any cow I have ever seen.

"Lately I have asked myself if it is not possible that the guinea is the ancestor of all domestic cows. Now and then one shows up, a throw-back, in every breed of cows.[4] The cattlemen have no time for her, since they are seeking heavier beef cattle all the time. I first noticed them because on my ranch, and no matter what the condition, she was always fat and healthy, when the feed was not sufficient for the others. And unlike many others, she can stand the Florida heat.

"Therefore, I see her as a primitive type. Look at that primitive head and navel that have bred out in larger cattle. There are many point to be considered in the survival of an animal and adaption to it's surrounding. Has it got a good mouth for foraging? The mouth is the cow's lawn-mower or power to gather in grass. It should be very broad. The lungs and liver together make up the cow's powerhouse. It is the machinery that keeps it going. Is it adequate? The guinea cow is well supplied in all these respects. And another thing, this guinea cow is not afraid of snakes and alligators like other breeds. By long centuries of adaptation, she can take care of herself in that respect too.

"And you will be surprised to find that they have developed a kind of *social organization. At calving time, they have an arrangement that I call baby-sitting. Two of the cows will look after and nurse the calves while the others take time out to grass. Then they are relieved and go to grass while two others take over the baby-sitting. I have taken a seat in the pastures many mornings and observed this arrangement. I like to watch nature at work.*

"Originally, all I hoped for was early maturity and fast fleshing for veal. I have that. My guineas have done much better than that. But at a meeting of the American National Livestock Association in Miami it came out that there is a growing demand among housewives for smaller beef cuts. Many markets in the North have little demand for animals topping a thousand pounds. The guinea cow can produce the small cuts that are growing in demand. In defense of smaller cuts Sexton says he has never known anyone who wanted to divide a T bone steak. These big steaks, in his opinion are vulgar and they passed out with the robber barons. He thinks the day of gout and big steaks that resembled washboards are over.[5]

"What is it then that I am work on now? That is where nangensis comes in. I am seeking some way to control the genes that determine the color of an animal. I want to produce a white cow, or one nearly white. Why? From my observation, I find that the lighter colored the cow, the less trouble she has with attacking insects, and the better she is adapted to withstand the warm climate. Notice that I have nearly every color in the rainbow now. The black cows are so attacked by flies that that they have to be sprayed. The heat worries them. I am looking to produce and fix the strain of white guinea cows. Then she will be the perfect animal for this climate."

Driving across one of the pastures of Treasure Hammock, he saw a small female turtle digging a hole in the dirt road to lay her eggs. Sexton remarked that she showed bad judgment, but he drove out of the road to avoid her. He was going to consult with Eddie, the Negro who had been with him for many years. Been with Sexton when the going was tough. Sexton wants everybody to meet his old employees. "Together, we gathered up the driftwood that went into building my hotel. Eddie and two other Negroes have been with me for many years and stuck with me through thick and thin. The others are not with me any more, but Eddie is, and he knows that I will keep faith with him.

"Tom got into a killing-scare a few years back. A contemporary worker took out after Tom's wife. Tom warned him that if he ever caught him around his house he was going to kill, but the man was not impressed, it seems. Well, Tom did catch him at his house late one night, and the next thing I knew, Tom was sending for me to get him out of the county jail. Naturally I was not *going to let Tom go to Raiford if I could help it. After Tom was freed of the charge, I asked him why he hit the man so hard. "A good beating would have been enough." "Yes, sir, Mr. Sexton, a good beating would have been a gracious plenty, and that is all I meant to do to him." "But you killed him dead, Tom, busted his skull." "That's right, Boss, I sure did." "What made you hit him so hard, then?" "Aw, I never hit him all that hard, Mr. Sexton, the trashy scamp just had one of them soft kind of heads."*

Mr. Sexton's son managed Treasure Swamp Ranch and he and his wife lived in a very interesting house out on the ranch. He had Eddie watering a pasture when we found him. Eddie was full of good humor and smiles and the incident of the soft head seemed forgotten.[6]

Back at the distinctive Sexton home, crammed with art objects and more curiosities from all over the inhabitable world, Mrs. Sexton turned out to be somewhat fabulous too, in the true Sexton tradition. She is a pretty kind of woman and had a fabulous white sweater of pure Angora wool, lavishly embroidered with jewels. Inside the house and everywhere around it were curiosities from everywhere. In a room adjoining the garage were numerous things, among them a high tall, elaborately decorated chair that had once been the property of Haile Selassie, King of Abbysinnia.

That got Waldo Sexton onto his love for fine and rare woods.

"I have a broad board and big table complex. I have one table down in the Hall of Giants at the McKee Jungle Gardens that is 35 feet long, 5 feet wide and four inches thick. It is one piece of solid mahogany. When I was asked its dimensions, I told people that I could not read and write, so I put 12 men, 12 horses and 2 chimpanzees up on the table at one time to give them an idea of its size. I also had twelve couples dancing at one time. We can comfortably seat fifty people around this table. It came from the Phillippine Islands, and was hewn out of a single log. It was first exhibited in this country at the St. Louis Exposition around the turn of the century where I first saw it. John D. Rockefeller tried to get his architects to incorporate this board into Rockefeller Center, but they did not have the imagination enough to just set it up as a table. It was exhibited in the Museum of Natural History in New York for twenty-five years as a piece of Redwood from California until a wood export came through and told them it was Philippine mahogany.

"The other table is circular. It is also one piece of solid Philippine mahogany and was taken out of the palace of the head of the Philippine government during the Spanish-American War by a Colonel. It is close to eight feet

in diameter, and two inches thick. I have nine other tables which I had cut out of one cypress log. The wood is crotch cypress, which is extremely rare."

But in no time at all Waldo Sexton was away from his tables and back to midget cows.[7]

"I always like to look in on the milking. Did you know that the feed the cow eats late in the afternoon makes the cream for your breakfast coffee? And by the way, I have introduced guinea cows into my dairy herd. They do not produce the volume of milk that a Holstein can, but it costs so much less to produce it with a guinea cow. Our profits last year would have amounted to $24,000 more than we did if my whole herd had been guineas."

Sexton has to have one last look for the dat (sic) at Double Muscle, and the very sight of the animal swelled his chest way out.

"Look at him! An AA guinea bull whose ancestry can be traced back to 1492. That's my "bragging bull." I would rather have produced Double Muscle than be governor of the State of Florida."[8]

ACKNOWLEDGMENTS

This project benefited greatly from the support of a cohort of historians and anthropologists who study the Native South, particularly scholars of Florida such as Andrew Frank, Denise Bossy, Alejandra Dubcovsky, Jason Herbert, Evan Nooe, Matt Jennings, and Christine Rizzi. This project is inspired by the excellent scholarship and collegiality of Jean O'Brien, Boyd Cothran, Jim Buss, James Brooks, Joe Genetin-Pilawa, Coll Thrush, Ian Saxine, Nate Osborn, Aubrey Lauersdorf, James Hill, Robbie Ethridge, and Greg Smithers. Our community of scholars has an incredible ally and colleague in Carol Higham, whose editing skills provided much-needed insight and clarity.

Research for this project was helped immensely by Ruth Stanbridge and Carolyn Bayless of the Indian River Historical Society who both patiently listened to my questions over the last several years as I worked through this project. I appreciate the generous support of my colleagues at the University of Southern Indiana, especially my chair, Jason Hardgrave, and my students. For Wes Durham, your patience and support are unmatched, thank you for your part in this project and its journey.

For Sean Sexton, my gratitude cannot be expressed in words, thank you for sharing family letters and stories with me and supporting the project, thank you for sharing Waldo's stories with me and for introducing me to Marvin Carter and Eugene Lyon whose knowledge of Vero and its history are unmatched. And for Waldo, I sit here in Indiana writing about this and dream of your Florida, it holds such a space in my heart, thank you for imagining it and building a world for my family to begin. There is no us without Vero.

No project would ever come to fruition without the support of my mother, Lynn, and my daughter, Annaliese, whose unwavering enthusiasm for my research is the foundation of my scholarship.

NOTES

Introduction

1 Athinodoros Chronis, "Heritage of the Senses: Collective Remembering as an Embodied Praxis," *Tourist Studies* (Vol. 6, No. 3, 2006, 267–296), 268–269.
2 Florida State Parks, "Ecology Indian River Lagoon," https://www.floridastateparks.org/learn/ecology-indian-river-lagoon Accessed November 1, 2022.
3 Jean O'Brien, *Firsting and Lasting: Writing Indians out of Existence in New England* (Minneapolis: University of Minnesota Press, 2010).
4 O'Brien, *Firsting and Lasting*, 52–53.
5 O'Brien, *Firsting and Lasting*, 107, 105.
6 O'Brien, *Firsting and Lasting*, 55.
7 Jean Delumeau, *History of Paradise: The Garden of Eden in Myth and Tradition* (Urbana: University of Illinois Press, 2000), 6.
8 Delumeau, *History of Paradise*, 109.
9 Delumeau, *History of Paradise*, 115.
10 James Baldwin, "The White Problem," in *The Cross of Redemption: Uncollected Writings*, ed., Randall Keenan (New York: Vintage International, 2011), 91.
11 Jean Ribault, *The Whole & True Discouerye of Terra Florida* [1563], Jeannette Thurber Connor (ed.). Gainesville: University Presses of Florida, 1974) Accessed via https://earlyfloridalit.net/jean-ribaut-the-whole-true-discouerye-of-terra-florida/
12 Nicholas Le Challeux, "Octet" [1565]. Trans. Maurice O'Sullivan. From *Discours de l'histoire de la florite contenant la trahison del Espangnols, contre les sujects du Roy* (1579) Accessed via https://earlyfloridalit.net/nicholas-le-challeux-octet/
13 Eugene Lyon, *The Enterprise of Florida: Pedro Menéndez de Aviles and the Spanish Conquest of 1565–1568* (Gainesville: University Presses of Florida, 1976), 12–13.
14 William E. Goun, *Southeast Florida Pioneers: The Palm and Treasure Coasts* (Sarasota, Florida: Pineapple Press, 1998), 122–123; Sidney Johnston, *A History of Indian River County: A Sense of Place* (Vero Beach, Florida: Indian River Historical Society, 2002), 8–10.
15 Sidney Lanier, *Florida: Its Scenery, Climate, and History: With an Account of Charleston, Savannah, Augusta, and Aiken; a Chapter for Consumptives; Being a Complete Hand-book and Guide* (New York: J. B. Lippincott & Company, 1875), 116; 140.

16 David Wrobel, *Promised Lands: Promotion, Memory, and the Creation of the American West* (Lawrence: University of Kansas Press, 2002), 13.
17 Frank Parker Stockbridge, *Florida in the Making* (New York: Debower Publishing Company, 1926), vii–viii.
18 Stockbridge, *Florida in the Making*, 1–2.
19 Edward King, "The Great South," *Scribner's Monthly: An Illustrated Magazine for the People* (New York: Scribner and Son; Volume 9, Issue 1, November 1874, 1–31), 2.
20 King, "The Great South," 2–3.
21 King, "The Great South," 3.
22 King, "The Great South," 28.
23 McGoun, *Southeast Florida Pioneers*, 122–123; Johnston, *A History of Indian River County*, 8–10.

Chapter 1. Vero Man to the Aís

1 Alejandra Dubcovksy, "When Archaeology and History Meet: Shipwrecks, Indians, and the Contours of the Early-Eighteenth-Century South," *Journal of Southern History* (vol. 84, no. 1 [2018]: 39-68), 60.
2 Bruce MacFadden, Barbara A. Purdy, Krista Church, and Thomas W. Stafford, "Humans were Contemporaneous with Late Pleistocene Mammals in Florida: Evidence from Rare Earth Elemental Analyses," *Journal of Vertebrate Paleontology* (Vol. 32 No 3, 2012, 708–716) http://www.jstor.org/stable/41515289.
3 Robert Davidson, *Indian River: A History of the Aís Indians in Spanish Florida* (West Palm Beach, Florida: Self-Published, 2001), 16.
4 The history of the Aís has been woefully neglected in the past, however, there is promising scholarship on the horizon, most importantly by Peter Ferdinando whose forthcoming work engages with the remarkable depth of the Aís connections with the Bahamas and their trading empires.
5 The archival holding shelves are over 9 kilometers in size, encompassing 43,000 volumes and 80 million pages worth of materials. See https://www.visitasevilla.es/en/monuments-and-culture/archive-indies.
6 With his detailed and intuitive understanding of the source materials, Lyon became an internationally renowned expert on Spanish colonial Florida and helped famed treasure diver Mel Fisher find two of the sunken treasure fleets, the Nuestra Senora de Atocha and Santa Margarita in the lower Florida Keys. Born in Miami, Lyon spent time in city politics before he became an academic, working as the Assistant City Manager for the city of Coral Gables (1950s) and as the City Manager of Vero Beach (1958–1961) before starting his doctoral study at the University of Florida in 1967. Lyon went on to run the St. Augustine Foundation at Flagler College where he oversaw the curation of thousands of reels of materials related to the study of Spanish Florida. He spent much of his career, working alongside his wife, Dorothy, who accompanied him on many of his archival trips providing insight as he collected materials not only related to St. Augustine but to the colony of Santa Elena (Parris Island, South Carolina) and remained an active advocate for greater awareness of history throughout his life, long after he retired to Vero Beach. Lyon passed away

on May 3, 2020, at the age of 91. I had the distinct honor of interviewing him at the beginning of this research project and learning about his wife Dorothy and their research adventures as well as their beautiful and loving courtship and life together. See Lyon, *The Enterprise of Florida,* 12–13.

7 Daniel S. Murphree, "Constructing Indians in the Colonial Floridas: Origins of European-Floridian Identity, 1513–1573," *The Florida Historical Quarterly* (Vol. 81, No. 2, Fall 2001, 133–154), 154.

8 Viviana Diaz Balsera, *La Florida: Five Hundred Years of Hispanic Presence* (Gainesville: University Press of Florida, 2014), 3.

9 Antonio de Herrera account quoted in Robert Davidsson, *Indian River: A History of the Ais Indians in Spanish Florida* (West Palm Beach, Florida: Self-Published, 2001), 12.

10 Davis T. Frederick, "The Record of Ponce de Leon's Discovery of Florida, 1513," *The Florida Historical Society Quarterly* (Vol. 11, No. 1, Jul. 1932, 5–15), 15.

11 Davidsson, *Indian River: A History of the Ais,* 18.

12 Louis J. Mendelis, "Colonial Florida," *Florida Historical Quarterly* (Vol. 3, No. 2, Article 5, 1924), 7.

13 Diaz Balsera, *La Florida,* 8.

14 Quoted in David B. Quinn, ed., *New American World: A Documentary History*, Volume 1, 247; Murphree "Constructing Indians in the Colonial Floridas," 139–140.

15 Ed Winn, *King Carlos of the Calusa Indians* (Winn Publishing, 2003), 26–27.

16 David O. True, ed., *Memoir of D. d'Escalante Fontaneda Respecting Florida, Written in Spain about the Year 1575* (Coral Gables, Florida: Glade House, 1945), 35; Jerald T. Milanich, *Florida Indians and the Invasion from Europe* (Gainesville: University of Florida Press, 1995), 42.

17 Eugene Lyon, "Pedro Menéndez's Strategic Plan for the Florida Peninsula," *The Florida Historical Quarterly* (Vol. 67, No. 1, July 1988, 1–14), 2.

18 Thomas Benjamin, *The Atlantic World: Europeans, Africans, Indians, and Their Shared History, 1400–1900* (New York: Cambridge University Press, 2009), 236–237.

19 J. Leitch Wright Jr., "Sixteenth Century English-Spanish Rivalry in La Florida," *The Florida Historical Quarterly,* (Vol. 38, No. 4, Apr. 1960, 265–279), 269–270.

20 Rouse, *Survey of Indian River,* 51; Hakluyt 1941: 48.

21 Brinton, *A Guidebook,* 34. Settler memory of Fort Caroline and the Huguenots tends toward the sympathetic particularly among the paraprofessional histories of the Gilded Age and Progressive eras who openly embraced an anti-Catholic sentiment. Presciently, Daniel Brinton wrote in 1869, the event was "not characterized by any greater atrocity than was customary on both sides in the religious wars of the sixteenth century, but it has been a text for much bitter writing since." Gloria Jahoda, *Florida: A Bicentennial History* (New York: W. W. Norton & Company, 1976), 31. In one Florida history written for the United States' bicentennial, the author was less sympathetic to the Spanish and fully jingoistic of the Anglo narrative, "Florida has always been a country of violent drama. Hapless French Protestants seeking religious freedom on the St. Johns had been handily slain 'as Lutherans.' Where the Massachusetts pilgrims had been friendly to Squanto, the conquistadores had cut

off the nose of Hirrigua. Where Virginia settled into the genteel piety of Anglicanism, Florida had a turbulent chronicle of martyrdoms." One should note, for clarity, that the Massachusetts pilgrims engaged in the massacre of the Pequot in the 1630s as well as praying town Natives in King Philips War and the Virginians conquered the Chesapeake through a series of devastating wars, kidnapped Pocahontas, and stole Native children for conversion and enslavement.

22 Quoted in Barcia 1973: 69; Davidsson, *Indian River*, 61–62.
23 Quoted in Fontaneda 1944, 33; Davidsson, *Indian River*, 62.
24 Davidsson, *Indian River*, 41.
25 Rough estimates in 1650 by one scholar indicated about 1,000 Natives in South Florida with the Aís numbering at 600, this number is questioned by scholars. Rouse, *Survey of Indian River*, 40.
26 Rouse, *Survey of Indian River*, 51; Barcia, 1723: 91.
27 Quoted in Bennett 1968: 168; Davidsson, *Indian River*, 62–63.
28 Quoted in Barrientos 1965: 75; Davidsson, *Indian River*, 63–64.
29 Quoted in Barrientos 1965: 75; Davidsson, *Indian River*, 63–64.
30 Quoted in Barrientos 1965: 72; Davidsson, *Indian River*, 63–64.
31 Quoted in Barrientos 1965: 73; Davidsson, *Indian River*, 65.
32 Lyon, *Enterprise of Florida*, 130.
33 Rouse, *Survey of Indian River*, 51.
34 In July 1654, a group of Indians from South Florida came to St. Augustine with ambergris that they used to trade with the Spanish for goods and tools. See James W. Covington, "Trade Relations between Southwestern Florida and Cuba: 1600–1840," *The Florida Historical Quarterly* (Vol. 37, No. 2, Oct., 1959, 114–28), 116; See also Peter Ferdinando, "Atlantic Ais in the sixteenth and seventeenth centuries: Maritime adaptation, Indigenous wrecking, and buccaneer raids on Florida's central east coast" (2015). *ProQuest ETD Collection for FIU*. AAI3721473. https://digitalcommons.fiu.edu/dissertations/AAI3721473
35 Lyon, *The Enterprise of Florida*, 129.
36 Gannon, *History of Florida*, "Eugene Lyon," 63; For a more detailed history of the Spanish missions, see Jerald T. Milanich, *Laboring in the Fields of the Lord: Spanish Missions and Southeastern Indians* (Washington D.C.: Smithsonian Press, 1999).
37 Jane Landers, *Black Society in Spanish Florida* (Urbana: University of Illinois Press, 1999), 14–15.
38 Quoted in Daniel S. Murphree, "Constructing Indians in the Colonial Floridas: Origins of European-Floridian Identity, 1513–1573," *The Florida Historical Quarterly* (Vol. 81, No. 2, Fall 2002, 133–154), 153. James W. Covington, ed., and A. F. Falcones, trans., *Pirates, Indians, and Spaniards: Father Escobedo's 'La Florida'* (St. Petersburg, Florida: Great Outdoors Publishing Co., 1963 [1598–1609]), 86–89. Writing about his rescue, the man said, "It was not an act of mercy by which they saved me but only a desire that I should be their silversmith . . ." and about his acts of carnal sin, "Those two girls that you see yonder are my daughters and they are Christians. If they are not beautiful to the human eye, they are beautiful in the eyes of our Lord. Although I may be a sinner, they are as pure as the stars in the sky." Classifying the

Aís language has been the subject of some debate among explorers and scholars as Bernard Romans translated Aís to mean deer (1775: 23) because of the close resemblance to the Choctaw word, Swanton included the language (1946, Table 1) in the Muskhogean linguistic stock, alongside the Calusa with a separate designation for the Timucua. Higgs (1942: 25–26) however suggested that Aís was derived from the Timucuan roisse, "meaning mother" See Irving Rouse, *A Survey of Indian River Archaeology, Florida* (New Haven: Yale University Press, 1951), 39.

39 Rouse, *Survey of Indian River*, 49.
40 Covington, ed., *Pirates, Indians, and Spaniards*, 91.
41 Rouse, *Survey of Indian River*, 66; See also Ferdinando.
42 Andrew K. Frank, *Before the Pioneers: Indians, Settlers, Slaves, and the Founding of Miami* (Gainesville: University Press of Florida, 2017), 46.
43 Quoted in Connor 1925: 55; Davidsson, *Indian River*, 76.
44 Gannon, *The History of Florida*, "Eugene Lyon," 71–72.
45 Charles D. Higgs, "Spanish Contacts the Ais (Indian River) Country," *The Florida Historical Quarterly* (Vol. 21, No. 1, Jul. 1942, 25–39), 27.
46 Hoffman, *Florida's Frontiers*, 87, 349.
47 Hoffman, *Florida's Frontiers*, 93–94.
48 Jason Daniels, "Shipwrecked in the Atlantic World: Reevaluating Jonathan Dickinson's Interactions with Native Peoples along Florida's Southeastern Coast," *The Florida Historical Quarterly* (Vol. 91, No. 4, Spring 2013, 451–490), 462.
49 Verne E. Chatelain, *The Defenses of Spanish Florida 1565 to 1763* (Washington, D.C.: Carnegie Institution of Washington Publication, 1941), 128 referencing Geiger, *Franciscan Conquest*, 177–178.
50 Quoted in Rouse, *Survey of Indian River*, 269–274.
51 Quoted in Rouse, *Survey of Indian River*, 269–274.
52 Rouse, *Survey of Indian River*, 54–56.
53 Alejandra Dubcovsky, *Informed Power: Communication in the Early American South* (Cambridge: Harvard University Press, 2016), 58–59.
54 Hoffman, *Florida's Frontiers*, 165.
55 Introduction by Bessie Wilson DuBois in the 300th anniversary printing. Evangeline Walker Andrews and Charles McLean Andrews, eds., *Jonathan Dickinson's Journal or God's Protecting Providence. Being the Narrative of a Journey from Port Royal in Jamaica to Philadelphia between August 23, 1696 and April 1, 1697* (Port Salerno, Florida: Florida Classics Library, 1985). Previously published by Yale University Press in 1945 and 1961.
56 Andrews and Andrews, eds., *Dickinson's Journal*, introduction.
57 Andrews and Andrews, eds., *Dickinson Journal*, 7.
58 Mary S. Mattfield, "Journey to the Wilderness: Two Travelers in Florida, 1696–1774," *The Florida Historical Quarterly* (Vol. 45, No. 4, April 1967, 327–351), 331.
59 Andrews and Andrews, eds., *Dickinson Journal*, 22–23.
60 Andrews and Andrews, eds., *Dickinson Journal*, 24–25.
61 Andrews and Andrews, eds., *Dickinson Journal*, 28–29; Amy Turner Bushnell, "The Wreck of the *Reformation*," *Humanities* (Vol. 34, No. 1, Jan./Feb. 2013).

62 Bushnell, "Wreck of the *Reformation.*"
63 Daniels, "Shipwrecked in the Atlantic," 463.
64 Mattfield, "Journey to the Wilderness," 332.
65 Mattfield, "Journey to the Wilderness," 336.
66 Daniels, "Shipwrecked in the Atlantic," 472.
67 Alejandra Dubcovsky, "When Archaeology and History Meet: Shipwrecks, Indians, and the Contours of the Early-Eighteenth-Century South," *Journal of Southern History* (Vol. 84, No 1, Feb. 2018, 39–68), 49–50.
68 Alexander Y. Sweeney, "Cultural Continuity and Change: Archaeological Research at Yamasee Primary Towns in South Carolina," in *The Yamasee Indians: From Florida to South Carolina,* edited by Denise I. Bossy (Lincoln: University of Nebraska Press, 2018), 99–131, 121.
69 Frank, *Before the Pioneers,* 35.
70 Paul E. Hoffman, *Florida Frontiers* (Bloomington: Indiana University Press, 2002), 22.
71 See Andrés Reséndez, *The Other Slavery: The Uncovered Story of Indian Enslavement in America* (New York: Houghton Mifflin, 2016).
72 Dubcovsky, "When Archaeology and History Meet," 50, 61.
73 Dubcovsky, "When Archaeology and History Meet," 50–51; Rouse, *Survey of Indian River,* 58.
74 Dubcovsky, "When Archaeology and History Meet," 39–40; Davidsson, *Indian River,* 89. Davidsson describes Darie as "wily . . . sensing the approach of a hurricane, he set a course away from the coast and saved his vessel from destruction," 90.
75 Dubcovksy, "When Archaeology and History Meet," 40.
76 Materials from the excavation ended up at Yale University's Peabody Museum of Natural History, at the University of Florida at Gainesville, and at the Florida Division of Historical Resources in Tallahassee.
77 Dubcovksy, "When Archaeology and History Meet," 40–41.
78 Dubcovksy, "When Archaeology and History Meet," 48.
79 Dubcovksy, "When Archaeology and History Meet," 54.
80 Davidsson, *Indian River,* 92. Earle 1980: 113, technique created by Richard Norwood, a former pirate and wrecker, in the Caribbean in 1612.
81 Dubcovksy, "When Archaeology and History Meet," 55–56.
82 Dubcovksy, "When Archaeology and History Meet," 57–58.
83 Dubcovksy, "When Archaeology and History Meet," 63.
84 Dubcovksy, "When Archaeology and History Meet," 65–67. In the mid-twentieth century, both amateur and professional salvage operations became a common sight along the Treasure Coast, the McLarty Treasure Museum along A1A is situated near the survivors' camp where salvage work offshore continues to this day, and in nearby Sebastian, the Mel Fisher's Treasures Museum hosts relics from the 1715 Fleet and the Atocha wreck off Key West. https://verobeach.com/vero-beach-community/mclarty-treasure-museum; https://www.melfisher.com/Sebastian/sebastian_museum.asp; for a history of the treasure hunt and Mel Fisher's role, see Eugene Lyon, *The Search for the Atocha* (New York: Harper & Row Publishers, 1979).

85 Charles D. Higgs, "Spanish Contacts with the Ais (Indian River) Country," *The Florida Historical Society* (Vol. 21, No. 1, Jul., 1942, 25–39), 28.
86 Rouse, *Survey of the Indian River*, 58.
87 Rouse, *Survey of the Indian River*, 59.
88 Rouse, *Survey of Indian River*, 59–60.
89 Jerald T. Milanich, *Florida Indians and the Invasion from Europe* (Tallahassee: University Presses of Florida, 1995), 231, xv.
90 Frank, *Before the Pioneers*, 8, 57.
91 Nathaniel Osborn, *Indian River Lagoon: An Environmental History* (Gainesville: University Presses of Florida, 2016), 2; on Bartram and failed plantations of the region, see Daniel L. Schafer, *William Bartram and the Ghost Plantations of British East Florida* (Gainesville: University of Florida Press, 2010).
92 Rouse, *Survey of Indian River*, 58; Bernard Romans, *A Concise History of East and West Florida* (Gainesville, University of Florida Press, 1962), 273, 284–285.
93 Landers, *Black Society in Spanish Florida*, 67; Matthew Jennings, ed., *The Flower Hunter and the People: William Bartram in the Native American Southeast* (Macon, Georgia: Mercer University Press, 2014), 34–35.
94 Anne E. Rowe, *The Idea of Florida in the American Literary Imagination* (Baton Rouge: Louisiana State University Press, 1986), 17.
95 Rouse, *Survey of Indian River*, 60.
96 T. D. Allman, *Finding Florida: The True History of the Sunshine State* (New York: Grove Press, 2013), 10, 124. Irving's nephew, Theodore Irving, wrote *The Conquest of Florida Under Hernando de Soto*, an account that Allman argues was "one of the most influential and untrustworthy books on Florida ever published . . . so abusive of the truth that it might have been written by Washington Irving . . . at the urging of his best-selling uncle, he too, took up the task of transforming Florida's chronicle of disaster, disease, and death into an adventure yarn," 13.
97 Daniel G. Brinton, ed., *A Guidebook of Florida and the South for Tourists, Invalids and Emigrants*, edited by William M. Goza (Gainesville: University Presses of Florida, 1978 [1869]), 32. Published originally in Philadelphia by George Maclean then later published in Jacksonville, Florida, by Columbus Drew.
98 C. Vickerstaff Hine, *On the Indian River* (Chicago: Charles H. Sergel & Company, 1891), 13, 61.
99 Louis J. Mendelis, "Publications of the Florida Historical Society," (Vol. 3, No 2, Oct. 1924, 4–15), 6.
100 Jennifer F. McKinnon, "The Archaeology of Florida's US Life-Saving Service Houses of Refuge and Life-Saving Stations," (PhD Dissertation Florida State University Department of Anthropology, 2010), 66.
101 Vero Beach was of course not the only town undertaking land reclamation in Florida; however, it was a place that actively advertised that its buyers should not purchase land sight unseen. This helped protect the Indian River Farms Company and the settlers of Vero from financial ruin with the collapse of the real estate market in Florida in other regions, including those to the south and in the Everglades. Other

factors were also in their favor, as storm surge and flooding proved to be a costly and disastrous problem for similar canal dredges and reclamation attempts to the north in the settlement of Fellsmere. See Gordon Patterson, "Ditches and Dreams: Nelson Fell and the Rise of Fellsmere," *Florida Historical Quarterly*, Vol. 76, No. 1, Summer 1997, 1–21; Christopher Knowlton, *Bubble in the Sun: The Florida Boom of the 1920s and How it Brought on the Great Depression* (New York: Simon and Schuster, 2020); Les Standiford, *Palm Beach, Mar-A-Lago, and the Rise of America's Xanadu* (New York: Atlantic Monthly Press, 2019).

102 Hrdlička's treatment of Indigenous remains as well as his controversial theories of human evolution and the Bering Strait theory remain contested to this day within academic and Indigenous communities.

103 Rody L. Johnson, *An Ice Age Mystery: Unearthing the Secrets of the Old Vero Site* (Gainesville: University Press of Florida, 2017), 41.

104 Jerald T. Milanich, "Revisiting the Freducci Map: A Description of Juan Ponce de Leon's 1513 Florida Voyage?" *The Florida Historical Quarterly* (Vol. 73, No. 3, Winter 1996, 319–328), 323–324.

105 Benjamin D. Brotemarkle, "The Florida Historical Society Present an Original Courtroom Drama: Ponce de Leon Landed HERE!!!" *The Florida Historical Quarterly* (Vol. 92, No. 1, Summer 2013, 106–127), 120–122.

Chapter 2. Settlers and Settler Colonialism of the Eighteenth and Nineteenth Centuries

1 See Alan Gallay, *The Indian Slave Trade* (New Haven: Yale University Press, 2002); Christina Snyder, *Slavery in Indian Country: The Changing Face of Captivity in Early America* (Cambridge: Harvard University Press, 2010); Kristalyn Marie Shefveland, *Anglo-Native Virginia: Trade, Conversion, and Indian Slavery in the Old Dominion, 1646–1722* (Athens: University of Georgia Press, 2016).

2 See James Taylor Carson, *Searching for the Bright Path: The Mississippi Choctaws from Prehistory to Removal* (Lincoln: University of Nebraska Press, 2003); Robbie Ethridge and Charles Hudson, eds., *The Transformation of the Southeastern Indians 1540–1760* (Oxford: University of Mississippi Press, 2002).

3 Osborn, *Indian River Lagoon*, 25, 28.

4 For a case study of the United States and the Creek relationship see Kathryn E. Holland Braund, *Deerskins and Duffels: The Creek Indian Trade with Anglo-America, 1685–1815*. (Lincoln: The University of Nebraska Press, 1993) and Robbie Ethridge, *Creek Country: The Creek Indians and Their World* (Chapel Hill: University of North Carolina Press, 2003), 13.

5 Maurice O' Sullivan and Jack C. Lane, eds., *The Florida Reader: Visions of Paradise from 1530 to the Present* (Sarasota, Florida: Pineapple Press, Inc., 2010 [1991]), 16–17; Frank, *Before the Pioneers*, 50.

6 Ethridge, *Creek Country*, 11.

7 Ethridge, *Creek Country*, 16.

8 Anthony F. C. Wallace, *Religion: An Anthropological View of the Death and Rebirth of the Seneca* (New York: Vintage Books, 1972).

9 Ethridge, *Creek Country*, 21; Wickman, *Osceola's Legacy*, 7.
10 Ethridge, *Creek Country*, 240–241; Wickman, *Osceola's Legacy*, 50–52.
11 O'Sullivan and Lane, eds., *The Florida Reader*, 16–17.
12 See James G. Cusick, *The Other War of 1812: The Patriot War and the American Invasion of Spanish East Florida* (Gainesville: University Press of Florida, 2003).
13 Frank, *Before the Pioneers*, 66, 80.
14 Allman, *Finding Florida*, 95.
15 Canter Brown Jr., "The Florida Crisis of 1826–1827 and the Second Seminole War," *The Florida Historical Quarterly* (Vol. 73, No. 4, Apr. 1995, 419–442), 421.
16 Allman, *Finding Florida*, 95.
17 *Niles Weekly Register*, March 11, 1837.
18 See Wickman, *Osceola's Legacy*, 10–23, 105.
19 Rowe, *Idea of Florida*, 10.
20 Patricia Riles Wickman, *Osceola's Legacy* (Tuscaloosa: University of Alabama Press, 2006, Revised Edition), 2.
21 Allman, *Finding Florida*, 122–123.
22 Rowe, *Idea of Florida*, 17, 21.
23 Albery Whitman, *Twasinta's Seminoles or Rape of Florida* (St. Louis: Nixon Jones Printing Co., 1885) 9, 13. https://archive.org/details/twasintassemino00whitgoog
24 Rowe, *The Idea of Florida*, 22.
25 Whitman, *Twasinta's Seminoles*, 56.
26 Ward et al., "The Disappearance of the Head of Osceola," 197.
27 Ward et al., "The Disappearance of the Head of Osceola," 197; Wickman, *Osceola's Legacy*, 140–141.
28 Walt Whitman, *Leaves of Grass*, ed. Malcolm Cowley (New York: Penguin, 1968), 463.
29 Wickman, *Osceola's Legacy*, 27, 163–164, 167, 172, 177.
30 Wickman, *Osceola's Legacy*, 187; Ward et al., "The Disappearance of the Head of Osceola," 197–200.
31 The violence of the colonial era can be seen in the settler reimagining of the death and beheading of Metacom, or King Philip, the subject of popular nineteenth-century plays and poems. As Jill Lepore has found, Indians emerge in histories in ways that are "cherished, romanticized, and fetishized," yet importantly, those roles are only present as a settler artifact of the distant past, "Indians themselves must exist only in the past, mute memorials, silent as a rock. Either that or else they could be far, far away—exiled west of the Mississippi." Jill Lepore, *The Name of War: King Philip's War and the Origins of American Identity* (New York: Vintage Books, 1998), 224. Washington Irving wrote sympathetically about Metacom and "urged his readers to see beyond the prejudices of the early historians of the war that they might better appreciate Philip's virtue . . ." 196–197. For discussion on settler scientific racism and the collection of skulls and human remains in the nineteenth and twentieth centuries see Ann Fabian, *The Skull Collectors: Race, Science, and America's Unburied Dead* (Chicago: University of Chicago Press, 2010); Samuel J. Redman, *Bone Rooms: From Scientific Racism to Human Prehistory in Museums* (Cambridge:

Harvard University Press, 2016), 3, 19. Redman, *Bone Rooms*, Aleš Hrdlička was responsible for the collection of many of the remains in the Smithsonian and collectors regularly sent unsolicited remains, which resulted in a case involving a Smithsonian impostor and the theft of Tom Tiger's remains, 70–71. By 1906, Aleš Hrdlička counted 8,000 skeletons at the Smithsonian, 83. And although it was illicit after the American Antiquities Act and Native communities began to fight back for their legal rights to ancestral remains, it continues to be an issue today.

32 Shire, *Threshold of Manifest Destiny*, 11.
33 Shire, *Threshold of Manifest Destiny*, 161, 192.
34 Wickman, *Osceola's Legacy*, 209–210. Weedon returned to St. Augustine after Fort Pierce burned down in December 1844. He died in 1857 in Key West. Cited from Weedon and Whitehurst Family Papers.
35 Joseph D. Cushman Jr., "The Indian River Settlement: 1842–1849," *The Florida Historical Quarterly* (Vol. 43, No. 1, Jul. 1964, 21–35), 22–25. Pineapples became a major crop in the Indian River economy after Thomas E. Richards planted them at his homestead later in the nineteenth century. See Osborn, *Indian River Lagoon*, 69.
36 Robert Ranson, *A memoir of Captain Mills Olcott Burnham, a Florida pioneer: written for members of his family and friends and all interested in the state's early history* (Tallahassee, Florida: T. J. Appleyard, Inc, 1927), 14.
37 Quoted in Cushman, "The Indian River Settlement," 26.
38 Edward Caleb Coker and Daniel L. Schafer, "A New Englander on the Indian River Frontier: Caleb Lyndon Brayton and the View from Brayton's Bluff," *The Florida Historical Quarterly* (Vol. 70, No. 3, Jan. 1992, 305–332), 305–306. Brayton's Bluff is in what is now Fort Pierce.
39 Quoted in Coker, "New Englander on the Indian River Frontier," 308.
40 Quoted in Coker, "New Englander on the Indian River Frontier," 312–315.
41 Charles Vignoles quoted in Osborn, *Indian River Lagoon*, 32.
42 Osborn, *Indian River Lagoon*, 35.
43 Quoted in Cushman, "The Indian River Settlement," 28. *Titusville Florida Star*, May 5, 1887; Robert Ranson, *Memoir of Captain Mills Olcott Burnham*, 10.
44 Ranson, *Memoir of Captain Mills Olcott Burnham*, 16.
45 Cushman, "The Indian River Settlement," 34–35; Osborn, *Indian River Lagoon*, 82.
46 Quoted in Coker, "New Englander on the Indian River Frontier," 321–322.
47 Ranson, *Memoir of Captain Mills Olcott Burnham*, 3.
48 Ranson, *Memoir of Captain Mills Olcott Burnham*, 12–13.
49 Osborn, *Indian River Lagoon*, 40.
50 Osborn, *Indian River Lagoon*, 43.
51 Bell, *My Pioneer Days in Florida*, preface written by Will Fee, historian of the *Old Timer's Association* of Fort Pierce, 1928.
52 Bell, *My Pioneer Days*, 6–8.
53 Bell, *My Pioneer Days*, 20.
54 The Bethel Creek house was located at what is now Jaycee Park. Sandra Henderson Thurlow, "Lonely Vigils: Houses of Refuge on Florida's East Coast, 1876–1915," *The Florida Historical Quarterly* (Vol. 76, No. 2, Fall 1997, 152–173), 152–154; McKinnon,

"The Archaeology of Florida's US Life-Saving Service Houses," 100–101. "Jaycee Park was visited with the intent to investigate the potential for research. Unfortunately, the construction of the park has drastically altered the original landscape. The entire park has been sculpted into a large grassy area with volleyball courts, picnic benches, a boardwalk, parking lots, and a restaurant. If the site were located within the park, there would be very little chance of finding subsurface remains. With this said, if it were located outside of the park there would be no chance of finding subsurface remains because the entire coastline within several miles has been developed with houses, marinas, golf courses, and resorts."

55 McKinnon, "Archaeology of Florida's US Life-Savings Service Houses," 66; No. 5 Indian River Inlet St Lucie County/Pepper Park, 1884.
56 McKinnon, "Archaeology of Florida's US Life-Savings Service Houses," 70, 78.
57 Bell, *My Pioneer Days*, 30.
58 Bell, *My Pioneer Days*, 31.
59 Bell, *My Pioneer Days*, 41
60 Bell, *My Pioneer Days*, 40–41.
61 Bell, *My Pioneer Days*, 42.
62 On the "Friends of the Indian," Reformers, and Federal Indian Policy see C. Joseph Genetin-Pilawa, *Crooked Paths to Allotment: The Fight over Federal Indian Policy after the Civil War* (Chapel Hill: University of North Carolina Press, 2012); Robert Mardock, *The Reformers and the American Indian* (Columbia: University of Missouri Press, 1971); Joseph E. Illick, "'Some of Our Best Indians are Friends . . .': Quaker Attitudes and Actions regarding the Western Indians during the Grant Administration," *Western Historical Quarterly* (Vol. 2, No. 3, 1971, 283–294); Cathleen Cahill, *Federal Fathers and Mothers: A Social History of the United States Indian Service, 1869–1933* (Chapel Hill: University of North Carolina Press, 2011); Carol Higham, *Noble, Wretched, and Redeemable: Protestant Missionaries to the Indian in Canada and the United States, 1820–1900* (Albuquerque: University of New Mexico Press, 2000); Francis P. Prucha, ed., *Americanizing the American Indian: Writings by the "Friends of the Indian" 1880–1900* (Cambridge: Harvard University Press, 1973); Francis P. Prucha, *American Indian Policy in Crisis: Christian Reformers and the Indian, 1865–1890* (Norman: University of Oklahoma Press, 1976).
63 Thurlow, "Lonely Vigils," 160.
64 One must consider the impact of national settler memory about Native peoples when examining pioneer remembrances and the choices they make related to Native speech patterns, see, Barbra A. Meek, "And the Injun Goes 'How!': Representations of American Indian English in White Public Space," *Language in Society* (Vol. 35, No. 1, 2006, 93–128).
65 Bell, *My Pioneer Days*, 43; McKinnon, "Archaeology of Florida's US Life-Savings Service Houses," 268.
66 Transcript, Alexander Linn, Oral History Interview with Tom King (March 23, 1974), Samuel Proctor Oral History Program Collection, P. K. Yonge Library of Florida History, University of Florida.

67 Harry A. Kersey, "The 'Friends of the Florida Seminoles' Society: 1899–1926," *Tequesta* (Volume 34, 1964, 3–20), 4.
68 Kersey, "Friends of the Florida Seminoles," 6–8.
69 Harry A. Kersey, "The Case of Tom Tiger's Horse: An Early Foray into Indian Rights," *The Florida Historical Quarterly* (Vol. 53, No. 3, Jan. 1975, 306–318), 307.
70 Kersey, "Friends of the Florida Seminoles," 14.
71 Kersey, "The Case of Tom Tiger's Horse," 309. Settler references to Tom Tiger first occurred in the 1880–1881 Smithsonian Institution Survey when Tom Tiger acted as informant for Reverend Clay MacCauley's survey. He appeared again in 1888 in Indian Agent A. M. Wilson's report about Seminole land relocation.
72 Quoted in Kersey, "The Case of Tom Tiger's Horse," 310; Harmon H. Hull to James M. Willson, May 29, 1898, James M. Willson Collection, University of Miami Library.
73 Kersey, "The Case of Tom Tiger's Horse," 313–314.
74 Kersey, "The Case of Tom Tiger's Horse," 313–314.
75 Quoting Frederick A. Ober who recalled Tiger in 1875. William E. McGoun, *Southeast Florida Pioneers: The Palm and Treasure Coasts* (Sarasota: Pineapple Press, 1998), 89.
76 McGoun, *Southeast Florida Pioneers*, 92.
77 McGoun, *Southeast Florida Pioneers*, 93; "Southeastern Indian Oral History Project—Interviewee Ada Williams; Interviewer Tom King" University of Florida December 14, 1973, http://ufdc.ufl.edu/UF00007983/00001 Tom Tiger's son was later murdered by the notorious Ashley Gang.

Chapter 3. The Indian River Farm Company's Booster Dreams of a Colonial Past

1 Indian River County Archives, Vero Beach Florida, "Vero" song in *The Riomar News*, February 10, 1921, Accession No. Rio 003.01, song by Abigail Evans Admire of Bloomington Illinois.
2 Indian River Farmer, Vol. 2 No 8 and 9, July and August 1914, 8. To be fair, the first commercial interest in Vero by settlers was the Redstone Lumber and Supply Company who began operations in the area in 1911.
3 T. Frederick Davis, "Early Orange Culture and the Epocal Cold of 1835," *The Florida Historical Quarterly*, (Vol. 15, No. 4, Apr. 1937, 232–241), 232–233.
4 Frank, *Before the Pioneers*, 68, 76–77.
5 T. Frederick Davis, "Early Orange Culture and the Epocal Cold of 1835," *The Florida Historical Quarterly*, (Vol. 15, No. 4, Apr. 1937, 232–241), 232–233.
6 Davis, "Early Orange Culture," 235, 239.
7 Jahoda, *Florida: A Bicentennial*, 106.
8 Ellen E. Stanley, *Pioneering Sebastian and Roseland* (Mount Pleasant, South Carolina: Fontill Media, Arcadia Publishing, 2017), 62–65.
9 Stanley, *Pioneering*, 65.
10 *The Indian River Farmer* (Vol. 2, No 8, October 1914, 14).
11 See works by Stephen Crane and Henry James, for example.

12 Tommy R. Thompson, "Florida in American Popular Magazines, 1870–1970," *The Florida Historical Quarterly* (Vol. 82, No. 1, Summer 2003, 1–15), 1–4; 14.
13 Quoted in Cox, *Dreaming of Dixie*, 112.
14 Cox, *Dreaming of Dixie*, 131.
15 Karen Cox, *Dreaming of Dixie: How the South was Created in American Popular Culture* (Chapel Hill: The University of North Carolina Press, 2011), 7.
16 Knight, *Tropic of Hopes*, 16–17.
17 Portions of this chapter appeared in Kristalyn Marie Shefveland, "Pocahontas and Settler Memorialization of 'Good Indians'" *The Western Historical Quarterly* (Vol, 52, No. 3, Autumn 2021, 281–303).
18 Wrobel, *Promised Lands*, 13.
19 Osborn, *Indian River Lagoon*, 3.
20 Johnston, *A History of Indian River County*, 56.
21 Indian River County Genealogical Society, *Postcard History Series: Indian River County* (Vero Beach: Indian River County Genealogical Society, 2007), 25.
22 *Indian River Farmer* (Vol. 2, No. 7, June 1914), 8.
23 Matthew F. Bokovoy, *The San Diego World's Fairs and Southwestern Memory, 1880–1940* (Albuquerque: University of New Mexico Press, 2005), 3, 13.
24 *Indian River Farmer* (Vol. 2, Nos. 8 and 9, July and August 1914), 4.
25 *Indian River Farmer* (Vol. 2, Nos. 8 and 9, July and August 1914), 5.
26 *Indian River Farmer* (Vol. 2, No. 6, May 1914), 18.
27 *Indian River Farmer* (Vol. 2, No. 6, May 1914), 2.
28 "Building Record for Six Months," *The Vero Beach Press*, 5 July 1923. Cost $18,000 to build.
29 "Large Force Works on New Apartments," *The Vero Beach Press*, 18 May 1926.
30 "The Pocahontas Apartments," *The Vero Beach Press*, 2 September 1926.
31 Suhi Choi, "Mythologizing Memories: A Critique of the Utah Korean War Memorial," *The Public Historian* (Vol. 34, No. 1 Winter 2012, 61–82), 64.
32 Faragher, "And the Lonely Voice of Youth Cries," 2–3.
33 For examples in New England, see Erika Doss, "Augustus Saint-Gauden's *The Puritan* Founders' Statues, Indian Wars, Contested Public Spaces, and Anger's Memory in Springfield, Massachusetts," *Winterthur Portfolio* (Vol. 46, No. 4, Winter 2012, 237–270), 243; David Wrobel, *The End of American Exceptionalism: Frontier Anxiety from the Old West to the New Deal* (Lawrence: University Press of Kansas, 1993).
34 See Boyd Cothran, *Remembering the Modoc War: Redemptive Violence and the Making of American Innocence* (Chapel Hill: University of North Carolina Press, 2014), 6. Of particular interest is the chapter on Winema (Toby Riddle) who used the Pocahontas myth to "become a national celebrity, earn a federal pension, and emerge as a local legend," 83, and even becomes a character in a novel that "portrays Winema as a model for civilizing Indigenous peoples through acculturation," 94.
35 Philip Young, "The Mother of Us All: Pocahontas Reconsidered," *The Kenyon Review* (Vol. 24, No. 3, Summer, 1962, 319–415), 415–416.
36 Young, "The Mother of Us All," 399.

37 Rayna Green, "The Pocahontas Perplex: The Image of Indian Women in American Culture," *The Massachusetts Review* (Vol. 16., No. 4, Autumn, 1975, 698–714), 703.
38 For a concise history of the varying historical treatments of the Pocahontas myth, see Rebecca K. Jager, *Malinche, Pocahontas, and Sacagawea: Indian Women as Cultural Intermediaries and National Symbols* (Norman: University of Oklahoma Press, 2015), 211–244; and Robert S. Tilton, *Pocahontas: The Evolution of an American Narrative* (New York: Cambridge University Press, 1994).
39 Kevin Bruyneel, *Settler Memory: The Disavowal of Indigeneity and the Politics of Race in the United States* (Chapel Hill: University of North Carolina Press, 2021), 152.
40 Philip J. Deloria, *Indians in Unexpected Places* (Lawrence: University of Kansas Press, 2004), 20.
41 See Cothran, *Remembering the Modoc War*; James Joseph Buss, *Winning the West with Words: Language and Conquest in the Lower Great Lakes* (Norman: University of Oklahoma Press, 2011). As Buss explains, "Art, science, and history mutually reinforced a concept of American progress and westward expansion that forecasted the erasure of America's indigenous peoples," 117.
42 Philip J. Deloria, *Playing Indian* (New Haven: Yale University Press, 1998), 21.
43 Lacy Cotton, "American Indian Stereotypes in Early Western Literature and the Lasting Influence on American Culture," (Masters' Thesis: Baylor University, Department of American Studies, 2008), 29; James K. Folsom, *The American Western Novel* (New Haven, CT: College & University Press, 1966), 145.
44 See Shephard Krech, *The Ecological Indian: Myth and History* (New York: W. W. Norton, 1999); Philip J. Deloria, *Indians in Unexpected Places* (Lawrence: University of Kansas Press, 2004).
45 Jean M. O'Brien, *Firsting and Lasting: Writing Indians out of Existence in New England* (Minneapolis: University of Minnesota Press, 2010), xiii.
46 On Pocahontas, see Helen Rountree, *Pocahontas, Powhatan, Opechancanough: Three Indian Lives Changed by Jamestown* (Charlottesville: University of Virginia Press, 2005); According to Clara Sue Kidwell, "Women, perceived as powerless by European men and voiceless in the historical records, are nevertheless powerful in the roles that they play in their own cultures, and even more powerful in the impact that they have on their own husbands or consorts and on the children of those liaisons." Clara Sue Kidwell, "Indian Women as Cultural Mediators," *Ethnohistory* (Vol. 39, No. 2, Spring 1992), 98; See also Juliana Barr, *Peace Came in the Form of a Woman: Indians and Spaniards in the Texas Borderlands* (Chapel Hill: University of North Carolina Press, 2007).
47 http://redmen.org/pocahontas/info/ Accessed 1/31/2017; For more on the Improved Order of the Redmen and monument building see Jean M. O'Brien and Lisa Blee, *Monumental Mobility: The Memory Work of Massasoit* (Chapel Hill: University of North Carolina Press, 2019).
48 George W. Lindsay, Charles H. Conley, Charles H. Lichtman, *Official History of the Improved Order of the Red Men* (Waco, Texas: Davis Brothers Publishing Co., 1964 [1892]), 757–758. There is another "Pocahontas story" in Florida. Settler Clarence Vandiveer opined, "Every school boy and school girl knows the story of Captain

John Smith and Pocahontas, but how many are acquainted with the far more authentic story of Juan Ortiz and Uleleh, the Indian Chieftain's daughter?" The story that Vandiveer is referencing comes from a Spanish survivor of the failed Narvaez expedition in 1528 who lived with Native Floridians until Hernando de Soto found him in 1539. Ortiz famously served as De Soto's interpreter before dying in Arkansas sometime during the winter of 1541-1542. Ortiz's time at the town of Uzita became part of the narratives chronicled from the De Soto expedition by all four of the accounts but most famously by the Inca, Garcilaso de la Vega (written from hearsay) and the Gentleman of Elvas (an actual member of the De Soto expedition). The story fits neatly into European traditions of princesses saving captives. In brief, on June 17, 1527, Panfilo de Narvaez, a one-eyed veteran of the Conquest of Mexico who had his hopes of wealth and notoriety destroyed by his rival, Hernan Cortes, started to make his way to explore Florida. Disaster quickly followed. During a layover in Santo Domino to resupply, 140 of his men deserted the expedition, deeming Narvaez as incompetent. He then lost two ships to a hurricane and had to winter in Cuba before finally arriving somewhere near Tampa in April 1528. The Narvaez expedition made themselves extremely unpopular as they moved up toward the panhandle burning Native burials that utilized wooden cargo cages from Spanish shipwrecks. Eventually choosing to face the Gulf of Mexico to escape the constant onslaught from aggrieved Native polities, many of the expedition died along the Louisiana coast. Ortiz, however, was already in the town of Uzita where he was shot with arrows and tied to a rack over a fire. The story is memorialized for the Anglo-American public by a 1908 edition of the *Publications of the Florida Historical Society*, alleging that the Natives thought he was the son of Narvaez, "the tortures of the unfortunate youth, who was but eighteen years of age, excited the pity of an Indian woman who hastened to the dwellings of the Casique and made known the situation to Uleleh the Chief's eldest daughter, then about sixteen years old." Moved to act, "the young princess thereupon threw herself at the feet of her father and entreated him to suspend the execution and release the victim." Ortiz suffered from severe burn wounds but eventually healed, and the people put him in charge of protecting the bodies of the dead from wolves. His life, however, was still in danger and allegedly, Uleleh warned him, and he ran away to her betrothed's village, Mocoso, "with a token of safety from her." See Charles Hudson and Jerald T. Milanich, *Hernando de Sot and the Indians of Florida* (Gainesville: University Press of Florida, 1993); John H. Hann, *Indians of Central and South Florida 1513-1763* (Gainesville: University Press of Florida, 2003); F. P. Fleming, "The Story of Juan Ortiz and Uleleh," *Publications of the Florida Historical Society* (Vol. 1, No. 2, Jul. 1908, 42–47), 43–45.

49   Nicole C. Cox, "Selling Seduction: Women and Feminine Nature in 1920s Florida Advertising," *The Florida Historical Quarterly* (Vol. 89, No. 2, Fall 2010, 186–209), 191.

50   See Clara Sue Kidwell, "Indian Women as Cultural Mediators," 97.

51   Mikaëla Adams, "Savage Foes, Noble Warriors, and Frail Remnants: Florida Seminoles in the White Imagination, 1865-1934," *The Florida Historical Quarterly* (Vol. 87, No. 3 Winter 2009, 404–435), 418.

52 Cox, "Selling Seduction," 204–206.
53 *The Indian River Farmer* (Vol. 2, No. 8, October 1914), 15.
54 Indian River County Archives, Vigorous Vero, *Fort Pierce News*, p 3, 20 July 1917.
55 Indian River County Archives, *Riomar News*, RIO-003-02.
56 Indian River County Archives, *Vero Beach Press*, "The Old Makes Way for the New," August 29, 1968.
57 Indian River County Archives, *The Vero Beach Press*, "Two Story Arcade Building Started," 17 Sept 1925, p 1.
58 Indian River County Archives, *The Vero Beach Press*, "Work Started on Office Bldg. Arcade Office Bldg. Latest Addition to City," 14 Jan 1926.
59 Indian River County Archives, *The Vero Beach Press*, "New Arcade Building for Vero Beach," 25 June 1925.
60 Indian River County Archives, Bob and Sandy Brackett, Pamphlet "Pueblo Arcade: A Blend of the Past and Present."
61 Anna Peal Leonard Newman, *Stories of Early Life Along the Beautiful Indian River* (Stuart Daily News, 1953), 31, 46, 51, 72.
62 Dorothy Fitch Peniston, *An Island in Time* (Orchid Oak Books, 1985), 151, 2.
63 Nixon Smiley, "When the Indians Mooched the Wyomy," *Miami Herald* from Indian River County Archives, Vandiveer Collection MSS0-VAN-054, Folder 4.
64 Smiley, "When the Indians Mooched the Wyomy."
65 Clarence Vandiveer, "Seminole Names," *Mimeo News* (Vol. 2, No. 5 October 1954), Indian River County Archives, Vandiveer Collection, MSS VAN 089, Folder 8.
66 Clarence Vandiveer, "Indians Traded at Wabasso in Pioneer Days," Indian River County Archives, MSS VAN-067, Folder 5.
67 Clarence Vandiveer, "History of Wabasso Dates Back to Pioneer Days and Relates March of Progress," Indian River County Archives, Vandiveer Collection, MSS VAN 068.
68 Fellsmere Sales Company, *Fellsmere Farms, Florida* (New York: Fellsmere Sales Co., 1913) 3, 22ff, 8; Jahoda, *Florida: A Bicentennial*, 163–164.
69 Gordon Patterson, "Ditches and Dreams: Nelson Fell and the Rise of Fellsmere," *The Florida Historical Quarterly* (Vol. 76, No. 1, Summer 1997, 1–19), 3–5.
70 Patterson, "Ditches and Dreams," 7.
71 Patterson, "Ditches and Dreams," 9.
72 Quoted in Patterson, "Ditches and Dreams," 10–11.
73 Patterson, "Ditches and Dreams," 11–13; See also Knowlton, *Bubble in the Sun*.
74 Patterson, "Ditches and Dreams," 17.
75 Gordon Patterson, "Raising Cane and Refining Sugar: Florida Crystals and the Fame of Fellsmere," *The Florida Historical Quarterly* (Vol. 75, No. 4, Spring 1997, 404–428), 411.
76 Patterson, "Ditches and Dreams," 2.
77 Quoted in Patterson, "Raising Cane," 414.
78 Patterson, "Raising Cane," 416, 418.
79 Patterson, "Raising Cane," 419, 421, 423, 428.
80 *The Indian River Farmer* (Vol. 2, No. 5, April 1914), 12.

81 *The Indian River Farmer* (Vol. 2, No. 5, April 1914), 15.
82 *The Indian River Farmer* (Vol. 2, No. 6, May 1914), 15.
83 Provided by Marvin Carter of Carter Associates, Inc., Consulting Engineers and Land Surveyors, Indian River Farms Drainage District, "First Bulletin of the Board of Supervisors and Engineer's Report Accompanying the Plan of Reclamation," April 1, 1920, 16.
84 Indian River County Archives, Vero Beach Florida, "Young, Anthony W. Family—Indian River Farms Drainage District, 1921," 3–5.
85 Young, "Indian River Farms Drainage District," 6–7.
86 Indian River County Archives, *The Indian River Farmer*, Oct 1914, 15.
87 Indian River County Archives, *The Indian River Farmer*, 4 May 1922, 6.
88 Indian River County Archives, *The Vero Beach Press*, "Newton R. Frost Landowner Here Dies in St. Paul," 5 Oct 1926.
89 Indian River County Archives, *The Vero Beach Press*, "Big Tract Here Being Prepared for Citrus Trees," 8 Dec 1926.
90 *The Indian River Farmer* (Vol. 2, No. 5, April 1914), 18–19.
91 Indian River County Archives, *The Vero Beach Press*, "Million Crates May Be Yielded By Tomato Crop," 19 Apr 1927.
92 Indian River County Archives, *The Vero Beach Press*, "Large Increase in Land Under Cultivation," 25 Jan 1929.
93 Provided by Marvin Carter, Carter & Associate, Indian River Farms Company "The Potato 'One of Mankind's Greatest Blessings' Its Successful & Profitable Cultivation in Indian River Farms at Vero Florida," 1.
94 Indian River Farms Company, "The Potato," 13.
95 Indian River Farms Company, "The Potato," 15.
96 Jerald T. Milanich, *Frolicking Bears, Wet Vultures, & Other Oddities: A New York City Journalist in Nineteenth-Century Florida* (Gainesville: University Press of Florida, 2005), 119.
97 Anna Pearl Leonard Newman, *Stories of Early Life Along Beautiful Indian River* (Stuart, FL: Stuart Daily News, Inc., 1953), 11.
98 *The Indian River Farmer* (Vol. 2, No. 5, April 1914).
99 Newman, *Stories of Early Life*, 28.
100 Newman, *Stories of Early Life*, 38.

Chapter 4. Citrus and Pineapple Dreams

1 *The Indian River Farmer* (Vol. 2, No. 5, April 1914), 12. "Put Your Shoulder to the Wheel," by a Subscriber.
2 Newman, *Stories of Early Life*, 63. An 1894 letter written by J. F. Mitchell, a Scottish immigrant who settled in the region in the 1880s.
3 Newman, *Stories of Early Life*, 68, 70. A letter written by J. F. Mitchell in 1894.
4 Newman, *Stories of Early Life*, 37.
5 Newman, *Stories of Early Life*, 49.
6 Newman, *Stories of Early Life*, 50.
7 Newman, *Stories of Early Life*, 51.

8 Newman, *Stories of Early Life*, 51.
9 Indian River County Historical Society, "History of the Hallstrom Farmstead Built in 1918," Pamphlet; Indian River County Historical Society, "100th Anniversary 1918-2018," Hallstrom House Pamphlet.
10 Indian River County Historical Society, "100th Anniversary 1918-2018," Hallstrom House Pamphlet. This home stands to this day, bequeathed to the Indian River County Historical Society by Ruth Hallstrom in 1999. Artisans from Norway and Sweden worked to complete the multi-story brick home with "10 ft ceilings, plaster walls, and ceiling, original oak floors," and red bricks from the state of Georgia. One can learn about this settler family thanks to the Indian River County Historical Society. It was Ruth's wish that they preserve the home and grounds as well as maintain the extensive collection of artifacts, documents, photographs, furniture, and family memorabilia from their transatlantic life.
11 Indian River County Historical Society, "100th Anniversary 1918-2018," Hallstrom House Pamphlet; Deborah C. Pollack, "A. E. Backus (1906-1990)—A Brief Biography," http://edwardanddeborahpollack.com/Backusbio.html; Sherrie Johnson, *A. E. Backus and the Backus School* (Stuart, FL: Marin County Council for the Arts, 2000).
12 Indian River County Historical Society, "100th Anniversary 1918-2018," Hallstrom House Pamphlet.
13 *The Indian River Farmer* (Vol. 2, No. 6, May 1914), 1. "Back to the Farm Famous Capitalist Says 'Turn to the Soil.'"
14 *The Indian River Farmer* (Vol. 2, No. 7, June 1913), "James J. Hill Persists," 10.
15 Al Burt, *Al Burt's Florida: Snowbirds, Sand Castles, and Self-Rising Crackers*, (Gainesville: University Press of Florida, 1997), 47.
16 *The Indian River Farmer* (Vol. 2, No. 5, April 1914), 16 "Suited to a Frazzle."
17 Indian River County Historical Society, "History of the Indian River Pineapple Industry." Display at Hallstrom House.
18 *The Indian River Farmer* (Vol. 2, No. 6, May 1914), "Nothing to it, Florida is All Right," 17.
19 *The Indian River Farmer* (Vol. 2, No. 7, June 1914), Jos. Hill, "Automobiling through St. Lucie County," 4.
20 *The Indian River Farmer* (Vol. 2, No. 5, April 1914), 16 "Suited to a Frazzle."
21 *The Indian River Farmer* (Vol. 2, No. 6, May 1914), "Views and Interviews Caught in the Hotel Lobby Throngs," 10.
22 *The Indian River Farmer* (Vol. 2, No. 8 and 9, July and August), 3. Indian River Farmer (Vol. 2, Nos. 8 and 9, July and August 1914), "How Pineapples Are Grown on East Coast of Florida," 3.
23 *The Indian River Farmer* (Vol. 2, Nos. 8 and 9, July and August 1914), "How Pineapples Are Grown on East Coast of Florida," 3.
24 *The Indian River Farmer* (Vol. 2, Nos. 8 and 9, July and August 1914), "Florida Products and Opportunities," 16.
25 *The Indian River Farmer* (Vol. 2, Nos. 8 and 9, July and August 1914), 17.

26 Nils G. Sahlin, ed., "Saga of a Florida Swede," *American Swedish Historical Foundation: The Chronicle* (Autumn and Winter 1955, Philadelphia, PA, 20–22), 20.
27 Nils G. Sahlin, ed., "Saga of a Florida Swede," *American Swedish Historical Foundation: The Chronicle* (Autumn and Winter 1955, PA, 20–22), 21.
28 Walter G. Nord, "Axel Hallstrom: In Memoriam," *American Swedish Historical Museum, Yearbook 1966*, 74–77, 74–75.
29 Indian River County Historical Society, Hallstrom House Collection, Lunds Botanical Garden, N. Hagman letter to Axel Hallstrom, Lunds Sweden, 25 February 1910, LTV3-27.
30 Indian River County Historical Society, Hallstrom House Collection, 18 January 1895, Alberta, Sweden LTV1-22.
31 Indian River County Historical Society, Hallstrom House Collection, Kirsti to Emely, 8 May 1904, Dalby Sweden, LTV1-37.
32 Indian River County Historical Society, Hallstrom House Collection Book 1 Letter to Axel, 9 August 1904.
33 Indian River County Historical Society, Hallstrom House Collection, Axel and Emily to Johanna, 21 June 1904.
34 Indian River County Historical Society, Hallstrom House Collection, Axel and Emily to Johanna, 21 June 1904.
35 Indian River County Historical Society, Hallstrom House Collection, Emely to Johanna, 13 October 1904.
36 Indian River County Historical Society, Hallstrom House Collection, Anna to Johanna, 12 November 1904.
37 Indian River County Historical Society, Hallstrom House Collection, Axel to Johanna, 8 December 1904, Viking, FL, LTV2-6.
38 Indian River County Historical Society, Hallstrom House Collection, Kirsti to Axel, 24 January 1904.
39 Indian River County Historical Society, Hallstrom House Collection, Emely to Johanna, 25 August 1904, Fort Pierce, FL, LTV1-4.
40 Indian River County Historical Society, Hallstrom House Collection, Axel to Johanna, 8 December 1904, Viking, FL, LTV2-9.
41 Indian River County Historical Society, Hallstrom House Collection, Axel to Johanna, 11 March 1905, Viking, FL, LTV2-13.
42 Indian River County Historical Society, Hallstrom House Collection, Axel to Johanna, 11 March 1905, Viking, FL, LTV2-13.
43 Indian River County Historical Society, Hallstrom House Collection, Axel to Johanna, 11 March 1905, Viking, FL, LTV2-13
44 Indian River County Historical Society, Hallstrom House Collection, Axel to Johanna, 26 March 1905, Viking, FL, LTV2-14.
45 Indian River County Historical Society, Hallstrom House Collection, Axel to Johanna, 5 April 1905, Viking, FL, LTV2-15.
46 Indian River County Historical Society, Hallstrom House Collection, Axel to Johanna, 6 July 1905, Viking, FL, LTV2-18.

47 Indian River County Historical Society, Hallstrom House Collection, Axel to Johanna, 6 July 1905, Viking, FL, LTV2-18.
48 Indian River County Historical Society, Hallstrom House Collection, Gottfried to Emely and Axel, 6 July 1906, Hogserod, Sweden, LTV3-4.
49 Indian River County Historical Society, Hallstrom House Collection, Gottfried to Emely and Axel, 6 July 1906, Hogserod, Sweden, LTV3-4.
50 Indian River County Historical Society, Hallstrom House Collection, Gottfried to Emely and Axel, 27 December 1906, Hogserod, Sweden, LTV3-8.
51 Indian River County Historical Society, Hallstrom House Collection, Gottfried to Emely and Axel, 27 December 1906, Hogserod, Sweden, LTV3-8.
52 Indian River County Historical Society, Hallstrom House Collection, Gottfried to Emely and Axel, 27 December 1906, Hogserod, Sweden, LTV3-8; On Müller see https://www.learntomuller.com/j-p-muller-a-danish-sportsman-world-famous-and-forgotten/.
53 Indian River County Historical Society, Hallstrom House Collection, Gottfried to Emely and Axel, 27 December 1906, Hogserod, Sweden, LTV3-8.
54 Indian River County Historical Society, Hallstrom House Collection, Gottfried to Emely and Axel, 27 December 1906, Hogserod, Sweden, LTV3-8.
55 Indian River County Historical Society, Hallstrom House Collection, Letter to Emely and Axel, 6 February 1908, Hogserod, Sweden, LTV3-14.
56 Indian River County Historical Society, Hallstrom House Collection, Axel letter to Johanna, 8 February 1908, Viking, FL, LTV3-15.
57 Indian River County Historical Society, Hallstrom House Collection, Axel letter to Johanna, 8 February 1908, Viking, FL, LTV3-15.
58 Indian River County Historical Society, Hallstrom House Collection, Axel letter to Johanna, 20 February 1908, Viking, FL, LTV3-16.
59 Indian River County Historical Society, Hallstrom House Collection, Par letter to Johanna, 13 May 1910, Sjobo, Sweden, LTV3-29.
60 Indian River County Historical Society, Hallstrom House Collection, Par letter to Johanna, Sjobo Sweden, May 13, 1910, LTV3-29.
61 Indian River County Historical Society, Hallstrom House Collection, Par letter to Johanna, 13 May 1910, Sjobo, Sweden, LTV3-29.
62 Indian River County Historical Society, Hallstrom House Collection, Johanna letter to Par, 3 June 1910, Lund, Sweden, LTV3-30.
63 Dick Lundin, "Axel Hallstrom's Career as Horticulturalist Traced," *The News Tribune*, July 19, 1973; Indian River County Historical Society, Hallstrom House Collection, Johanna letter to Par, 3 June 1910, Lund, Sweden, LTV3-30.
64 Indian River County Historical Society, Hallstrom House Collection, Johanna letter to Par, 3 June 1910, Lund, Sweden, LTV3-30.
65 Indian River County Historical Society, Hallstrom House Collection, Johanna letter to Par, Lund Sweden, June 3, 1910, LTV3-30.
66 Indian River County Historical Society, Hallstrom House Collection, Kjersti letter to Johanna, 5 July 1910, Dalby, Sweden, LTV3-31.

67 Indian River County Historical Society, Hallstrom House Collection "Oral History Matilda Miller Marshall, Interviewed by Pearl McKenzie," 2008. Indian River County Historical Society, Hallstrom House Collection, "Information about workers at the Hallstrom House." Known laborers at the Hallstrom Farm—Frederick V. Skow, b. 1916–d. 1987, race—white, originally from Iowa; Rosemary C. Skow b. 1913; Riley L. Shaw, b. 1913–d. 1994, race—white; James Alfonzo Albury, b. 1933–d. 1985, race—black; Hugh Lewis, b. 1921–d. 1996, race—black; Arthur Lattimore, b. 1914–d. 1982, race—black; Willie James Royals, d. 1954, race—black; Isaac Vogt Troutman, b. 1914–d. 1996, race—black, originally from Pennsylvania; Alice Jane Sexton, b. 1942–d. 1990, race—black; Christine Rita Johnson, d. 1957, race—white; Jacob Shaw, b. 1921–d. 1981, race—black; Alfred T. Yount, b. 1910–d. 1985, race—white, originally from Michigan; Amos Bennefield, b. 1916, originally from Georgia. Enar Hallstrom—manager of the farm; Johanna Hallstrom—responsible for house, garden, and family orchard; Fred Sodeberg—nursery manager. Questions remain about the Hallstrom farm laborers—Was it a community before its time? Did Axel Hallstrom have a unique attitude toward labor and race relations?
68 Indian River County Historical Society, "History of the Indian River Pineapple Industry." Display at Hallstrom House.
69 Newman, *Stories of Early Life*, 51. Dr. Inga Olla Helseth; Burt, *Al Burt's Florida*, 47. "Nematode infestations ruined the pineapple business and competition from Cuban pineapples discouraged any revival." That said, in the last several years, Vero farmers have brought small harvests of pineapples to various markets in the region.
70 "Saga of a Florida Swede," 21–22.
71 Indian River County Historical Society, "100th Anniversary 1918–2018," Hallstrom House Pamphlet.
72 Indian River County Historical Society, "100th Anniversary 1918–2018," Hallstrom House Pamphlet.

Chapter 5. Memory and the Built Environment

1 Allman, *Finding Florida*, xiii.
2 Gary Backhaus and John Murungi, *Symbolic Landscapes* (New York: Springer Press, 2009), 5, 9.
3 Jane D. Brush, "Tales of Old Florida," *The Florida Historical Quarterly* (Vol. 40, No. 3, Jan 1962, 300–310), 302.
4 Burt, *Al Burt's Florida*, 13.
5 Jahoda, *Florida: A Bicentennial History*, 3.
6 Barr, "How do you get from Jamestown to Santa Fe," 559.
7 Barr, "How do you get from Jamestown to Santa Fe," 561.
8 Johnson, *An Ice Age Mystery*, 72–73.
9 *Vero Beach Press Journal*, 23 December 1932, quoted in Johnson, *An Ice Age Mystery*, 73.
10 Johnson, *An Ice Age Mystery*, 74–75.
11 Wrobel, *Promised Lands*, 25.

12 Johnson, *An Ice Age Mystery*, 76, Regarding Vero Man and paleontological work in Florida, a 1941 report from the Museum of Comparative Zoology at Harvard College, "from Vero Beach representative materials were presented by Mr. Waldo Sexton and a series of teeth by Mr. Frank Ayers: further specimens were obtained by purchase." Thomas Barbour, Annual Report of the Director of the Museum of Comparative Zoology at Harvard College to the President of Harvard College for 1940–1941 (Cambridge: Harvard University Press, 1941), 30.

13 *Encyclopedia of Cleveland History*, "Arthur Glenn McKee," http://case.edu/ech/articles/m/mckee-arthur-glenn/ Waldo was involved in almost every enterprise in the development of the town—from citrus groves, the Vero Beach Dairy, golf courses, and real estate. His most conspicuous mark was the building of his family home and later tourist resort, the Driftwood, and then the McKee Jungle Gardens. Anna Pearl Leonard, *Stories of Early Life Along Beautiful Indian River* (Vero Beach, FL: APL Newman, 1953), 59.

14 Andrew Frank, "Authenticity for Sale: The Everglades, Seminole Indians, and the Construction of a Pay-Per-View Culture," in *Destination Dixie: Tourism & Southern Culture* edited by Karen L. Cox (Gainesville: University Press of Florida, 2014), 285–300, 285.

15 See Breslauer, *Roadside Paradise*, 12.

16 George W. Gross and Ralph Sexton, *Tales of Waldo Sexton: An Eccentric Pioneer* is remembered, using his anecdotal tales which were often embroidered with colorful exaggerations (Vero Beach, FL: Coastal Graphic Fine Printing, Sexton, Inc., 2001), 14. The collection of stories was edited by Gross alongside Waldo's son, Ralph.

17 Newman, *Stories of Early Life*, 59.

18 Gross, *Tales of Waldo Sexton*, 21.

19 Gross, *Tales of Waldo Sexton*, 22, 24.

20 Gross, *Tales of Waldo Sexton*, 89–90.

21 Gross, *Tales of Waldo Sexton*, 25–27.

22 "Interview with Walter Buckingham and John Wheeler" *Indian River County Oral History Collection* University of Florida George A. Smathers Library Digital Collections, 20 May 1967.

23 Gross, *Tales of Waldo Sexton*, 96–98.

24 Sidney Philip Johnston, *A History of Indian River County: A Sense of Place* (Vero Beach, FL: Indian River County Historical Society, 200), 101.

25 Waldo Sexton to Elsebeth Martens, 4 May 1918, courtesy of Sean Sexton.

26 Waldo Sexton to Elsebeth, Monday, 1918, courtesy of Sean Sexton.

27 Waldo Sexton to Elsebeth, Monday 1918, courtesy of Sean Sexton.

28 Waldo Sexton to Elsebeth, 6 May 6 1918, courtesy of Sean Sexton.

29 Waldo Sexton to Elsebeth, 13 June 1918, courtesy of Sean Sexton.

30 Waldo Sexton to Elsebeth, 13 June 1918, courtesy of Sean Sexton.

31 Waldo Sexton to Elsebeth, 16 June 1918, courtesy of Sean Sexton.

32 Waldo Sexton to Elsebeth, 2 July 1918, courtesy of Sean Sexton.

33 Waldo Sexton to Elsebeth, 2 July 1918, courtesy of Sean Sexton.

34 Waldo Sexton to Elsebeth, 2 July 1918, courtesy of Sean Sexton.

35 Waldo Sexton to Elsebeth, 2 July 1918, courtesy of Sean Sexton.
36 Waldo Sexton to Elsebeth, undated letter, likely early July 1918, courtesy of Sean Sexton.
37 Waldo Sexton to Elsebeth, 10 July 1918, courtesy of Sean Sexton.
38 Waldo Sexton to Elsebeth, 10 July 1918, courtesy of Sean Sexton.
39 Waldo Sexton to Elsebeth, 31 July 1918, courtesy of Sean Sexton.
40 Waldo Sexton to Elsebeth, 6 August 1918, courtesy of Sean Sexton.
41 Waldo Sexton to Elsebeth, undated letter, likely late July early August 1918, courtesy of Sean Sexton.
42 Waldo Sexton to Elsebeth, 18 August 1918, courtesy of Sean Sexton.
43 Waldo Sexton to Elsebeth, 18 August 1918, second letter, courtesy of Sean Sexton.
44 Waldo Sexton to Elsebeth, undated letter, likely late July early August 1918, courtesy of Sean Sexton.
45 Waldo Sexton to Elsebeth, second undated letter from Summer 1918, courtesy of Sean Sexton.
46 Waldo Sexton to Elsebeth, letter dated Saturday night (could be 1918 or 1919), courtesy of Sean Sexton.
47 Augustus Mahew III, "Family saves Mizner treasures from rubble," *Palm Beach Daily News* 27 May 2007; See also, Gross, *Tales of Waldo Sexton*, 84–85.
48 Gross, *Tales of Waldo Sexton*, 84–85.
49 Gross, *Tales of Waldo Sexton*, 85.
50 Drye, *For Sale American Paradise*, 10.
51 Quoted in Drye, *For Sale American Paradise*, 14.
52 Gross, *Tales of Waldo Sexton*, 14.
53 Gross, *Tales of Waldo Sexton*, 59, *Miami Herald*, 2 August 1961, 4c quoted.
54 Gross, *Tales of Waldo Sexton*, 80–82, 125–127.
55 Jay Clarke. "They Call It 'The Damndest Place You Ever Saw' On the Beach. Where Turtles Come to Cry" *New York Times* 12 December 1971 https://www.nytimes.com/1971/12/12/archives/they-call-it-the-damndest-place-you-ever-saw-on-the-beach-where.html.
56 Gross, *Tales of Waldo Sexton*, 73.
57 Johnston, *A History of Indian River County*, 102; Hutchison, Hubbard "Florida's Jungle Garden of Rare Plants: In the McKee Park the Riotous Blooms of Tropical Lands Have Been Added to the Native Growths with Unique Effect," *New York Times* 11 September 1932.
58 Gross, *Tales of Waldo Sexton*, 105.
59 Gross, *Tales of Waldo Sexton*, 65.
60 Portions of this chapter appeared in Kristalyn Marie Shefveland, "Remembering an Indigenous South: Regional Identity, Vero Beach, and Settler Tourism" *Florida Historical Quarterly* (Vol. 100, No. 1, Summer 2021, 106–127).
61 Gross, *Tales of Waldo Sexton*, 106–107.
62 John Troutman, "'The Overlord of the Savage World': Anthropology, the Media, and the American Indian Experience at the 1904 Louisiana Purchase Exposition," Mas-

ter's Thesis, University of Arizona, 1997, UMI Number: 1385757, 70. *Pennsylvania Ledger* January 23, 1904, quoted in Troutman.

63 Mikaëla M. Adams, "Race, Kinship, and Belonging among the Florida Seminole," in *The Native South: New Histories and Enduring Legacies*, edited by Tim Alan Garrison and Greg O'Brien (Lincoln: University of Nebraska Press, 2017), 150. Descendants of Nagey Nancy, an African slave, some tribal members referred to these children as belonging to the "Little Black Snake Clan."

64 Mikaëla Adams, Email message to author, April 22, 2019. Adams consulted the Reconstructed Florida Seminole Census of 1914 (reconstructed in 1977) in the National Archives in D.C. (NARA, Washington, D.C., RG 75 Records of the Bureau of Indian Affairs. Records of the Statistics Division. Census Rolls and Supplements, 1885–1940. Reconstructed Florida Seminole Census of 1914. Box 846. PI-163. Entry 964).

65 Gross, *Tales of Waldo Sexton*, 113. Suzan Philips, *The Miracle of McKee* (Vero, FL: McKee Botanical Garden Incorporated, 2007), 34. See Nancy J. Parezo and Don. D. Fowler, *The 1904 Louisiana Purchase Exposition: Anthropology Goes to the Fair* (Lincoln: University of Nebraska Press, 2009); Jose D. Fermin, *1904 World's Fair: The Filipino Experience* (Diliman: University of the Philippines Press, 2004), 27, "The emphasis at the Louisiana Purchase Exposition was on the 'civilized' versus the 'primitive,' resulting in the reinforcement of racial stereotypes," 150; Discovery Institute, "Inhumane Zoos," 2019 https://humanzoos.org/category/explore/st-louis-worlds-fair/; Missouri Historical Society, "1904 The World's Fair: Looking Back at Looking Forward," 2004, https://mohistory.org/exhibitsLegacy/Fair/WF/HTML/index_flash.html.

66 In later years, Waldo would also become a patron to famed author Zora Neale Hurston when she was experiencing final hardships. Kathy Oristaglio, "Waldo Sexton's Successful Business Legacy Continues," *Treasure Coast Palm*, October 14, 2009, http://archive.tcpalm.com/news/waldo-sextons-successful-business-legacy-continues-ep-396963220-347295732.html

67 Roy Nash, *Survey of the Seminole Indians of Florida* (Washington D.C.: United States Department of the Interior Office of Indian Affairs, 1932), 41, http://ufdc.ufl.edu/FS00000029/00001.

68 Nash, *Survey*, 87.

69 "McKee Jungle Gardens—Vero Beach, Florida" 1941 park flier, author personal collection.

70 Ken Breslauer, *Roadside Paradise: The Golden Age of Florida's Tourist Attractions 1929–71* (St. Petersburg, FL: RetroFlorida, 2000), 6; Gross, *Tales of Waldo Sexton*, 109.

71 Breslauer, *Roadside Paradise: The Golden Age of Florida's Tourist Attractions 1929–71*, 6.

72 Oristaglio, "Waldo Sexton's Successful Business Legacy Continues."

73 Breslauer, *Roadside Paradise: The Golden Age of Florida's Tourist Attractions 1929–71*, 59–60.

74 Gross, *Tales of Waldo Sexton*, 127.

75 Gross, *Tales of Waldo Sexton*, 75. Not a member of any organized church but helped build churches in town, Waldo still made frequent reference to sin and to God.
76 Gross, *Tales of Waldo Sexton*, 76.
77 Gross, *Tales of Waldo Sexton*, 76–78. Originally, thought by the Exposition to be a slab of California redwood, later experts from Yale University determined that it was Philippine mahogany.
78 Gross, *Tales of Waldo Sexton*, 111.
79 Gross, *Tales of Waldo Sexton*, 137.
80 Gross, *Tales of Waldo Sexton*, 142–143.
81 Gross, *Tales of Waldo Sexton*, 143.
82 Gross, *Tales of Waldo Sexton*, 144.
83 Sean Sexton, *Waldo's Mountain: A brief history of a small elevation* (Orlando: Waterview Press, 2002, 19–36), 68.
84 Sexton, *Waldo's Mountain*, 69.
85 Gross, *Tales of Waldo Sexton*, 146.
86 Sexton, *Waldo's Mountain*, 69–70; *Tales of Waldo Sexton*, 146.
87 Gross, *Tales of Waldo Sexton*, 146.
88 Sexton, *Waldo's Mountain*, 71.
89 Sexton, *Waldo's Mountain*, 72.
90 Waldo Sexton, "Sexton's Mountain: Hanging Gardens of Vero Beach," *Vero Beach Press Journal*, 14 July 1960.
91 Gross, *Tales of Waldo Sexton*, 146–149.
92 Gross, *Tales of Waldo Sexton*, 65.
93 Gross, *Tales of Waldo Sexton*, 124.
94 Gross, *Tales of Waldo Sexton*, 68.
95 Gross, *Tales of Waldo Sexton*, 68–69.
96 Gross, *Tales of Waldo Sexton*, 69.
97 Gross, *Tales of Waldo Sexton*, 70–71.
98 Breslauer, *Roadside Paradise*, 6, 9, 59–60.
99 Mays, "Gatorland," 520.
100 Mays, "Gatorland," 510–512. Through ingenious leadership committed to evolving to the changing tourist landscape, Gatorland is one of the few attractions that survived and continues to operate to this day.
101 Gross, *Tales of Waldo Sexton*, 67.
102 University of Florida Libraries, "Richard Treadway April 28, 1988" (Indian River County Oral History Collection), 5. http://ufdc.ufl.edu/UF00007804/00001.
103 Breslauer, *Roadside Paradise*, 6, 9, 59–60.
104 Breslauer, *Roadside Paradise: The Golden Age of Florida's Tourist Attractions 1929–71*, 6; IRC Oral Histories #8, University of Florida Libraries, Richard Treadway April 28, 1988, p 5.
105 Colleen Wixon, "Vero Beach trying last-ditch effort to save historic Szechuan Palace Building," *Treasure Coast Palm*, February 6, 2020, https://www.tcpalm.com/story/news/local/shaping-our-future/growth/2020/02/05/vero-beach-making-last-ditch-try-save-szechuan-palace-demolition/4665127002/.

106 Willi Miller, "The Walls According to Waldo," *Vero Beach Magazine*, September 2005; Willi Miller, "What Would Waldo Do? Or, Hold That Wrecking Ball, Please, Mister," Vero Beach Arts Blast, Volume 2 No7b, February 11, 2020, https://willimiller.com/what-would-waldo-do-special-edition.html.

107 Florida Department of State, "James F. Hutchison—Painter," Florida Artists Hall of Fame, dos.myflorida.com/cultural/programs/florida-artists-hall-of-fame/james-f-hutchison. Accessed May 7, 2020.

108 Miller, "What Would Waldo?"

109 Miller, "What Would Waldo?"

110 Knight, *Tropic of Hopes*, 12.

111 Kothari, "Reworking Colonial Imaginaries," 252–253.

Chapter 6. Guinea Cows, Landscape Paintings, Waldo, and Zora

1 James A. Lewis, "Cracker: Spanish Florida Style," *Florida Historical Quarterly* (Vol. 63, No. 2, October 1984, 184–204), 185–188.

2 Burt, *Al Burt's Florida*, 109, 104.

3 Burt, *Al Burt's Florida*, 103.

4 Milanich, *Frolicking Bears, Wet Vultures*, 37–39.

5 Milanich, *Frolicking Bears, Wet Vultures*, 44.

6 Benjamin F. Rogers, "Florida Seen Through the Eyes of Nineteenth Century Travellers," *The Florida Historical Quarterly* (Vol. 34, No. 2, October 1955, 177–189), 186. In this essay, the author also posits that the Southern Frontier is just as an important as the Western Frontier, "there should be a footnote to remind us that although Florida was the first of the forty-eight states to see an attempt at colonization, it was one of the last frontiers to be developed; and that although it has a long and interesting history, the accomplishments of the past one hundred years dwarf those of the preceding three centuries," 188.

7 Susan A. Eacker, "Gender in Paradise: Harriet Beecher Stowe and Postbellum Prose on Florida," *The Journal of Southern History* (Vol. 64, No. 3, August 1998, 495–512), 497.

8 Alisha Norwood, "Zora Hurston," National Women's History Museum, 2017. www.womenshistory.org/education-resources/biographies/zora-hurston, Accessed May 14, 2020.

9 Elvin Holt, "Zora Neale Hurston," ed., M. Thomas Inge, *Literature* The New Encyclopedia of Southern Culture Volume 9, (Chapel Hill: University of North Carolina Press, 2008), 327–328.

10 There's a telegraph and the March 3, 1954, letter about her writing a story about the Brooklyn Dodgers, https://ufdc.ufl.edu/AA00009755/00148.

11 Paige Van Antwerp, "Unlikely Friendship of Waldo Sexton, Zora Neale Hurston will come to life at Charter High," *TCPalm*, November 14, 2017, tcpalm.com/story/specialty-publications/vero-beach/2017/11/14/unlikely-friendship-waldo-sexton-zora-neale-hurston-come-life-charter-high/850272001/.

12 Gordon K. Hurd, "1941–1970 Alfred Hair: A charismatic businessman who created a movement for Florida's black artists," *The New York Times*, 2019, nytimes.com/

interactive/2019/obituaries/alfred-hair-overlooked.hmtl; see also Chapter 4 and the Hallstrom connection to Backus and the Highwaymen.
13 Zora Neale Hurston, "The Tripson Story: Milk of Human Kindness," *The Chronicle* (Vol. 2, No. 12, Fort Pierce, FL, February 6, 1959).
14 https://www.saturdayeveningpost.com/2016/11/the-conscience-of-the-court/
15 Zora Neale Hurston letter to Waldo Sexton, 22 May 1953, Eau Gallie, FL. Sexton Family Collection, courtesy of Sean Sexton.
16 Hurston letter to Waldo Sexton, 22 May 1953, Eau Gallie, FL.
17 Hurston letter to Waldo Sexton, 22 May 1953, Eau Gallie, FL.
18 Letter from Waldo Sexton to Zora Neale Hurston, 23 May 1953, Eau Gallie, FL, courtesy of Sean Sexton.
19 Sexton Letter to Hurston, 23 May 1953.
20 Sexton Letter to Hurston, 23 May 1953.
21 Sexton Letter to Hurston, 23 May 1953.
22 Zora Neale Hurston Letter to Waldo Sexton, 28 May 1953.
23 Hurston to Sexton, 28 May 1953.
24 Waldo Sexton Letter to Zora Neale Hurston, 28 May 1953.
25 Sexton to Hurston, 28 May 1953.
26 Sexton to Hurston, 28 May 1953.
27 Sexton Letter to Hurston, 28 May 1953.
28 Waldo Sexton Letter to Zora Neale Hurston, 2 June 1953, courtesy of Sean Sexton.
29 Waldo Sexton Letter to Zora Neale Hurston, 2 June 1953, courtesy of Sean Sexton.
30 Waldo Sexton Letter to Zora Neale Hurston, 2 June 1953, courtesy of Sean Sexton.
31 Waldo Sexton Letter to Zora Neale Hurston, 2 June 1953, courtesy of Sean Sexton.
32 Waldo Sexton Letter to Zora Neale Hurston, 2 June 1953, courtesy of Sean Sexton.
33 Waldo Sexton Letter to Zora Neale Hurston, 2 June 1953, courtesy of Sean Sexton.
34 Zora Neale Hurston Letter to Waldo Sexton, 13 June 1953, courtesy of Sean Sexton.
35 Zora Neale Hurston Letter to Waldo Sexton, 13 June 1953, courtesy of Sean Sexton.
36 Waldo Sexton Letter to Zora Neale Hurston, 23 June 1953, courtesy of Sean Sexton.
37 Waldo Sexton Letter to Zora Neale Hurston, 23 June 1953, courtesy of Sean Sexton.
38 Waldo Sexton Letter to Zora Neale Hurston, 3 March 1954, courtesy of Sean Sexton.
39 Waldo Sexton Letter to John D. Pennekamp, 15 March 1960, courtesy of Sean Sexton.
40 Waldo Sexton Letter to John D. Pennekamp, 15 March 1960, courtesy of Sean Sexton.
41 John E. Rouse, *The Criollo: Spanish Cattle in the Americas* (Norman: University of Oklahoma Press, 1977), 3–4.
42 Rouse, *The Criollo*, 74.
43 Rouse, *The Criollo*, 75.
44 Jason Herbert, "Beast of Many Names: Cattle, Conflict, and the Transformation of Indigenous Florida, 1519–1858," PhD Dissertation, University of Minnesota, Department of History, 2022.
45 Rouse, *The Criollo*, 7.
46 Rouse, *The Criollo*, 186–187.

47 Judy King article quoted in Gross, *Tales of Waldo Sexton*, 94.
48 Gross, *Tales of Waldo Sexton*, 94.
49 Channing Cope, "Down our Way" *Farm and Ranch Southern Agriculturalist* August 1952, quoted in Gross, *Tales of Waldo Sexton*, 94.
50 Kristin G. Congdon, "Stories about the Highwaymen: Insights About All of Us," *Visual Arts Research* (Vol. 30, No. 1 Diverse Populations, 2004, 13–21), 18.

Conclusion

1 Sean Sexton, *Portals: Poems* (Winston-Salem, NC: Press 54, 2022), 16. Reprinted with permission by the author.
2 John Mack Faragher, "And the Lonely Voice of Youth Cries 'What is Truth?': Western History and the National Narrative," *Western Historical Quarterly* (Vol. 48, Spring 2017), 12.
3 O'Brien, *Firsting and Lasting*, 55.
4 Gross, *Tales of Waldo Sexton*, 61–62.
5 Gross, *Tales of Waldo Sexton*, 74.

Appendix A

1 Zora Neale Hurston, "Double Muscle and his Pappy Too," unpublished manuscript 1954, courtesy of Sean Sexton.
2 Hurston, "Double Muscle," 2.
3 Hurston, "Double Muscle," 3.
4 Hurston, "Double Muscle," 4.
5 Hurston, "Double Muscle," 5.
6 Hurston, "Double Muscle," 6.
7 Hurston, "Double Muscle," 7.
8 Hurston, "Double Muscle," 8.

INDEX

African Americans, 23, 32, 45, 47, 49, 75, 79, 94, 120, 127, 140, 142–46, 149–50, 193n67, 196nn63,64
Aís, 2, 7–8, 12, 15–33, 38, 82, 135, 161, 176n38
American Revolution, 34, 42–43
Apalachee, 8, 28, 41–42
Armed Occupation Act, 9, 13, 52
Ayers, Frank, 37

Backus, A. E. "Beanie," 94, 139–40, 146–47, 157
Bartram, William, 33–34, 49
Bell, Emily Lagow, 56–59
Bjorkelund, Gottfrid, 104–6
Boosters, 1, 4, 10, 13, 38, 53, 68, 70, 72, 74–78, 84, 87, 89–90 112–13, 141, 160
Brayton, Caleb Lyndon, 53–55
Bryan, William Jennings, 123, 125

California, 70–71, 79, 112, 140, 168
Calusa, 23–24, 29, 32, 176n38
Cattle (Guinea/Cracker Cows) 3, 19, 34, 40, 58–60, 63, 82, 92, 141–45, 152, 155, 163–69
Citrus, 3, 52–54, 64–66, 69, 71, 77–78, 81, 85–86, 92, 94, 99, 103, 109–10, 114, 136, 159, 161
Civilization Program, 44–45
Coacoochee (Wildcat), 47–48
Creek Indians, 32, 41–42, 44–45, 47–48, 180n4

d'Escalante Fontaneda, Hernando, 19, 21
Dickinson, Jonathan, 8, 24, 26–28
Divine Providence, 5, 10, 28, 52, 63
Driftwood Inn, 13, 115, 122–26, 130–33, 135–37, 139, 148, 150–52, 164 194n13

Eden, 3–9, 20, 34, 36, 38–39, 49, 53, 56, 67, 70, 74, 84, 92–93, 112–13, 117, 123, 126–28, 133–34, 142, 152

English colonization, 7, 15, 25–29, 32–33, 40–42, 65, 73, 76, 161
Everglades, 10, 39, 82–83, 111, 113, 139, 179n101

Fellsmere, 38, 61, 81, 179n101
Fellsmere Farms Company, 82–84, 86
Fenimore Cooper, James, 50, 74
Firsting and Lasting, 1, 5–6, 10, 59, 77
Flagler, Henry, 12, 61, 81, 87, 91, 93, 109, 125–26
Fort Capron, 48
Fort Pierce, 48, 52–53, 57–58, 60–63, 83, 91, 93–94, 97, 100, 110, 145–46, 182n38
Fountain of Youth, 35, 70, 135
French Huguenot settlement, 6–7, 19–21, 175n21
Friends of the Seminole, 59–62, 183n62

Georgia, 12, 32, 43, 45, 143, 146, 150

Hallstrom, Axel, 92–94, 99–110
Hallstrom, Emily Bjorkelund, 92–94, 100–101, 104–7
Hallstrom, Johanna, 93–94, 100–104, 106–9
Hallstrom, Ruth, 92–94, 102–4, 106–10, 190n10
Havana, 21–24, 30–32, 95
Highwaymen, ix, 94, 132, 146, 156–57
Houses of Refuge, 57, 59, 183n54
Hrdlička, Aleš, 37, 180n102, 182n31
Hurston, Zora Neale, 94, 143–55, 162

Improved Order of the Red Men, 76, 186n47
Indian Removal Act, 46–48, 52, 55, 63, 68, 140
Indian River Farmer (journal), 71, 84, 87, 95–97
Indian River Farms Company, 3, 13, 36, 61, 69, 72, 83–85, 87, 93–94, 113–16, 126, 151, 179n101
Indian River Lagoon, 2–4, 7, 15, 32, 34–35, 39, 42, 66, 71, 91–92

Indian slavery, 2, 7, 17, 19, 25–26, 28–29, 40–41, 49, 63, 175n21
Irving, Washington, 34–35, 48–49, 70, 179n96, 181n31

Jackson, Andrew, 45–47
Jece, 8

Key West, 54, 125, 178n84

Lake Okeechobee, 10
Lyon, Eugene, 16–17, 171, 174n6

Manifest Destiny, 2, 4–5, 10, 52, 56, 63
McKee, Arthur, 14, 113–15, 126, 129, 138
McKee Jungle Garden, 110, 113–14, 123, 126–29, 133, 136–38, 148, 151, 164, 168
Méndez de Canzo, Gonzalo, 24
Menéndez de Avilés, Pedro, 7–8, 17, 19, 22, 65
Miami, 67, 95, 98, 111, 113, 123, 126, 137, 153, 167, 174n6
Mizner, Addison, 122–23, 132, 152
Mosquito County, 8

New Smyrna, 42, 57, 65
1904 Louisiana Purchase World's Fair Exposition, 125–26, 130, 195n62, 196n65
Noble savage, 2–3, 34, 48–49, 51, 62, 67–68, 74, 77–78

Old Florida, ix, 2–3, 14, 39, 111, 113, 132, 140, 149
Orchid Isle, 8
Osceola, 45–46, 48–51, 59, 77–79, 139, 156, 159

Paradise, 10, 19–20, 23, 36, 38, 49, 53, 56, 66, 70, 74, 82, 92–93, 96, 104, 108, 110–11, 116, 118, 122, 130, 134
Phillips, William Lyman, 126, 138
Pineapples, x, 13, 90–97, 104, 193n69
Pioneer memory. *See* Settler memory
Piracy and privateering, 19–20, 32, 153
Plantation economy, 40–41
Pocahontas, 67–69, 72–77, 175n21, 185n34, 186nn46,48
Pocahontas Building, 72, 75, 79–80
Pocahontas Park, 70, 123

Ponce de León, 16, 18–19, 29, 34–35, 38, 70, 135, 155
Pueblo Arcade, 75, 79–80

Queen Anne's War, 28, 30, 42

Red Stick War, 45, 47
Riomar, 8, 16

Sebastian, 7, 9, 16, 30, 34, 52, 55, 61, 66, 81–82, 178n84
Sellards, E. H., 36–37
Seminole, 43, 45–63, 75, 77–82, 85, 89, 92, 110, 113, 126–30, 138–40, 142–43, 155, 196nn63, 64
Seminole Building, 75, 79
Seminole Wars, 8–9, 13, 43, 45–49, 53, 56, 63, 68, 77
Settler innocence, 1, 27, 46, 48, 55–56, 73–74, 160
Settler memory, 1, 14, 26, 34–35, 38–39, 46, 51, 54, 68, 73, 77, 79, 92, 110, 130, 132, 139, 143, 149, 159–60, 175n21, 183n64
1715 Treasure Fleet, 30–33, 178n84
Sexton, Elsebeth, 116–22, 124, 128, 136–37
Sexton, Waldo Emmerson, x, 12, 14, 74, 79, 85, 94, 109, 113–40, 143–57, 161–62, 163–69, 171, 194n16
Sleepy Eye Lodge, 69–70, 75, 79, 115, 120, 123, 165
South Carolina, 28–30, 41, 174n6
Spanish colonization, 7–8, 14, 17, 19, 22, 65, 70, 143, 161
Spanish missions, 8–9, 15, 19, 22–24, 26, 28, 31–33, 65, 70–72, 125, 155, 176n36
St. Augustine, 8, 17, 20, 22–33, 38, 41–42, 51, 55, 70, 155
St. Lucie River settlement, 53, 55–56, 97
Surruque, 23–27
Susanna, 9

Tarzan Park, 112–13
Tequesta, 8, 22–24, 32–33
Tiger, Tom, 61–63, 150, 184n71
Tiger Hammock, 79, 85–86, 89, 92–93, 110, 150
Timucua, 8, 20–21, 23–24, 29, 31, 38, 42, 177n38
Treasure fleets, 4, 21, 23, 30, 33, 174n6, 178n84

Tucker, Lewis, 59, 113, 127, 130
Tuscarora War, 41

Vero Beach, ix, 2–3, 7, 12, 22, 30, 57, 61, 68, 78, 80, 111, 113, 125, 135, 138, 154, 160, 165, 174n6, 179n101
Vero Man, 13, 15, 36, 116, 194n12
Viking, 13, 86, 91–93, 97, 100, 103, 108, 110

Wabasso, 12, 81–82, 89, 136
Waldo's Mountain, 115, 132–36

War of 1812, 45–46
Weedon, Frederick, 50–53, 182n34
Wells, Isaac, 37
Wreckers, 4, 23–24, 141–42

Yamasee, 29–31, 41–42

Zeuch, Herman J., 69, 71, 85–86, 92, 113, 151

Kristalyn Marie Shefveland is associate professor of history at the University of Southern Indiana where she teaches courses on Settler and Indigenous America, the American South, and topics in Colonial North America and the Atlantic World. She is the author of *Anglo-Native Virginia: Trade, Conversion, and Indian Slavery in the Old Dominion, 1646–1722* and became interested in settler memory due to her family's long history with Vero Beach. Her essay, "Remembering an Indigenous South: Regional Identity, Vero Beach, and Settler Tourism," was part of a special edition of the *Florida Historical Quarterly* on Indigenous Florida that won the Arthur W. Thompson Award from the Florida Historical Society in 2022.

Florida in Focus

Edited by Andrew K. Frank

Books in this series provide original and lively introductions to a range of topics in Florida history. Written by established scholars and using original research, the books draw upon current scholarly developments to situate subjects in a broad historical context.

Before the Pioneers: Indians, Settlers, Slaves, and the Founding of Miami, by Andrew K. Frank (2017)
Millard Fillmore Caldwell: Governing on the Wrong Side of History, by Gary R. Mormino (2020)
Tampa Bay: The Story of an Estuary and Its People, by Evan Bennett (2024)
Selling Vero Beach: Settler Myths in the Land of the Ais and Seminole, by Kristalyn Marie Shefveland (2024)